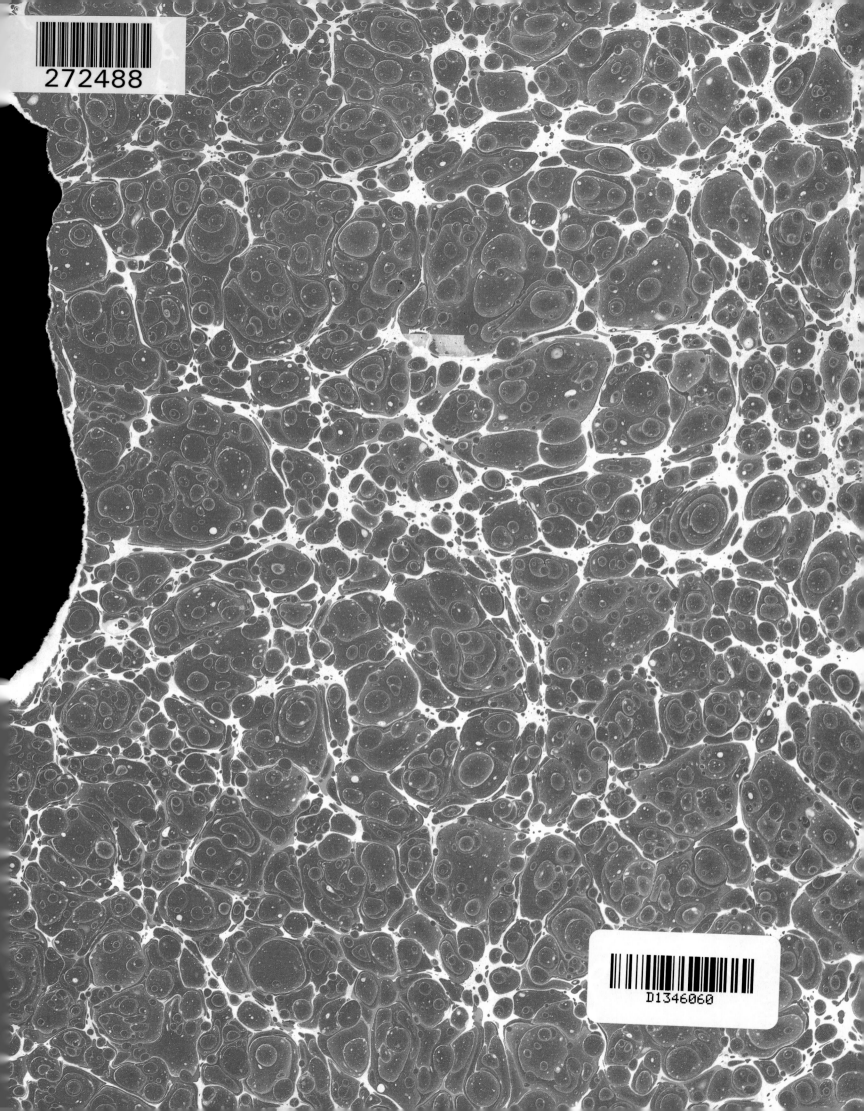

Nineteenth Century Lighting

Candle-powered Devices: 1783-1883

Nineteenth
Century Lighting

Candle-powered Devices: 1783-1883

H. Parrott Bacot

Schiffer Publishing Ltd

West Chester, Pennsylvania 19380

Printed in the United States of America.
ISBN: 0-88740-098-1
Published by Schiffer Publishing Ltd.
1469 Morstein Road, West Chester, Pennsylvania 19380

This book may be purchased from the publisher.
Please include $2.00 postage.
Try your bookstore first.

To Barbara

Contents

Acknowledgments 11

Introduction 17

Candleholders...................21

Girandoles.....................153

Candle Powered Chandeliers

and Sconces 199

Glossary 253

Index 256

Acknowledgments

It will become immediately apparent that this volume dealing with candle-powered lighting devices manufactured between roughly 1783 and 1883 is not only a compilation of photographs of objects from many diverse public and private collections, but also a collation of the research and thoughts concerning these devices by numerous minds.

Gratitude, like most things, properly begins at home. My almost obsessively orderly wife, Barbara, has borne with patience the tremendous litter of papers, piles of photographs, stacks of books and dusty boxes under beds (and underfoot) that the writing of this book has brought to her ordinarily neat home. Of course, it was she in league with publisher Peter B. Schiffer who convinced me to tackle this monumental project. She has not flagged in her support and enthusiasm, and for this I am grateful.

I count myself fortunate to work at an enlightened university which has museums and encourages research and publication. It is my privilege to direct Louisiana State University's Anglo-American Art Museum, one of the few university-related art museums in the United States that collects both fine and decorative arts. The Museum is operated under the aegis of the Office of Research directed by Vice-Chancellor Sean P. McGlynn, a research chemist, who understands the importance of humanities collections and research in the curriculum of a great university. Throughout this endeavor, it has been business as usual at the Art Museum and I have had the good fortune of having Mibs Bartkiewicz to sustain the entire operation as my secretary. Student help has played a significant role in this undertaking. Hearty thanks is owed my graduate assistant, Maureen Baker, and my undergraduate assistant, Mark LeFeaux, for aid with research, proof reading and other mechanical details. My former student worker, Lyn Wyble, is a gifted graphic artist and he has rendered the handsome illustrations of prism types seen in these pages. Through the Office of Public Relations, I have had access to the superior photographic abilities of Jim Zietz and Prather Warren. They have photographed all the Museum's lighting devices with consummate artistry.

The *raison d'etre* for this book being done at this time and place is the rather extraordinary collection of nineteenth-century lighting devices that has been formed at the Anglo-American Art Museum through the generous funding of the Friends of the Museum. The current president of the Friends, C. C. Coles, M.D., and the immediate past-president, Stephen G. Henry, Jr., have been champions of patronage in endorsing this accessions policy.

A plethora of kindnesses have been extended to me by a host of antique dealer-interior designer friends throughout the eastern half of the United States. Heading this list is the Pennsylvania interior designer, Samuel J. Dornsife. He has cared about, nay loved, the nineteenth century when that century's artifacts were being confined to the dust-bins. He can be credited with converting a whole generation or more of art and architectural historians to a genuine appreciation of the nineteenth century. His marvelous library, now largely housed in The Athenaeum of Philadelphia (also the home of the Victorian Society in America) will be relied on heavily in future lighting device research.

Another of the scholar-collector-dealers is Garrison Grey Kingsley of Greenville, Delaware. Gary Kingsley, as he is known to his friends, is one of the principal evangelists for decorative arts made during the first sixty years of the nineteenth century. His special interest is that period's lighting devices. He not only permitted the photographing of his extensive collection of candle, oil and gas-powered lighting devices, but offered instruction on the finer points of Philadelphia, New York and Boston styles, construction and finishes. In the same vein, Craig Littlewood, the widely acclaimed restorer of early lighting devices in Palmyra, New Jersey, tutored me from his vast wealth of knowledge about the subject. He and his partner J. Craig Maue permitted the photographing of a number of superior examples in their collections.

One simply cannot discuss lighting devices of the eighteenth and nineteenth centuries without the assistance of Albert Nesle of Nesle, Inc. in New York. More exceptional lighting devices dating from those centuries have probably passed through his showrooms than any other dealership in America. Mr. Nesle opened his extensive photographic files and shared, from his storehouse of fifty years of collecting and dealing in the best quality fixtures, the knowledge that he has gleaned. His expeditions in quest of the finest lighting devices have led him all over Britain, continental Europe and even to India at the end of the British Raj. Mr. Nesle is a superb teacher and in his shop-classroom one can learn the subtle differences between Scandanavian and Russian work, as well as begin to understand the nuances of differences between French designs and those of French-inspired work executed elsewhere.

I am much in the debt of Jonathan Snellenburg and Dean Failey of Christie, Manson and Woods International, Inc. in New York for opening the photographic files of that old-line auction house. The much younger auction firm of Neal Alford Company in New Orleans has extended a similar courtesy. Neal Alford and Della Graham of that organization have been particularly helpful.

Other dealers furnishing photographs from their files or allowing pieces from their stock to be photographed for publication include Joan Bogart of Rockville Centre, New York, Ronald Bourgeault of Hampton, New Hampshire, Philip H. Bradley Company of Downingtown, Pennsylvania, and David Calcote of Natchez. My friend from graduate school days, D. Roger Howlett of Childs Gallery, Boston, provided pictures of objects from his stock and private collection. Special thanks go to J. Donald Didier, David Wojciechowski, Nicholas Barras and James Anderson of Didier, Inc. in New Orleans for allowing the photography of objects in their stock and offering encouragement as this project has moved forward.

Cary Long and Douglas Wink of Goudeau Antiques in Baton Rouge and James E. Guercio in Natchez have allowed me to disrupt their shops several times to photograph items in their stock. Several objects are illustrated through the courtesy of Joe Kindig Antiques in York, Pennsylvania. Bernard and S. Dean Levy in New York continued their long tradition of assisting scholars with both their own extensive knowledge and access to their incredible photographic files. C. Neri, proprietor of the Neri Collection in Philadelphia, has also provided photographs and permitted photography of objects in his showroom. Gothann Oertling of the 18th Century Shop in New Orleans knows as much about prisms as anyone in the world and has been a god-send in matching prisms for several incomplete fixtures in various collections in the region before photography was done. M.S. Rau Antiques, also in New Orleans, permitted photography of objects in their shop. Herbert Schiffer in West Chester, Pennsylvania, graciously provided photographs from his files as did David Stockwell of Wilmington, Delaware. Jack McGregor of Buena Vista Galleries in Houston also has a keen interest in nineteenth century lighting devices and shared his knowledge with me.

Numerous institutions ranging from historic house museums to art museums to private library companies have allowed objects from within their collections to be studied and illustrated in this book. Included are pages from pattern books as well as actual lighting devices.

The institutions in the lower Mississippi River Valley have been especially liberal in providing staff-time in assisting me in the examination of objects within their collections. In New Orleans, I am grateful to the current director, Ann Masson, her predecessor, Karen Wade, and Carolyn Bercier, the assistant director at the Gallier House. At the Hermann-Grima House, the present director, Charles L. Mackie, and his predeces-

sor, Ann Durant, and the curator, Jan Bradford, all have cheerfully allowed me to trespass on their time. E. John Bullard, director of the New Orleans Museum of Art graciously consented to allow that institution's curator of decorative arts, John W. Keefe, time to review the attributions made in this entire volume. Mr. Keefe's expertise in the field of European and American glass, as well as French decorative arts made his help invaluable. The present director, Dode Platou, the former director Stanton Frazar, chief curator John Mahé, II and curator John Lawrence at the Kemper and Leila Williams Foundation's The Historic New Orleans Collection all have dealt with my requests in the courteous manner for which that institution is justly recognized. Timothy Chester, formerly the chief curator at the Louisiana State Museum and now assistant director for the Grand Rapids Public Museum, guided me to some particularly interesting fixtures and pattern books within the massive holdings of the State Museum.

In Baton Rouge, I am indebted to my colleagues John Dutton, director of Louisiana State University's Rural Life Museum, and to Timothy J. Mullin, the former director of Magnolia Mound Plantation House and now the director of the George Read House in New Castle, Delaware. St. Francisville with its fabled Rosedown Plantation and Gardens is less than an hour from Baton Rouge. Mr. Ormond Butler, overseer of the property, and the owners, Mr. and Mrs. David Underwood, and the fantastic staff of docents allowed me to interrupt the efficient running of that historic house museum several times to examine and photograph the extraordinary collection of lighting devices there.

Mississippi institutions that have extended many niceties are headed by the wonderful group of ladies who compose the Pilgrimage Garden Club of Natchez. Stanton Hall, the Club's first acquired historic house, is a veritable treasure house of lighting devices ranging from candleholders through one of the finest suites of gasoliers and gas brackets surviving in the United States. Rosemont Plantation at Woodville, owned by Percival T. Beacroft, Jr. and administered by Ernesto Caldeira, opened its doors to hours of photography on both a torrid summer day and another chilling winter one. The Mississippi Department of Archives and History in Jackson has the happy burden of administering the handsome Mississippi Governor's Mansion. The director of the Department, Elbert R. Hilliard and the Mansion's former curator, Anne D. Czarniecki have been most accommodating colleagues. Katherine S. Howe, curator of decorative arts at the Museum of Fine Arts, Houston, has assisted in many other ways including pointing me toward several Gothic Revival objects.

Turning to the east coast, I could not ask for a better personal friend and colleague than Roger William Moss, director of the venerable The Athenaeum of Philadelphia. Dr. Moss has made his institution a major American center for nineteenth century art and architectural studies. The collection of wonderful lighting devices is exceeded by the staggering holdings of nineteenth-century pattern books, sale catalogues and manuscripts. While she is not affiliated with her husband's library company, one must mention the benefits of discussions with art and architectural historian, Gail Winkler Moss. Her lightning-quick perception of several questions greatly assisted in their resolution.

The Henry Francis duPont Winterthur Museum in Delaware and more especially its curator of metals, Donald L. Fennimore, has provided a myriad of answers to questions from his own vast experience and he has spent not a little time doing research for this book in his institution's library. At the Index of American Design, housed in the National Gallery of Art in Washington, every possible courtesy was extended by the Index's curator, Lina Steele, and assistant curator, Lisa Fukui.

Further north at the New York State Office of Parks, Recreation and Historic Preservation more professional friends of long standing, James and Cheryl Gold, gave access to many objects at several of their glorious Hudson River sites. Paul G. Schneider, Jr. provided beautiful photographs of those objects needed for this book. Boscobel at Garrison-on-Hudson is one of the country's most magnificent Federal period houses and its furnishings are equally outstanding. Frederick W. Stanyer, the director, has provided beautiful photographs and precise information concerning several of Boscobel's candelabra and chandeliers.

It is fortunate for historians that New England's climate is conducive to the preservation of man-made culture and that New Englanders in general have a natural predilection for saving old things. Old Sturbridge Village in Massachusetts owns the only known surviving copy of the 1856 trade catalogue of the New York firm of Starr, Fellows and Company and the 1859 catalogue of its successors, Fellows, Hoffman and Company. Without it many attributions could not have been made. My very helpful friends and colleagues at Old Sturbridge Village are John O. Curtis, director of the Curatorial Department, and their former curator of textiles and ceramics, Jane Nylander, who subsequently has become the director of Strawbery Banke, Inc. in Portsmouth, New Hampshire. At the Essex Institute in Salem, Massachusetts, another of those key documents in the study of nineteenth-century American lighting fixtures is to be found. At this time, that Museum possesses the only known copy of an illustrated catalogue by the prominent Boston firm of Henry N. Hooper and Company. At the Essex, former curator John Wright and Marylou Birchmore of the photography department have cheerfully provided requested materials. Richard C. Nylander, curator of the Society for the Preservation of New England Antiquities in Boston has willingly given of his time.

Private collectors, especially in the lower Mississippi River Valley have welcomed the invasion of their privacy by me, photographers and all the accompanying photographic paraphernalia. Photographs of objects from the collections of Emily J. Jones in Baton Rouge, the Messers Eugene D. Cizek, Lloyd L. Sensat, Frederick Lee Lawson and Mr. and Mrs. George Crounse, Jr. of New Orleans are reproduced through their courtesy. Mr. and Mrs. Frank W. Wurzlow, Jr. and Russell B. Wilkes are other Louisiana collectors who have allowed reproduction of their fixtures for this book.

Natchez friends have been equally kind and supportive. Chief among my Natchez coterie is Bethany B. Lambdin, a fine scholar in her own right and my collaborator and co-author in several Mississippi decorative and fine arts projects. Mr. and Mrs. John Callon of Melrose have allowed the illustration of some of the marvelous pieces that have come down in their remarkable Greek Revival house, as well as lighting devices they have added to the Melrose Collection. A number of prime fixtures from the collection of Mr. and Mrs. William McGehee and Mr. and Mrs. Raymond St. Germain appear through their courtesy.

Finally and certainly not least, publisher Peter B. Schiffer has been forbearing over more years than he should have been with me and this undertaking. He has been more of a midwife in the birth of this book than can rightfully be expected of a publisher. His talent with the camera under every imaginable condition that the weather and locations north and south could offer appear in part in these pages. His good humor rarely deserted him even after having to photograph the umpteenth chandelier in the middle of the night, balanced atop a twelve foot ladder. Peter Schiffer is teamed with his equally resourceful and dedicated wife, Nancy, who has been an encouraging and obliging friend. Without their dogged perseverance, this project would not have come into fruition.

H. Parrott Bacot,
Baton Rouge.

Introduction

There have been numerous books published over the past twenty years dealing in whole or part with lighting devices ranging from the American Federal Period, or in the broader sense, the Neoclassical period, through the late Victorian era. There has, however, been no general work that has attempted to cover that period of slightly over one hundred years in which more inventions were developed and more improvements were made in lighting than during the entire previous history of man.

In 1783, the Franco-Swiss chemist Ami Argand invented a successful lamp employing new scientific principles of combustion. Argand's burner and oil reservior arrangement triggered an extraordinary series of inventions and improvements that culminated in the invention of the incandescent electric light by the American scientist Thomas Alva Edison in 1879. The appropriate place to begin a history of nineteenth century lighting devices in the Western world is therefore 1783.

The vastness of the array of lighting devices made during this span of one hundred years has assisted in making the decision to limit this volume to candle-powered fixtures. Candles were the principal means of artificial light during the first forty or fifty years of this period. This book will therefore survey the devices made in northern Europe and the British Isles, as well as those made in America. As an American author, I have chosen to concentrate on candle-powered fixtures ranging from the humblest "hogscraper" candlesticks to the most *soigne* table and hanging fixtures that could have been used in the United States during the late eighteenth and nineteenth centuries. Many lighting devices were imported from Europe, so most European readers should find this work useful.

The study focuses primarily on those lighting devices which were used in domestic situations, although there will be some examples that were used both domestically and in public places. It is my intent to advance chronologically with the inventions and modifications in lighting without forgetting that the new devices did not immediately supercede the old ones. Obviously, the more urban, sophisticated and wealthy areas would be the first to make use of new methods of lighting. The use of lighting principles dating from the Middle Ages endured in lesser houses and on the frontier. Even in great houses, where the finest, most up-to-date fixtures were used in the primary rooms, simple candleholders might still be found in secondary and tertiary chambers.

This study will then survey the various types of devices from common sheet iron candlesticks to magnificent candlesticks and chandeliers—wrought in silver, ormolu and cut glass. Care will be taken to explain in laymen's terms the basic principles of advancing technology and emphasis will be placed on dating the various fixtures. The nineteenth century begins the efflorescence of the trade catalogue and pages from rare surviving catalogues are reproduced both as an aid in dating and to show pieces as originally made. Some fixtures have been changed from candle to oil to gas or electricity as each new improved burner or fuel was introduced. Older devices that have been adapted at later dates will be noted.

An apologia is here offered for any of this work's deficiencies. In a work covering so vast a topic both time and expense have made it impossible to dedicate equal time to each type of device. Decisions to emphasize those groups of devices which seem more important from both technological and aesthetic points of view have been made. As much as possible I have endeavored to provide illustrations of objects not illustrated before and to give dimensions of pieces.

This volume will deal only with the primary source of lighting that was already on the scene when Argand's revolutionary new oil burners and fonts were invented— candlepower. During this period of incredible advances in lighting technology, the candle remained a popular source of light for dining in even the finest residences and for use in lesser rooms of well-to-do houses. In frontier areas candle fixtures continued to be used by all classes of people. The romance associated with the flickering flame of candles, therefore, is not exclusively a modern phenomenon.

It is my fervent hope that this volume will benefit all students of material culture, private collectors and antiquarians, as well as curators.

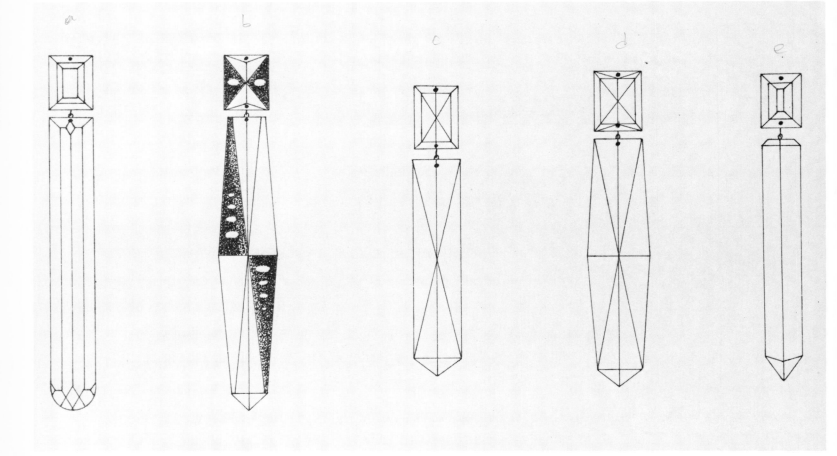

Schematic Drawings of Prisms Used in the Nineteenth Century, Drawings by Lyn Wyble
These drawings illustrate in basically chronological order most of the kinds of prisms used on metal and glass fixtures during the nineteenth century. Note that the term pyriform or pear-shaped so well describes the form that it is unnecessary to illustrate an example of the pyriform model in a drawing.

Plate 1

(a.) Many-faceted straight prism (referred to by antique dealers as "Georgian" prisms). These are appropriate for use on English lustre candleholders and sconces of the early nineteenth century as well as on English and American-made argand lamps dating as late as 1840.

(b.) Coffin-shaped prism with frosting and oval cuts in the frosting. This is a relatively rare model and when seen is in the larger size for use on solar lamps. Used during the 1840-1860 period.

(c.) Modified coffin-shaped prism. The straight sides of this prism achieve the coffin effect by the deep cutting of its face which provides a high relief on that surface. This model is appropriate for use on argand and solar lamps and oil chandeliers dating from the early to the mid-nineteenth century. Also, they are found on girandoles.

(d.) Coffin-shaped prism. These prisms are so cut that they are widest in the center, which gives the full effect of a coffin. This type of prism is correctly used on argand and solar lamps as well as oil chandeliers from the early nineteenth century to as late as 1870. This is a particularly popular model for girandoles.

(e.) Straight spear-tip prism. This basically long narrow, triangular type of prism can be found properly used on chandeliers from the 1830s to the 1850s.

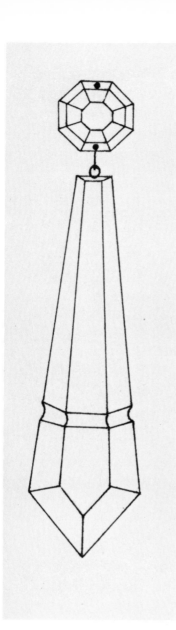

Plate 2

(f.) Spear-point prism. This type of prism which tapers upward has a deeply cut necking above the spear tip. This type of prism is seen on English-made candleholders and argand lamps and in the United States on girandoles made in Boston. This style of prism was used from the 1820s through the 1860s.

Plate 3

(g.) Broad spear-tip prism. Dealers frequently refer to this form as "colonial" prisms. They were used during the 1840 to 1875 period on all types of oil lamps, candle and oil chandeliers and on girandoles.

(h.) "C" prism. This is like the preceding prism only it is etched with a "C" motif. This model is appropriate for use in better quality girandoles, solar lamps and chandeliers as well as on some candle-powered chandeliers.

(i.) Interlocking "C" and star prism. In configuration this model is like (g) and (h), only rarer. It looks well on the finer girandoles and would not be inappropriate for use on solar lamps and chandeliers as well as candle chandeliers.

(j.) Snowflake prism. Of the decorated broad spear-tip models this is the most common and is available in fine quality reproductions. It is seen in trade catalogues of the period on girandoles and certainly is appropriate for solar lamps and chandeliers, as well as candle chandeliers. Note that plain faceted headers can be used as well as the matching snowflake models. This model also was made with stars.

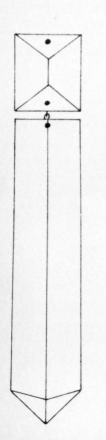

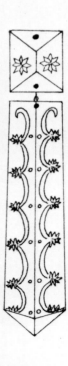

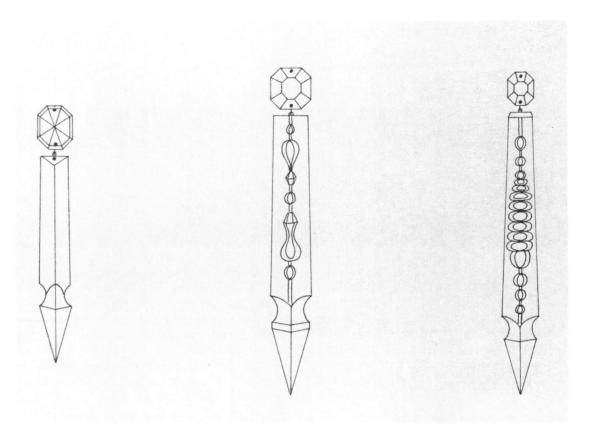

Plate 4

(k.) Plain "Albert" prism. Named for Queen Victoria's consort, this is the simplest design of the model. All "Alberts" have a necking between their shafts and their several pointed spear tips. "Albert" prisms usually have octagonal headers in contrast to the square and rectangular ones seen on the other models illustrated here. This type of prism is seen on post 1855 gas fixtures and on lustres made from that period forward. They are used on late candle-lighted chandeliers.

(l.) Back-cut "Albert" no. 1 prism. In this model the leading edge between the two narrowest of the three sides is cut in baluster and sphere patterns. These are used on the finer lines of lustres and chandeliers from 1855 forward.

(m.) Back-cut "Albert" no. 2 prism. Rarer than the no. 1 model, this pattern features cojoining cut circles and spheres. It was employed on the same lighting devices as the back-cut "Albert" no. 1.

Series of Four Glass Bobeches, American, Victorian style, circa 1840-1870. Left to right: 1) clear glass, Diam: 3-½ in. 2) opaque white glass, Diam: 3 in. 3) clear glass with gilding, Diam. 3-⅜ in. 4) frosted green glass, Diam: 3-½ in. Collection of Frederick Lee Lawson.

Inexpensive detachable glass bobeches were made in fairly large numbers in many patterns and colors for use on gilded girandoles, chandeliers and other metal candleholders whose finishes needed protection. They have not survived in sizeable quantities because of their fragile nature and the hard service which they received. The four shown here provide only a sampling of the range of patterns and colors in which these pieces were produced. Both of the clear pieces are examples of fairly heavy American pressed glass.

20

Candleholders

This chapter concerns itself with all the lighting devices powered by candles, with the exception of chandeliers, sconces and girandoles which are treated in two separate chapters. Although the period from 1783 to 1883 witnessed the invention of lighting improvements ranging from the argand burner through gas lighting to electric lighting, candles were greatly improved and remained an important source of domestic lighting. The illustrations in this chapter will make it readily apparent that some of the most handsome candleholders ever produced were manufactured during the hundred year period that began in 1783.

Those of us living in the rapidly changing, electrically lighted, late twentieth century need some perspective to appreciate the candle as a means of illumination. Perception is clouded by present-day use of candles for decoration at parties to lend a festive or romantic air to those social occasions. Western man's other current use of candles is for religious and secular ceremonies. In the slower moving late eighteenth and nineteenth centuries, the latest technological advances did not reach all parts of the western world in a matter of weeks or months as happens today. The problems of transporting fuel for some of the lamps developed during that period prevented their instant popularity. Gas required a central gas manufacturing plant in urban situations or an expensive private plant for country houses, in addition to pipes to move the gas. Electricity must both be generated and transported by wire. Even in the twentieth century some rural areas did not receive electricity until as late as 1940. Coal-oil lamps and even candles, for example, were the sources of illumination in many rural districts in the southern United States until the government's rural electrification projects were begun as a part of President Roosevelt's New Deal programs.

The earliest candles were rush piths which were dipped in tallow. These rush lights were used in humbler homes into the nineteenth century. The true wax candle, in the cylindrical shape and made of materials such as tallow and beeswax enclosing and saturating a fibrous wick, dates to the beginning of the Christian era. The Greeks and Romans coated flax threads with pitch or wax. Oil lamps were more popular until the medieval period when the candle came into prominence. The tallow candles were by no means easy to use since they required wick trimming every five to thirty minutes, depending on the quality of the wax. Scissor-like snuffers with boxes to catch the charred wick ends had to be used to keep those particles from falling into the molten tallow. Wick debris caused "guttering," that is to say, gullies of molten tallow would run down the side of the candle from the pool of liquefied tallow beneath the flame. Left untended, the majority of the candle would go to waste.[1]

Finer candles were commercially made from the seventeenth century forward, but it was the advent of whaling as a major industry in the late eighteenth century that led to the discovery of a new candle-making material. Spermaceti, which came from the head cavity of the sperm whale, could be made into a white candle that burned with a clear, steady flame. The light provided by a spermaceti candle weighing one sixth of a pound and burning at a rate of 120 grains an hour was regarded as "one candle power" and was the international standard measurement for artificial light until well into the twentieth century.[2]

The twenty-year period from 1820 to about 1840 witnessed phenomenal improvements in candles and in their manufacture. Up until 1820, all candle wicks had been made by twisting flax or cotton together. In that year the Frenchman, Jean-Jacques Cambaceres, discovered that plaiting cotton produced a wick that would bend into the outer part of the flame where it would be consumed. At the same time Michel-Eugene Chevreul, a French chemist, was doing research concerning fatty acids. His paper "Recherches Chimiques sur les corps gras d'origine animale" was published in 1823. This research led another French scientist, Gay-Lussac, in 1825 to separate the fatty acid from the glycerin of fat to produce stearic acid. The Englishman Milly not only helped to commercially establish this even-burning material in candle manufacture, but in 1831 he introduced the impregnation of wicks with boric acid which virtually eliminated guttering.[3]

Improvements in the machinery to manufacture candles began as early as 1801, which led to the modern methods of chandlering. Thomas Binn, a "water-closet maker," was granted a British patent in that year for his invention of a water-coiled mould. In 1823 Joseph Morgan devised a movable piston to eject the cooled candle.[4] By the mid 1830s these developments had been incorporated into a full-fledged machine consisting of rows of moulds set in a metal tank which was heated and cooled alternately. Wicking located on spools below the machine was fed through the pistons which ejected the candles from the moulds after the moulds were cooled.[5] These candles which did not need their wicks trimmed or in the terms of the day were "snuffless" could be bought for a shilling a pound in 1840.[6] The discovery of oil in both Canada and the United States in the late 1850s[7] realized as a by-product, paraffin. When made into a wax, a better and cheaper candle could be made. Termed variously paraffin oil, coal oil or kerosene, this oil was a superior burning fluid for lamps. Inexpensive kerosene which could be easily transported by expanded railway systems and gas-fired lighting devices are the reasons for the rapid decline in candle use that began in the 1860s.

The majority of the candleholders illustrated in this chapter are fabricated from metal. A number of the earlier pieces have stems or shafts made by the seamed construction method.[8] In that process the stems are cast in two halves and brazed together before being joined to a core or solid cast base. The seamed method was used in Britain and on the Continent from the late seventeenth century through the 1790s as a means of reducing the amount of raw material needed in the fabrication of candle shafts and similar objects. After that time the raw materials were readily available and the less labor intensive core cast method was employed. In the United States the seamed construction technique was still being employed in the manufacture of such articles as andiron shafts and finials and lamp standards through the 1840s.

In this chapter the objects have been arranged chronologically except where comparisons seemed necessary. Liberty has been taken additionally to group compatible materials such as glass and ceramics together for ease in seeing relationships in candleholders made in the same material over a time range of up to forty years. The candleholders are grouped generally into national types. The French as the tastemakers of the western world in the decorative arts come at the head of each category. Then come the other continental pieces with an emphasis placed on the Germanic and Scandinavian contributions. The contributions made by the English and Americans have been grouped together in each category because of the close cultural and commercial ties that those two nations have historically enjoyed.

French-made candlesticks begin the chapter followed by continental candlesticks and chambersticks. Next in order are the Anglo-American candlesticks, chambersticks and wax jacks. They are followed by all the candelabra beginning with the French-made pieces, the other continental styles and ending with Anglo-American examples. A small number of pavement lights or *torcheres*, which were used in only the most luxurious of settings, follow the candelabra. Finally, there are the candle lamps which are divided into French and Anglo-American examples.

1. Pair of Single Socket Candleholders, French, *Directoire* style, marble and ormolu, circa 1793-1800. Courtesty Nesle, Inc., New York. Photo by Helga Photo Studio.

The reeded and fluted candle sockets, the foliate ormolu border at the base of the cylindrical plinth and the beading of the base are all very crisply cast. The ununusual two-tailed mermaid is, however, not quite as well porportioned and detailed as most *Directoire* pieces are. This gives some credence to the possibility of these objects having been made during the revival of the late eighteenth century that took place in the 1870s up through 1900. The *Directoire* era was a turbulent period and some documented pieces from that time exhibit some of the same inconsistencies seen here.

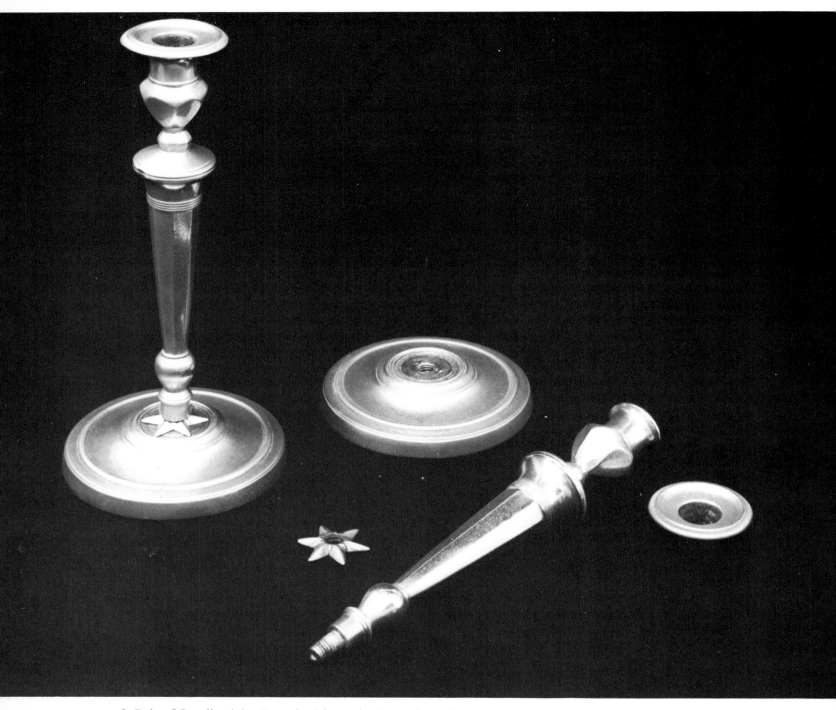

2. Pair of Candlesticks, French, *Directoire*-Consular style, core cast and seamed construction brass, circa 1795-1804. H: 10-⅞ in. Diam. of base: 5-⅛ in. Collection of Mr. and Mrs. Frank Wurzlow, Jr. Photo by Prather Warren.

This handsome pair illustrates the elegance that was achieved during the late eighteenth century and opening years of the nineteenth century through chaste designs. Low, broad, circular bases were a particular favorite with the French from the *Directoire* through the *Restauration* periods. Cabling is used for the principal borders on the bases and the edges of the bobeches, as well as on the upper and lower knops of the shaft. Another French design predilection is that of the long tapered shaft. Here the shafts are hexagonal and match the faceted candle cups. From the *Directoire* period through the *Restauration*, there was an increasingly noticeable narrowing of the elements between the candle cup and the shaft and between the shaft and the base. These candlesticks, like so many French examples, were originally silvered.

The photograph shows one candlestick disassembled so the construction can be better understood. There are actually five separate castings. The base, star, and detachable bobeche elements are core cast, while the shaft has been cast in halves and brazed together. The French and continental-made candlesticks rely on threading the lower part of the shafts to fit threads in the center of the bases. British construction, in contrast, during the eighteenth century usually used a brass rod which was flattened on the bottom end by tamping to hold the base and shaft together. Fairly early in the nineteenth century the British switched to tangs as the connecting elements between shaft and base.

3. Pair of Candlesticks, French, *Directoire*-Consular style, core cast and seamed construction brass, circa 1795-1805. H: 10-⅞ in. Diam. of Base: 5 in. Private Collection.

The photograph hardly does justice to this pair which is engraved with bands of chevets, bells, rosettes and foliate designs in the best neoclassical manner. In construction this model is precisely like the previous pair. With the exception of the bobeches, each piece is stamped with an "F" which could have something to do with the name of the maker, the engraver or the first owner. On the underside of each separately cast foliate necking element and inside the socket of each base, wherein the necking and the shaft are seated, there are three matching punch marks. These candlesticks were originally silvered and should either be replated with silver or gilded to preserve the engraving which can be removed by overly zealous polishing.

4. Pair of Candlesticks, French, *Directoire*-Consular style, core cast and seamed construction brass, circa 1795-1805. H: 11 in. W: 5 in. Courtesy Magnolia Mound Plantation, Recreation and Park Commission, Baton Rouge, Louisiana. Photo by Prather Warren.

Perhaps the most restrained of the *Directoire-Consular* examples shown, this pair features a handsome band of anthemia on the cylindrical candle cups and a palmette border on the bases. The lower part of the plain tapered shafts have been ornamented with raised fluting. Originally the candle cups would have been outfitted with detachable bobeches which are now missing.

5a. Single Candlestick, French, *Directoire* to First Empire style, core cast and seamed construction brass, circa 1795-1810. H: 9-1/16 in. Diam: 4-1/2 in. Courtesy Magnolia Mound Plantation, Recreation and Park Commission, Baton Rouge, Louisiana. Photo by Prather Warren.

This is a more ordinary design from the French brass founders of the latter part of the eighteenth and early nineteenth centuries. Through polishing, much of the beading on the bold circular base and the beading on the knop of the stem have been worn away. The bobeche is detachable. This candlestick bears on the underside of its base traces of its original silver-plated finish.

5b. Detail of Single French Candlestick disassembled.

Very noticeable in this view is the single punch mark which can be either a foundry worker's punch or may be a secret owner's mark.

6. Candlestick (one of pair), French, Consular-Empire style, patinated bronze and ormolu, circa 1800-1815. H: 10-5/8 in. Diam: 4-1/2 in. Courtesy Rosedown Plantation and Gardens, St. Francisville, Louisiana.

Here the French tapered stem candlestick has been carried to its greatest refinement. The perfect balance between the dark bronze and the ormolu has been established. The large, strong border of anthemia on the stepped base is repeated on the cap of the stem in reduced scale. That element is additionally enriched with cast tassels which are suspended from it. There is a beaded ormolu necking around the middle of the stem and the stem is seated in a socket formed by palmettes. The socket is held by a foliate decorated knop.

7. Two Candlesticks, French, Consular-First Empire style, core and seamed construction brass, circa 1800-1815. Dimensions L to R: H: 10-3/8 in. Diam: 4-3/4 in.; H: 8-1/8 in. Diam: 4 in. Collection of Frederick Lee Lawson.

The taller candlestick has a seamed construction stem raised on a core cast base and probably dates to 1800-1805. Its shaft is a hexagon which tapers down to a nest of cojoining eagle talons. The broad base is bordered with palmettes. The other example is core cast entirely and is very much neo-Egyptian, having three pharaonic heads atop a tapering column. The column is almost like a skirt from which three pairs of feet emerge at the bottom. The upper surface of the circular base is decorated with laurel, whereas there is a band of anthemia on the ovoid candle cup. Both pieces have traces of their original silverplated finishes and are missing their detachable bobeches. The shorter example is marked in script on the bottom "A3"—perhaps indicating that it is the third in a set.

8. Candlestick, French, First Empire style, ormolu and glass, circa 1810. Courtesy Nesle, Inc., New York. Photo by Helga Photo Studio.

All of the magnificence associated with the bronze founders of First Empire is embodied in this candlestick. Two neoclassical female figures dance in perfect harmony with their backs to each other and against a baluster-shaped stem while one hand of each figure helps to support an inverted bell-shaped blown glass shade. The figures are mounted on a pierced drum which is supported by freestanding griffins. The animals are joined together by ormolu swags composed of fruit and floral devices.

Opposite page:

9. Pair of Single Light Candleholders, probably French, Empire style, patinated bronze, circa 1810. Courtesy Bernard and S. Dean Levy, Inc., New York. Photo by Helga Photo Studio.

The spread eagle was one of the principal emblems of Napoleonic France. The candleholders can be attributed to French manufacturers on the basis of the wide-mouthed campana-shaped candle cups. Many French candlesticks dating from the late eighteenth and early nineteenth centuries have these flared candle cups with broad apertures. The French also show a strong predilection for high circular bases which are frequently embellished with an overall cast pattern border. Here the border is a punchwork design. Applied cabling has been used on the foot, on the necking of the shaft and on the circular plinth supporting the eagle. The prism supports are inverted "J"-shaped wires which are usually associated with Scandinavian work. They are seen in French work—especially when the larger part of each inverted "J's" staff is soldered to the principal shaft. The candlesticks suffer from someone in the past having attempted to polish them.

10. Pair of Single Light Candleholders, French, First Empire style, ormolu and patinated bronze, circa 1810. H: (female) 13-½ in. H: (male) 13-⅜ in. W: 14-½ in. D: 5-¾ in. Courtesy Dornsife Collection.

Magnificent is the best descriptive word for this large pair of candleholders which evoke all the splendor associated with the imperial France of Napoleon I. The enormous size of the fixtures almost makes the fact that each device holds but one candle ridiculous. The proportions and balance, however, are perfect and make one realize immediately that the functional aspect is secondary to the decorative purpose. Each patinated bronze lamp of learning rises from a square ormolu foot and ormolu lobes embellish the lower half of the bowl of the lamp. The exposed ormolu candle cup is cast as a perpetual flame and conceals a simple, cylindrical candle socket. The youthful classical scholars in patinated bronze recline atop each lamp reading gilded pages.

12. Single Candlestick, French, First Empire style, core and seamed construction brass, circa 1810. H: 8-5/16 in. Diam: 4-5/16 in. Courtesy Lambdin Collection.

This pleasant candlestick having a slightly tapered baluster-type stem combines two principal decorative motives—cabling and beading. Cabling alternates with strong beading from the top of the candle cups to the base except on the principal knop where a pair of beaded borders run. Another interesting feature is the lion's mask seen on the base.

11. Pair of Candlesticks, French, First Empire style, patinated bronze and ormolu, circa 1805-1815. H: 23-7/8 in W: 5-1/2 in. D: 5-1/2 in. Courtesy Dornsife Collection.

Rather than the more usual goddess, this handsome pair employs a Pan or putto figure in the stem of each shaft. The combination of ormolu and patinated bronze is most effectively used here. The podium base has a crisply cast egg and dart moulding above the foot and a companion border of palmettes at the head of the plinth. The principal face of each plinth displays a separately cast and applied ormolu motif which features a classical lyre with swans supports, set against a matte finish gold ground. Each plinth supports a bright ormolu foliate element which in turn is the frame for a golden sphere. A winged putto literally dances on one foot atop each globe and holds a wreath of ormolu rosettes above his head. A trumpet-shaped element embellished with lotus leaves and palmettes springs from each wreath to hold a cylindrical candle cup.

13. Pair of Candlesticks, French, First Empire style, core cast and seamed construction, red brass, circa 1805-1815. H: 10-⅝ in. Diam: 5 in. Collection of Mr. and Mrs. Raymond St. Germain.

This pair is a classic example of French First Empire baluster-type candlesticks. Cabling appears as a border on the edge of the base and on the knop of the candle cup. Bands of diapering are on the knop at the head of the shaft and on the upper part of the baluster above a broad band consisting of ten rows of rosettes set within circles. These candlesticks are missing their original detachable bobeches and were silverplated originally.

14. Two Single Candlesticks, French, First Empire style to *Restauration* style, Left: copper and brass originally gilded, circa 1810. H: 9-½ in. Diam: 4-⅞ in.; Right: core cast brass, circa 1810-1820. H: 9-½ in. Diam. 4-½ in. Collection of Frederick Lee Lawson.

The taller candlestick bears the engraved legend, "MINORET, RUE St HONORE' No 58 PARIS" on its underside. Whether Minoret was a founder or a retailer is not known. The candlestick is another variation of the baluster shaft-circular based Empire model. It also has a very wide-mouthed candle cup. The relationship between these two candlesticks is closer than casual study would suggest. The lower base and domed plinth of the right-hand candlestick resembles English designs. Close examination of the band of decoration on the base of the stem of the left candlestick and of the border of the plinth on the right fixture reveals that both are spiral twists consisting of plain stripes alternating with beaded spirals. This border is almost invariably French.

15. Pair of Candlesticks, French, *Restauration* style, core cast brass, circa 1820. H: 9-⅞ in. Diam: 4-¾ in. Courtesy Magnolia Mound Plantation, Recreation and Park Commission, Baton Rouge, Louisiana. Photo by Prather Warren.

The overall heavier appearance of these candlesticks as well as their construction being exclusively core cast removes them from the Empire period. The columnar shafts are not dissimilar from English-made examples of the Regency-George IV era. The handling of the circular base, the method of screwing the shaft into the base and the decorative band on the base and candle cup are French. The decorative borders consist of rows of circles and each circle contains a Gothic style rosette. The finishing of the underside of this pair's bases is perfectly smooth and traces of their original silvering remain.

16. Pair of Candlesticks, French, *Restauration* style, core cast brass and iron, circa 1816-1825. H: 7-⅞ in. Diam: 3-⅝ in. Collection of Mr. and Mrs. Raymond St. Germain.

These candlesticks are somewhat deceptive for dating purposes. On a quick glance they would pass for *Directoire* or early First Empire. The shafts are thicker and the broad, flat bases associated with the *Directoire*—First Empire candlesticks are missing here. The brass elements are fitted over a drawn iron rod—a construction technique associated with the *Restauration* and later periods. The foliate devices directly below the campana-shaped candle cups are separately cast and look much like the elements seen directly above the base of the *Directoire*-Consular pair shown as Ill. 3.

17. Pair of Candlesticks, French, *Restauration* style, core cast brass, circa 1820-1830. H: 11-¼ in. Diam. of base: 4-¾ in. Courtesy Magnolia Mound Plantation, Recreation and Park Commission, Baton Rouge, Louisiana. Photo by Prather Warren.

These columnar candlesticks owe much to the First Empire style, but are a little more highly ornamented. They are also made in a different way. The circular bases actually rise to a small nipple element and that element is threaded to receive a drawn iron rod which functions as a concealed shaft holding the seven individually cast elements of each shaft together. Counting the base and bobeche, each candlestick has nine separately cast elements. The majority of the late neoclassical decorative vocabulary is brought into play. Two variations of palmettes appear on the base along with a laurel wreath border and the vertical cabling so often used by the French founders. The necking elements which fit over the nipples on the bases also have that type of cabling. The columnar shafts have a lower drum embellished with scaling and a fluted element which is capped with a capital composed of a band of three rows of rosettes set within circles. The candle cup itself is almost barrel-shaped with the cabled decoration appearing almost like the staves of barrels. The bobeches are bordered with anthemia.

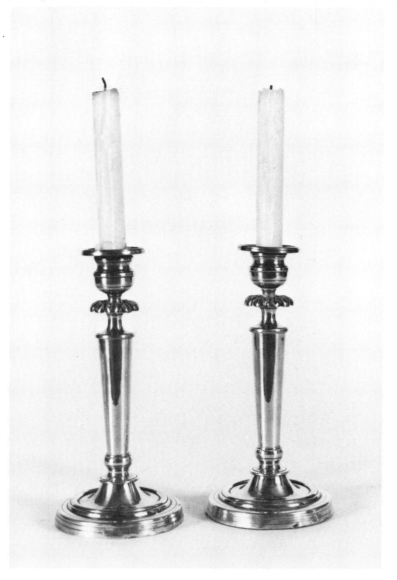

18. Pair of Candlesticks, French, *Restauration* style, ormolu and iron, circa 1816-1830. H: 11-¼ in. Diam: 4-⅞ in. Courtesy Hermann-Grima House, New Orleans.

This variation on the French columnar model features fluted columns with Corinthian capitals and knopped bases on the columns which are decorated with diapering. The diapering is repeated on the campana-shaped candle cups. Note that the elements below the columns are actually a slightly bulbous campana shape. Each stepped base has acanthus leaves as its main border motif and the smaller border is a row of palmettes. The ormolu elements fit over a drawn iron rod.

19. Pair of Candlesticks, French, *Restauration* style, core cast and sheet brass, circa 1830-1840. H: 8-⅞ in. Diam: 4 in. Courtesy Magnolia Mound Plantation, Recreation and Park Commission, Baton Rouge, Louisiana. Photo by Prather Warren.

These candlesticks are made in almost the same manner as the preceding two pairs in that there are numerous elements of brass fitted over a drawn wire. The fluted columns are, however, thin-gauge sheet brass as is indicated by the number of dents in those elements. The cabling seen above and below the columns, as well as the diaper and rosette pattern on the lowest knop and the beaded spiral twist on the candle cups, are derived from First Empire sources. The ornate band of foliage, flowers and acorns seen on the base are neo-rococo.

20. Pair of Candlesticks, French, *Restauration*-Louis Philippe style, patinated bronze, ormolu and iron, circa 1825-1840. H: 12 in. Diam: 5-½ in. Collection of Mr. and Mrs. Raymond St. Germain.

The more florid appearance of the ormolu candle cups, bobeches, capitals and bases of the fluted, patinated bronze shafts is an indication of *Restauration* or Louis Philippe manufactory date for the candlesticks. The more domical tops of the bases are another later feature. These candlesticks' elements fit over a drawn iron rod.

21. Pair of Candlesticks, French or possibly English, *Restauration* style, patinated bronze, circa 1830. H: 4-⅜ in. W and D: 3 in. Collection of Frederick Lee Lawson.

These charming candlesticks combine a canted hexagonal and concave base and plinth with an urn-shaped candle cup. The cabbage rose and foliage on the front of each plinth and the heavily cast roses of each detachable bobeche are moving in feeling toward the floridness of the Victorian period. While probably made in France, these could have easily been made in Britain and reflect the influence of the taste makers in Paris.

22. Pair of Candlesticks, French, *Restauration*-Louis Philippe style, ormolu, patinated bronze and iron, circa 1825-1840. H: 13-⅛ in. W: 5-⅜ in. D: 5-⅜ in. Collection of Frederick Lee Lawson.

This type of standard is more frequently encountered in candelabra, but numerous examples were also made as single-light candlesticks. A hexagonal, ormolu base with concave sides provides the support for the three patinated bronze lion legs that form the plinths. An ormolu socket decorated with anthemia holds the patinated bronze column which is capped with a sumptuous, flaring Corinthian-type ormolu capital. The patinated bronze candle cup is very much in the classical urn shape and has an ormolu bobeche. The shaft elements are fitted over a drawn iron rod.

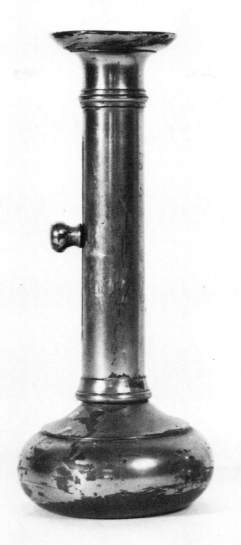

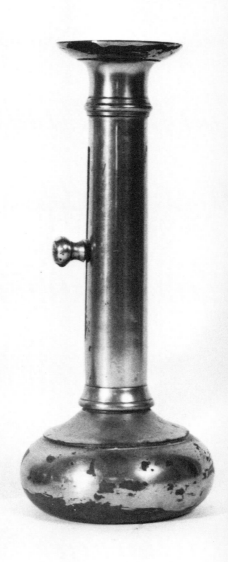

24. Pair of Candlesticks, French or possibly English, *Restauration* style, gilded core cast brass, circa 1820-1840. H: 8-½ in. Diam: 3-½ in. Collection of Frederick Lee Lawson.

An unusual variation on the model with side pushups, this pair has weighted bun-shaped feet. Perhaps intended for use on shipboard where the weighted bases would assist in keeping them upright, these candlesticks survive with a great deal of their original inexpensive gilded and lacquered finish.

23. Candlestick, French, *Restauration* style, core cast brass, circa 1820-1840. H: 7-¼ in. Diam: 3-¼ in. Courtesy Goudeau Antiques, Baton Rouge, Louisiana. Photo by Jim Zietz.

While a number of this general model of candlestick were made in England as well as France, this example with its double stepped base and continuous bead for a foot is in the French taste. Also, it has a large threaded element at the base of the stem for the joining of the stem to the base in the French manner. With its handy side pushup candle ejector, this candlestick blends well with neoclassical continental and Anglo-American furniture.

25. Candlestick (one of a pair), French (probably made by the Baccarat Works), early Rococo Revival style, green and clear glass, circa 1840-1850. H: 14-⅜ in. Diam: 6-½ in. Courtesy Gallier House, New Orleans.

The Baccarat Works in conjunction with Cristalleries de St. Louis was the largest producer of fine glass in France during the nineteenth century. The pale emerald green of the swirl or spirally twisted foot and shaft combine most effectively with the clear glass prism ring and vase-shaped candle cup. The prism ring and candle cup also employ the spiral twist decoratively. Square, faceted headers are used with snowflake pattern prisms.

26. Pair of Candlesticks, French, Rococo Revival style, ormolu, circa 1840-1860. H: 10-½ in. Diam: 4-¾ in. Courtesy Rosedown Plantation and Gardens, St. Francisville, Louisiana.

Europeans have always been fascinated by the exotic aspects of the native populations of Asia, Africa and America. Here an American Indian brave and maiden are modestly dressed and have facial features closer to the Victorian concept of the ancient Roman rather than American Indians. Indeed, the only aspects of their costume to identify them as Indians are their curious feathered head dresses, beads, arm bands, the feathered overdress that the brave wears and the fringe of the maiden's skirt. The casting, finish work and detail are all of superior quality.

27. Pair of Candlesticks, French, Louis XV Revival, ormolu and porcelain, circa 1865-1880. H: 9 in. W: 3-½ in. D: 3-½ in. Courtesy Dornsife Collection.

These candlesticks date from the latter part of the rococo revival period and were a part of a larger mantel garniture. In France during the post-1865 period, the revival of the great decorative-arts styles of the eighteenth century ranging from Louis XIV to Louis XVI was becoming more scholarly. Furniture, in particular, became reproductions rather than the inventive selective borrowing of old designs which were reinterpreted during the early rococo period. This happened to a lesser extent in the area of metalwares. These candlesticks capture the spirit of the eighteenth century rococo in the lightness and delicacy of the swirling, three-footed bases which rely on "C" scrolls and shell devices in creating that effect. In the same manner, the downturned drip pans and the candle cups with their foliate "C" borders and irregular striated lines help to promote that illusion. The baluster-shaped porcelain stems and their metal mounts are not copied from rococo designs. The diapered bezel supporting the lower part of the stem and the beaded one at the top were prompted by designs originating during the First Empire period. The painting on the stems was inspired by both Louis XV and Louis XVI examples. The favorite ground colors for this type of porcelain were pink or blue-green. Here it is blue-green. Reserves are formed on each candlestick by a chain of elliptical medallions in the Louis XV taste. Each of the medallions contains a sprig of flowers. One candlestick's reserve contains a standing lady in a garden situation while her gentleman companion is framed in the other candleholder's reserve. They are dressed in the Louis XV mode.

28. Pair of Candlesticks, French (possibly one of the Paris factories), Rococo Revival style, porcelain, circa 1850-1865. H: 8-¼ in. W: 5-¾ in. D: 5 in. Collection of Frederick Lee Lawson.

In polychrome and gilt the candlesticks can truly be considered a revival of the eighteenth-century rococo which took great delight in porcelain figurines. Here we have the eighteenth-century gentleman in striped knee breaches and patterned waistcoat standing on a canted and serpentine plinth raised on four button feet. The coy female wears the striped and floral dress of a peasant girl. Both figures stand in front of and are discreetly joined to the foliate stems of each candlestick. The candle cups are embellished with niches and pairs of gilded scrolls and have attached scalloped bobeches.

29. Pair of Table Candlesticks, Italian (made by Giuseppe Grazioni of Rome), Neoclassical style, silver, circa 1790. Courtesy Christie's, New York.

These candlesticks relate closely to Germanic work of this period and to that of the mid-eighteenth century. The large circular, stepped bases are certainly old fashioned, as is the bold, almost baroque handling of the vitruvian wave borders set against punchwork grounds on the base and knop. The leaf borders against punchwork grounds appearing on the foot and the bottom of the candle cup are also reminiscent of the treatment given this motif earlier in the eighteenth century. The tapered stems engraved with swags and festoons of laurel are neoclassical. The fluting of the bell-shaped plinth is handled in a manner not unlike decorations in the English Adam taste.

30. Pair of Table Candlesticks, Belgian (maker's mark C enclosing a star), Neoclassical style, sterling silver, circa 1815. H: 11-¾ in. Courtesy Christie's, New York.

In silver, the tapered stem is a form used both on the Continent and in Britain. This Belgian-made pair follows the French tradition in overall design and decoration. The circular base is broad and has the flattish top favored by the French. The heavy beading and striation seen on the base, as well as the large and small beading on the knop and the large beading on the bobeche, all follow French stylistic predilections.

41

Opposite page:

31. Two Pair of Table Candlesticks, Spanish (the taller by Daguer of Barcelona; the shorter possibly by Rosel of Barcelona), Neoclassical style, silver, circa 1815. Taller pair-H: 8-7/8 in.; shorter pair-H: 8 in. Courtesy Christie's, New York.

The Iberian Peninsula was not a style pacesetter during the late eighteenth or the nineteenth century; however, handsome decorative arts made there were inspired by both French and British fashions. These two pair relate best to French Empire examples with their broad, circular bases with corded borders and their finely chased, vertical acanthus leaves at the center of each base. The octagonal columnar stems, having capitals with corded or continuous beaded borders and detachable bobeches, are severely neoclassical.

32. Pair of Table Candlesticks, Middle European, Renaissance Revival, rock crystal and silver-gilt, circa 1840-1860. H: 7-1/8 in. Courtesy Christie's, New York.

Bohemia in particular, but other Germanic and Slavic areas of middle Europe as well, had a great tradition going back to the late medieval period of making various decorative arts from rock crystal mounted in silver-gilt. These candlesticks build on that tradition and are rather similar in feeling to Plate 61, an English silver-gilt pair by Paul Storr. This set, however, was made in the midst of the romantic renaissance revival. The slightly stepped, low hexagonal bases are framed with silver-gilt borders consisting of cabling and vertical leaves. Those same framing devices assist in holding the two hexagonal, curved, rock-crystal elements in the shaft. The candle cups are cylindrical and have cabled borders. A brass rod runs from the inside of each candle cup through the base to actually hold all the components together.

33. Pair of Table Candlesticks, Polish (made by LHF of Lemberg), Neoclassical style, silver, circa 1807. H: 7-1/2 in. Courtesy Christie's, New York.

Characteristic of many candleholders made in the Germanic and Slavic countries are ones such as these where the conical stems flow directly from low square bases without benefit of transitional elements. The edges of the bases tend to be flared, as is the case here. The vase-shaped candle cups have plain fixed bobeches. Like most Germanic, Scandinavian and Slavic silver these candlesticks are not sterling standard.

34. Candlesticks, probably Russian or middle European, Baroque Revival style, core cast brass, circa 1810-1860. H: 10-¾ in. W: 4-¹³/₁₆ in. D: 4-¹¹/₁₆ in. Collection of Emily S. Jones. Photo by Jim Zietz.

Baluster stemmed candlesticks such as this one have long been misrepresented as dating from the seventeenth and early eighteenth centuries. They are extremely heavy— this example weighs 5-½ pounds. They employ the technique favored in continental Europe since the Middle Ages of threading the lower part of the shaft so that it will screw into the base. The underside of the base of this example and others like it exhibits the roughest of casting marks which are totally out of character for candlesticks made in the seventeenth and eighteenth centuries. While not having the most harmonious proportions these are none the less pleasant. Many collectors find them desirable based on the strength of weight alone.

35. Table Candlestick, probably Dutch, Neoclassical style, painted pewter, circa 1820. H: 8-⁹/₁₆ in. Diam. of base: 3-¼ in. Courtesy of James E. Guercio Antiques, Natchez, Mississippi.

The Dutch are quite well-known for their painted pewter, especially the pyriform urns having brass spigots. The fat baluster-shaped stem raised on a square base, as seen here, has been associated with Dutch work. Making this candlestick exceptional is the fact that it survives with most of its original paint. The serious collector will not want a piece which has lost all of its original paint or has been so poorly restored that it displays little of the design as conceived by the artisan who first painted the piece. Here the ground color is black, while the necking of the baluster is decorated with gilt foliage and lines. The base also has gilt lines, stylized gilt anthemia at each corner and gilt palmettes on the circular plinth. The polychrome scene on the baluster features a man in early nineteenth-century dress with sheep, a cow and trees.

36. Pair of Lustres, Bohemian, early Victorian style, clear glass with red and white paint, circa 1840-1865. H: 12-¼ in. Diam. at Lip: 7 in. Courtesy Dornsife Collection.

Colored lustres observed a great vogue throughout the entire Victorian period. Nowhere was their popularity greater than in Britain and the United States. The majority were probably made in Bohemia for that market. This pair are especially grand and would have originally graced an important mantel, pier table or dining table. To their octagonal baluster-shaped stems, domed circular feet and scallop edged prism rings, have been added painted decorations consisting of Gothic revival trefoils, quatrefoils, ogee arches and fleurs-de-lis. Appropriately, the prisms are of the "back-cut Albert" variety used on most fine lustres of the 1840 to 1880 period.

37. Lustre, Bohemian, Rococo Revival style, cranberry and clear glass, circa 1860. H: 9-⅛ in. Diam. of lip: 5-⅛ in. Collection of Eugene D. Cizek, Ph.D. and Lloyd L. Sensat, Sun Oak House, New Orleans.

Thousands of lustres were made in clear glass and various colored glass from the early nineteenth century through the 1880s. Used in pairs, these pieces were especially popular in Britain and the United States as garniture for mantels and pier tables. This shape, having the large bowl acting as a bobeche, employing an inverted bowl as a foot and using the "back-cut Albert" type of prism, is a typical Victorian form of lustre. This attractive example decorated with an etched and cut vintage pattern and a scalloped lip should date from somewhere after the mid-nineteenth century to as late as the 1870s. The Bohemian glass works specialized in colored glass, much of which has been intended for export since the eighteenth century.

38. Set of a Pair of Candlesticks and a Pair of Two Light Candelabra (one shown), Bohemia, clear glass, stained red glass with white enameling and gilding, Rococo Revival style, circa 1850-1870. Candelabra H: 23-¼ in. W: 12 in. Diam: 5 in.; Candlesticks H: 10-½ in. Diam: 5 in. Collection of Mr. and Mrs. John Callon, Melrose, Natchez, Mississippi.

Photography simply does not do justice to this extraordinary large set of lighting devices. The enameled white flowers and gilding are not readily apparent. The baluster-shaped stems are hexagonal and the round bases are divided into hexagonal sections by the raised roundels. Each foot has a heavily beaded border. Note that the diameters of the feet of the single candleholders and the candelabra are the same, but the single candlesticks have a lower dome as opposed to the very high dome of the candelabra. The shafts of the candelabra are attenuated, whereas those of the single candlesticks are compressed. The lobed prism and "back-cut Albert" prisms are similar to other Bohemian work. The candle cups are almost in the shape of a ruffled tulip. The branches of the candelabra are clear scrolling glass. Rather than having a third candle socket, each candelabrum has a flared bouquet holder.

39. Tinder Box-Candlestick, Continental, Empire Revival style, sheet brass and felt, circa 1870. H: 5-½ in. Diam: 3-½ in. Courtesy James E. Guercio Antiques, Natchez, Mississippi.

This piece is included as one of the many curiosity pieces that occur in nineteenth century-made candleholders. The style of the bold baluster shaft and the use of stamped brass with much cabling suggest a continental European origin for this piece. It could have been made anywhere from Holland to Russia. Calling this a tinder box is probably a misnomer since this piece was made after matches were developed. Very likely there was another more appropriate surface for striking matches originally used in place of the felt.

40. Chamberstick, French (made in Paris but maker's marks are rubbed), *Restauration* style, silver-gilt, 1819-1838. Length: 11-¼ in. Courtesy Christie's, New York.

A circular, footed dish having a guilloche border provides the support for a vase-shaped candle cup having a detachable bobeche with a palmette and berry border. The long down-curved side handle also has the palmette and berry border. The upper part of the handle has an applied silver coat of arms of an unidentified cardinal.

41. Chamberstick, probably Scandinavian, Neoclassical style, sheet brass, brass wire and iron wire, circa 1825-1840. H: 5-⅞ in. Diam. 4-¾ in. Courtesy Lambdin Collection.

The use of thin sheet brass for the stem, handle and the well articulated, pierced gallery identify this piece as dating from the nineteenth century. The use of the scrolling brass wire for the handle of the candle ejector suggests Scandinavia as the place of origin for this piece. The pattern of rings looped together is not dissimilar from some decorative patterns seen on Scandinavian chandeliers.

42. Chamberstick, Italian (made by Guadagni), Neoclassical, silver, circa 1805-1820. L: 12-¾ in. Courtesy Christie's, New York.

The heavy silver chamberstick has a most unusual trough-like element going from the dish to the handle. The lower bulbous section of the vase-shaped candle cups is reeded and a handsome, boldly cast anthemion appears at the head of the trough. The slightly tapered, cylindrical handle looks back to seventeenth century designs.

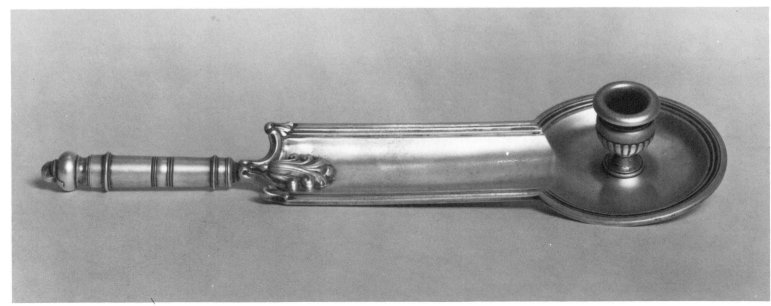

48

43. Two Pairs of Single Light Candleholders, English, Adam style, (left pair) ormolu, blue jasper Wedgwood porcelain, and glass, (right pair) Derby feldspar, glass and brass, circa 1795-1805. Courtesy Nesle, Inc., New York. Photo by Helga Photo Studio.

The left pair with the blue jasper-ware Wedgwood-made drum-type plinth is an especially rich example. Each drum has four different bas relief, classical oval-shaped vignettes set against the famous Wedgwood blue ground. The drums are mounted in simple, circular, ormolu bezels. Each upper bezel is domical and supports an egg-shaped element of cut glass which serves as each candleholder's shaft. Graduated circular prisms hang from the edges of the Van Dyke-style candle cups, while alternating large and small circular prisms are attached to the star-shaped prism rings.

The other pair is a variation on the theme. Here the drum-shaped plinths, circular bases and domical caps for the drums have been turned from single blocks of subtly mottled, greyish colored feldspar. The shaft is a ribbed piece of pear-shaped glass having ormolu fittings. The star-shaped prism rings hold graduated pyriform prisms. The candle cups are campana shaped and ribbed to match the glass shaft.

44. Pair of Candlesticks, English, Neoclassical style, amber and clear glass, circa 1800-1815. H: 12-½ in. Diam.: 5-½ in. Collection of Mr. and Mrs. Raymond St. Germain.

The amber colored shafts, candle cups and bobeche cum prism rings of this pair are uncommon. The heavy, diaper cut baluster-formed shaft and thick base suggest an early nineteenth century date for this pair. The Van Dyke candle cups, star-shaped prism ring/bobeche and tear-drop prisms harken back to the late eighteenth century.

50

45. Candlestick, English or American (upper East Coast), traditional or folk style, unidentified hardwood and tin, circa 1800-1840. H: 6-¼ in. Diam. 4-¼ in. Courtesy Herbert Schiffer Antiques, West Chester, Pennsylvania.

Numerous examples of these lathe-turned candlesticks are to be found both in Britain and America. When found in the United States, they are, with rare exception, identified as American-made. The design of this candlestick is not unlike those made in pewter. The circular base is turned out of one piece of wood and screwed to the shaft which is turned from another piece of wood. The tin lining of the cylindrical candle cup is an uncommon, but not rare, feature of this sort of candlestick.

46. Pair of Table Candlesticks, English (made by Robert Bush and Richard Perkins of Bristol), *Retardataire* Baroque style, pewter, circa 1775-1781. H: 9-½ in. Diam. 6-⅜ in. Courtesy Herbert Schiffer Antiques, West Chester, Pennsylvania.

Pewter is an alloy whose principal element is tin which is combined with copper and/or lead and/or antimony. The alloy has a very low melting point and for that reason it is rather simple to cast in bronze or copper moulds. It was a material that was popular for the utensils used by the more traditional, less fashion-conscious stratas of society. Without the marks, "London/B&P" with the Britannia, leopard's head and rosette symbols, it would be impossible to say whether this pair of candlesticks had been made in 1730 or as late as 1800. The bold circular bases, broad reel elements and the bulbous baluster are not far removed from designs popular in the seventeenth century. While there are notable exceptions, pewter candlesticks made in Britain, continental Europe and America during the late eighteenth and early nineteenth centuries generally were composed of some sort of circular foot used in conjunction with a baluster shaft.

47. Pair of Candlesticks, English, Neoclassical style, core cast and seamed construction brass, circa 1790. H: 9-½ in. W: 5-½ in. D: 3-¾ in. Lambdin Collection.

This is an exact copy of a model seen in silver and Sheffield plated silver on copper. The bases, knops, candle cups and detachable bobeches are all boat-shaped.

48. Two Pairs of Table Candlesticks, English (made by John Parsons and Co. of Sheffield), Neoclassical style, sterling silver, 1793. H: 11-¾ in. Courtesy Christie's, New York.

These two pair make a fine set of four since only minor differences occur between them. The broad, circular bases have only a reeded border and an engraved crest for decoration. The upper part of each base is spool-like in the English taste. Each tapered stem begins as a spool. Each shaft and vase-shaped candle cup is fluted and has palmettes on its lower section. This motif is a popular one and is seen in both sterling and plated wares. Each candlestick has a plain, detachable bobeche.

52

49. Two Almost Identical Pairs of Candlesticks, English or American, Neoclassical style, core cast and seamed construction brass, circa 1785-1815. H: 10-¼ in. Diam. at base: 4-³/₁₆ in. Collection of Eugene D. Cizek, Ph.D. and Lloyd L. Sensat, Sun Oak House, New Orleans.

The fact that few British brass candlesticks are signed and signed American ones are practically non-existent makes the exact place of manufacture of these neoclassical devices impossible to pinpoint. Most experts choose to credit them to Britain where the majority of them were doubtlessly manufactured. This, however, denies the existence of a substantial brass manufacturing industry in the United States that arose after the Revolution. Signed American andirons offer ample evidence of the quality of brass founding in the United States. The American founders of the late eighteenth and early nineteenth century did not have access to large supplies of copper and zinc since the discovery of those raw materials on American soil did not come until much later. They therefore elected to continue the much more labor intensive process of casting shafts of andirons and candlesticks in two pieces and seaming them together in order to save brass. The British brass foundries gradually switched from seamed construction exclusively to core casting beginning around 1780. The process of seamed shafts had probably disappeared entirely from Britain by 1800, but was still being used in the United States into the 1840s. These two pairs of candlesticks with their seamed construction urn-shaped candle cups, attached bobeches and tapering stems raised on circular core cast bases could just have easily have been made in Boston, New York or Philadelphia as in Birmingham, England.

50. Two Pairs of Candlesticks, English, Neoclassical style, taller pair made of core cast red brass, the other of standard yellow brass, circa 1790-1810. Dimemsions L to R H: 11-¼ in. Diam: 5-³/₈ in.; H: 10-³/₈ in. Diam: 4-³/₈ in. Lambdin Collection.

While the circular bases were not so popular with English brass founders as they were with the French brass founders of the neoclassical period, many were made. In contrast with the French candlesticks to be seen elsewhere in this chapter, the circular English bases have lower rims and are generally not so broad as their French counterparts. Both pairs have tapered, fluted shafts. The pair on the right has the additional distinction of having beading set within its flutes, but is missing its detachable bobeches.

The left pair is made of what is frequently called bell metal. Bell metal is properly a bronze alloy, whereas red or pink brass simply is brass with a slightly higher content of copper than occurs in yellow brass. Red and pink brass are less common than yellow brass and, therefore, more highly prized by many collectors. The collector who likes his metals brightly hand polished should be warned that red or pink brass does tarnish more quickly than yellow brass.

51. Pair of Candlesticks, English, Neoclassical style, core cast brass, circa 1800-1815. H: 5-½ in. Courtesy Philip H. Bradley Company, Downingtown, Pennsylvania.

These short candlesticks have a long faceted candle cup which literally serves as a shaft. They are elegant and originally may have been intended for use on the more confined spaces of ladies' desks and dressing tables.

52. Pair of Table Candlesticks, English, Neoclassical style, pewter, circa 1800-1830. H: 9-½ in. Diam. 4-⅜ in. Courtesy Herbert Schiffer Antiques, West Chester, Pennsylvania.

This attractive pair of pewter candlesticks has the delicacy associated with the neoclassical period. The circular feet are low and dished and have handsome gadrooned borders. The gadrooning is repeated at the lower end of the stems and as a border on the bobeches. The stems are a baluster shape with a concave spool above and a large knop near the bottom of each stem. The candle cups are plain vase forms with incurved sides.

53. Pair of Table Candlesticks, English, Neoclassical style, pewter, circa 1810-1830. H: 8-⅜ in. Diam. 4-¼ in. Courtesy Herbert Schiffer Antiques, West Chester, Pennsylvania.

This pair might be slightly newer than the previous pair because of the heavier stems. Here the bases are stepped domes having a gadrooned border. The gadrooning is repeated at the base of each stem and as a border edging the bobeches of the urn-shaped candle cups. The cylindrical spool-shape in each stem is another form that appears often in circa 1810 to 1860 candlesticks.

54. Pair of Traveling Candlesticks, English, Neoclassical style, core cast brass, circa 1790-1820. Diam: 3-5/8 in. Courtesy Antiques Guercio. Photo by Prather Warren.

This type of candlestick is the rare exception to the rule of British founders not making candlesticks whose bases and shafts screw together. Not commonly seen today, many examples of the form were doubtless made for the British military and civil servants who were building, protecting, and administering the Empire. The hard use that they received accounts for their paucity today. Brass is not the hardest of metals and threads that are constantly used will wear out. When the candle cups are unscrewed and fitted into one base and the other base screwed on top for travel, the resulting configuration is that of a bun. In Britain they are sometimes referred to as ''Brighton buns.''

55. Four Candlesticks, L to R - (1) English, Neoclassical style, core cast, red brass, circa 1785-1815, H: 5-1/4 in. Diam: 3-1/2 in.; (2) French, Consular-First Empire style, core and seamed construction, brass, circa 1800-1810, H: 6-1/2 in. Diam: 3-3/8 in.; (3) English, Regency style, core cast brass, circa 1805-1820, H: 6 in. W and D: 3-1/4 in.; (4) English, George IV-William IV style, core cast brass, circa 1820-1840, H: 6-1/4 in. W: 3-1/8 in. D: 2-3/4 in. Collection of Frederick Lee Lawson.

This grouping of candlesticks offers a contrast between the English and French styles of neoclassicism during the late eighteenth century and opening years of the nineteenth century and the slightly later Regency and George IV-William IV models. The short English red brass candlestick is another of those examples where a large candle cup functions both as candle socket and stem. The French example displays the typical broad base with the low domed upper surface preferred by that nationality. The square-based English Regency example with the baluster base is a common model. It illustrates the slight change in the shape of the base and the beginning of the preference for bulbous balusters and spool turnings in stems that the English turned for most of the rest of the nineteenth century. The final example displays the form that many of the candlesticks of the 1830 to 1860 period assumed. The square base with ovolo corners is, however, still in the Regency mode.

57. Pair of Candlesticks, English, Neoclassical style, core cast brass, circa 1790-1820. H: 10-⅜ in. W: 4-⅛ in. Lambdin Collection.

The square base with concave sides and two rows of beading is one of the more popular English forms of neoclassical candlestick bases. These bases are used in conjunction with a variety of columnar and tapered shafts. Here a fluted column with a Tuscan capital is employed. Originally this pair would have had detachable bobeches. Core casting suggests an early nineteenth century date of manufacture. One candlestick is upturned to reveal the relatively smooth base as well as the hand-hammered head of the rod that has been tamped in to join the shaft to the base. This model and other similar designs were so numerous that it was natural for the foundries to copy them from the beginning of the Adam Revival in the 1870s to the present time. The reproductions are heavier and exhibit rough undersides. Usually the casting of the beading is not as crisp. Variations on this model are being made today for the gift shop trade.

56. Pair of Candlesticks, English, Neoclassical style, core cast brass, circa 1790-1815. H: 11 in. W. and D: 4-⅛ in. Lambdin Collection.

Semi-ovoid, fluted and reeded candle cups can be seen in English brass founders' catalogues dating from about 1780. The fluting of the candle cups is the one design element that sets this example apart from thousands of candlesticks having square stepped bases with beading and tapered shafts. The core casting of this pair points toward a late eighteenth or early nineteenth century date of manufacture. Models similar to this were reproduced from the beginning of the Adam Revival in the 1870s into the twentieth century. These candlesticks exhibit the same relatively smooth undersides of bases and the same juncture between bases and shafts as seen in illustration 57.

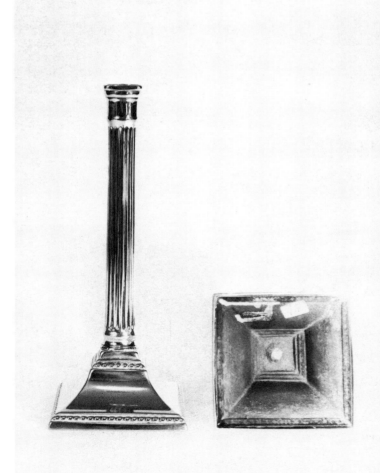

58. Group of Four Candlesticks, English, Neoclasssical style, core cast brass, circa 1800-1825. Dimensions L to R, H: 10-¼ in. W and D: 3-¾ in.; H: 9-⅜ in. W and D: 3-¾ in.; H: 6-⅞ in. W and D: 3-½ in.; H: 5-⅛ in. W and D: 2-½ in. Lambdin Collection.

This ballet of candlesticks gives some idea of the combinations of shafts and sizes of shafts that can be placed on a square concave base either with or without beading. The tallest example has reeding on the lower part of its column as well as a detachable bobeche. The other examples have candle cups with bobeches that are cast as part of the cup. This is typical of most nineteenth century base metal candlesticks.

59. Pair of Candlesticks, American or English, Regency or late Federal, core cast and seamed construction brass, circa 1815-1835. H: 8-⅞ in. Diam of base: 4 in. Collection of Eugene D. Cizek Ph.D. and Lloyd L. Sensat, Sun Oak House, New Orleans.

On the basis of style and construction this pair was almost certainly made in the United States. The spool-like turning of the stem relates closely to the turnings seen on American made andirons of the late 'teens to mid-1830s. In conjunction with this style is the fact that the shafts are of seamed construction. The candlestick on the right has a very pronounced split on one of its seams which should be rebrazed. Like all seamed construction candleholders the underside of the core cast bases are lathed smooth of the impression of the sand casting marks. The reclamation of the metal for future use was the prime concern rather than the finishing of the bottom.

57

60. Pair of Candlesticks, English, Regency style, core cast brass, circa 1820-1835. H: 6-⅜ in. W and D: 3-½ in. Collection of Eugene D. Cizek, Ph.D. and Lloyd L. Sensat, Sun Oak House, New Orleans.

Plain brass candlesticks were not the lighting devices of high fashion rooms in the nineteenth century, but were rather for use in the tertiary rooms of the great houses and in the better rooms of the middle classes. Patterns therefore generally had long periods of production. Here the founder has combined the then old-fashioned slim urn-shaped candle cup and upper shaft of the neoclassical period with the new stepped, octagonal foot that was introduced around 1820.

Opposite page:
61. Pair of Table Candlesticks, English (made by Paul Storr of London), Regency period in the seventeenth century taste, silver-gilt, 1807. Courtesy Christie's, New York.

The eccentric Englishman, William Beckford, commissioned architect James Wyatt to build a romantic "Gothick" Revival pile in Wiltshire in 1795. The finished product was the cruciform-plan Fonthill Abbey, completed in 1807. It was so flimsily constructed that the 278 foot tall central tower collapsed in the year that the house was completed. Fonthill was the largest house to be built in the Gothic style since medieval times, but Beckford's interest in the antique did not stop with the medieval. These candlesticks, commissioned by Beckford from the great Paul Storr, are in the seventeenth century French style—a style that was not generally revived until the Victorian period. The broad, low, octagonal bases have acanthus leaf borders with overall rinceaux designs of foliage and rosettes surrounding phoenix birds in various positions. That motif is repeated on the sides of the candle cups. The baluster stems are composed of knops and spools decorated with acanthus leaves and scaling.

62. Set of Four Table Candlesticks, English (made by Paul Storr of London), Regency style, sterling silver, 1808 (one bobeche 1809). H: 13-½ in. Courtesy Christie's, New York.

Paul Storr deservedly holds a high place of honor among English silversmiths and is undoubtedly the best known practitioner of the craft during the Regency-George IV period. The candlesticks, while not as lavish as some of his epergnes and presentation pieces, are apogees of English candlestick making of the period. Each candlestick rests on a spreading circular base with a foliate border set against a matte ground. The upper part of each base is chased with acanthus leaves situated below a fluted knop. Each tapered stem has at its lower end a broad band of vertical palmettes, while the upper part is decorated with a band of anthemia which alternate with lilies on a matte ground. Each stem is crowned with a highly articulated, convex band of foliate and floral devices as a knop. The vasiform sockets are partially reeded and broadly banded with a detailed basket weave pattern. The detachable bobeches have ovolo borders. Both bases and bobeches are engraved with crests.

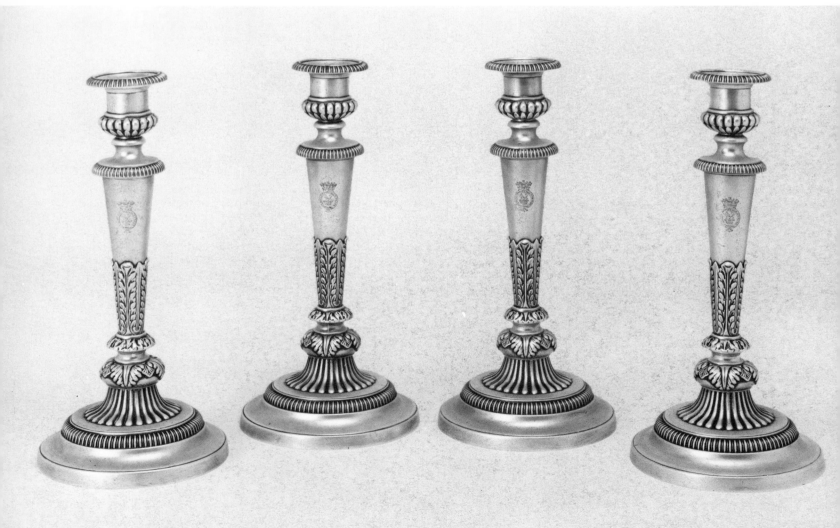

Opposite page:

63. Pair of Table Candlesticks, English (made by Matthew Boulton of Birmingham), Regency style, sterling silver, 1809. H: 14 in. Courtesy Christie's, New York.

While Paul Storr is heralded as the most famous of silversmiths of Regency England, Matthew Boulton's firm was the largest manufacturer of silverplated wares and other elegant metal "toys" in England. Boulton's firm also made fine sterling silver objects as is attested by this pair of candleholders. Each circular base is chased with a band of acanthus foliage with a bold reeded knop above, where each reed is embellished with a small leaf. These small leaves are repeated on the reeds of the vase-shaped candle cups. The tapered stems are plain save at the bottom, where vertical acanthus leaves provide elegant decoration. Both the upper knop and the edge of the detachable bobeches have finely executed foliate borders. Both bobeches and bases bear engraved crests.

64. Set of Four Table Candlesticks, English (made by Matthew Boulton of Birmingham), Regency style, sterling silver, 1817. H: 13-1/8 in. Courtesy Christie's, New York.

This handsome set bears the engraved Royal Badge, Garter and Crown on the upper part of each stem as well as on the detachable bobeches. The stepped, circular bases are treated in that powerful manner associated with the Regency designs of such men as Thomas Hope and George Smith. Here the vertical gadrooning seen on each foot is repeated in a reduced scale at the upper knop and on the edge of the bobeche. Heavy reeding decorates the center of each, while naturalistic acanthus leaves alternate with a stylized foliate device on the lower knop. The lower part of each tapering stem has vertical acanthus leaves as ornamentation in the same manner as the previous set by Boulton. Note too that the reeds decorated with individual leaves appearing on the vase-shaped sockets here are identical to those seen on the previous Boulton set.

65. Set of Four Table Candlesticks, English (made by Paul Storr of London), Regency style, silver-gilt, two made in 1812, two made in 1813. H: 13 in. Courtesy Christie's, New York.

One hesitates to describe this magnificent set as Regency style since it really relates more to the rococo and should perhaps be termed early rococo revival. Each rests on a shaped circular domed base which has been both cast and chased with flowers and foliage sprays within scrolls. The baluster stems are chased with acanthus foliage, flutes and foliate festoons. It is indeed the symmetry and almost neoclassical feeling of that decoration that separates these candlesticks from the eighteenth century rococo and rococo revival that will begin in earnest in British silver during the 1820s. The detachable bobeches are fluted and sit in vase-shaped candle cups chased with foliage and scrolls. The engraved crest and coronet on the bases and bobeches are those of either the Dukes of Abercorn or Hamilton.

66. Pair of Table Candlesticks, (from a set of four), English (made by Joseph Cradock and William K. Reid of London), George IV style, sterling silver, 1824. H: 11 in. Courtesy Christie's, New York.

The rococo revival in English silver manifests itself during the reign of that most taste conscious of British monarchs of the last two hundred years, George IV. This pair of candlesticks was obviously inspired by the work of such eighteenth century masters as George Wickes, Ebenezer Coker and John Cafe, all candlestick specialists. This set is, however, no patent copy of any known eighteenth century set, but rather employs the rococo vocabulary in slightly different ways. Each candleholder begins on a shaped circular base which is cast and chased with four grotesque masks, flowers, foliage and scrolls. Each fluted, baluster stem is chased with flowers on a matte ground and has masks at the shoulders. The candle cups are of the bulbous vase type in a matte finish with an unusual set of four equidistantly placed series of graduated shells. The detachable bobeches have cast masks for decoration.

67. Single Light Candleholder (one of a pair), English, Regency style, giltwood, marble and ormolu, circa 1805-1820. H: 12-5/16 in. W: 4-1/8 in. D: 4-1/8 in. Courtesy Rosedown Plantation and Gardens, St. Francisville, Louisiana.

A modestly clad giltwood putto stands on a circular plinth of the same material, both raised on a square base of white marble. The tapering, spirally twisted torch standard which the putto holds is probably a wire with applied carved gesso. It terminates in a foliate giltwood necking in which an ormolu drip pan is situated. From the drip pan a vase-shaped candle cup with reeded sides rises to a plain bobeche. While this piece lacks the sophistication of detailed execution and the use of materials seen in the candelabrum example by Hopper (p. 125, ill. 177), this piece and its matching companion have a naive charm of their own.

68. Candleholder, English, Neoclassical style, mahogany and gilt brass, circa 1795-1820. H: 8-5/8 in. Private collection.

This candleholder which is missing its shade permits a view of the simple, cylindrical candle cup as well as the shade holder. Refinement is brought to the shade holder by the bold beaded border on its lower edge and the band around its principal element.

70. Two Candle Shades, probably American (Pennsylvania), Neoclassical style, blown flint glass, Left: circa 1780-1810, Right: circa 1810-1835. Left: H: 21-¹³/16 in. Diam. at base: 8 in. Width at bulge: 8-⅝ in. Right: H: 22 in. Diam. at base: 7-³/16 in. Width at bulge: 8-⅞ in. Collection of Anglo-American Art Museum, Louisiana State University, Baton Rouge.

These two undecorated candle shades contrast the earlier and later form of blown shades. The earlier model has a less pronounced baluster shape and its fold-over foot is low. In contrast the later model has a great bulge in its middle and its base is much higher than the pre-1810-made models. A comparison of the right example with the following etched pair will show that these three shades are of the same construction and general configuration. The refinement of the etched decoration makes the succeeding pair both finer and probably a little later in date.

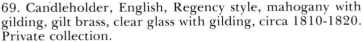

69. Candleholder, English, Regency style, mahogany with gilding, gilt brass, clear glass with gilding, circa 1810-1820. Private collection.

Candleholders with shades to protect the flame from drafts date back into the eighteenth century, but were especially popular during the first half of the nineteenth century. This is a quite spectacular example of the form having a turned mahogany base and baluster-shaped shaft, both of which have been gilded with fern-type fronds. The brass socket which holds both the candle and the shade is decorated with a band of cast cabbage roses and foliage and is edged with downturned leaves. The inverted, waisted bell-shaped hurricane shade is of generous proportions and gilded all over with rosettes situated between borders composed of vertical fern fronds and trailing vines.

71. Pair of Shades, American (possibly Pennsylvania), American Empire style, copper wheel engraved and etched flint glass, circa 1840. H: 25 in. Courtesy Christie's, New York.

In the later form of shades, the central part of the baluster has a more pronounced bulge as is seen here. The etched and engraved designs of swags, stars, garlands and shields are much bolder than the copper wheel engraved shades of the Federal period. American glass houses such as those at Pittsburg were quite capable of producing pieces of this quality by the 1830s.

72. Pair of Candleholders, English, Regency style, ormolu and glass, circa 1820. Courtesy Bernard and S. Dean Levy, Inc., New York. Photo by Helga Photo Studio.

These candleholders merit close scrutiny for full appreciation of the fine quality of the bronze casting and the double gilding. The sockets which hold the cut glass shades have a brightly gilded Greek key motif set against matte finished areas which are striated. The rings of palmettes which is applied to the domed part of the upper base as well as the cabled border are sharp and crisp. The upper face of the square plinth has separately cast and applied ormolu fleurs-de-lys affixed to the matte finished square and ormolu foliate feet with rosette supports. The cylindrical shades with their pair of diaper cut borders and copper wheel cut vertical gouges are seen on many English ormolu, silver and silverplated candleholders from the Regency period.

73. Pair of Candleholders, English, George IV-William IV style, silverplated copper with etched and gilded glass, circa 1820-1835, and circa 1865-1880. H: 20-¾ in. Diam: 5-¾ in. Collection of Frederick Lee Lawson.

Most of the candleholders with hurricane shades, dating from the 1820s forward, have ventilators in the shade holders to admit more oxygen for the proper burning of the candles. The circular bases have lobed or melon-shaped borders and those devices are repeated as knops at the base and head of the columnar stem. The attenuated, inverted, waisted bell-form shades are not original to these candleholders. While they make an acceptable substitute for the broader originals, these shades with their etched and gilded horizontal lines, interlocking diaper pattern and foliate border appear to date from the Victorian period.

74. Set of Three Candlesticks, English (made by "CU" of London), Adam Revival style, sterling silver and glass, 1875. H: 20-¹³/₁₆ in. Diam. of base: 4-¾ in. Collection of Mr. and Mrs. John Callon, Melrose, Natchez, Mississippi.

Inspired by late eighteenth-century models, these candlesticks incorporate those forms with nineteenth-century interpretations of those designs and the technology of the latter century. Each of these candlesticks begins on circular bases whose upper edges are bordered by profuse foliage and interlocking "C" scrolls. These decorations which are studied and executed in a nineteenth-century manner appear three more times on each candlestick—first, on a small concave necking below each upwardly tapering stem, second, as a broad band on the lower part of each stem, and finally on a knop at the head of each stem. The broad flutes appearing on the upper part of the bases and on the upper part of each stem remind one more of the decoration seen on some nineteenth-century argand lamp standards. The vase-formed candle cups are decorated with vertically placed leaves and the ventilated shade holders are made as one with the candle cups. This sort of construction does not occur until about the 1820s. The clear, inverted, waisted bell-shaped shades have assumed more of the form of the late eighteenth and early nineteenth-century examples. They are late nineteenth-century interpretations rather than reproductions. Note that the shoulders are narrower and the flare of the lip a little too pronounced in relation to the earlier examples that have survived with their original shades.

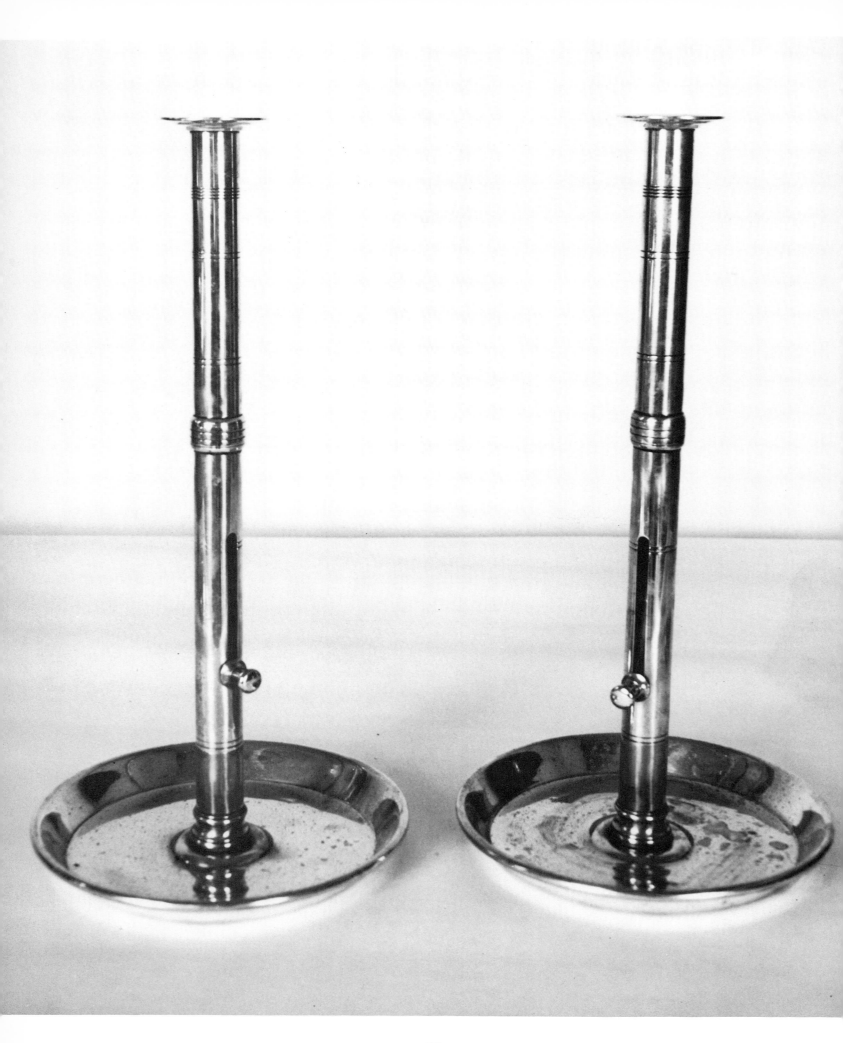

75. Pair of Candlesticks, English, late Georgian style, core cast brass, circa 1800-1850. H: 16-½ in. Courtesy Herbert Schiffer Antiques, West Chester, Pennsylvania.

While called "pulpit" candlesticks in the antique trade, there is little documentation to support an ecclesiastical use of this form. The extra long candles and side pushups to control the exact amount of candle needed probably made these candleholders useful in counting houses, legal firms and other commercial and governmental offices. Decorated with scribed lines which are seen on other Regency to early Victorian models, the earliest possible date of manufacture would be 1800, but the later date would be more likely. The band placed around the center of each stem appears to be a strengthening element for these tall shafts and may hide a joint line. The bases are quite heavy.

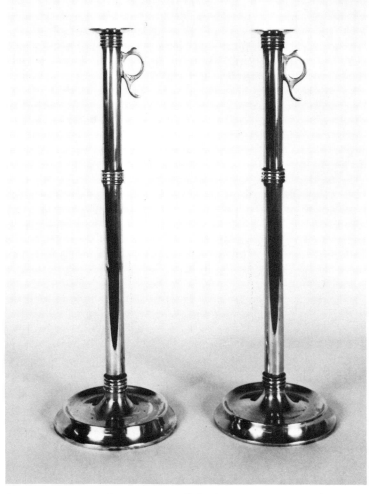

76. Pair of Candlesticks, English, late Georgian style, core cast brass, circa 1800-1850. H: 21 in. Courtesy Herbert Schiffer Antiques, West Chester, Pennsylvania.

This variant on the "pulpit" model has a dished base as opposed to the pan of the previous example. Reeded bands appear at the head and base of the stem and almost two-thirds above the center. The side pushup candle ejectors have looped and hooked handles for easy carrying. Height was obviously the desired effect here since the pushups rise only at the top of the stem.

77. Candlestick (one of a pair), English, William IV-early Victorian style, core cast brass, circa 1830-1860. H: 8-½ in. Diam. 4-½ in. Courtesy James E. Guercio Antiques, Natchez, Mississippi.

This is a very pleasing model employing a low circular base with knop and spool turnings combined with a cylindrical candle cup having an attached flaring bobeche. A pattern such as this one could easily have been manufactured over a thirty year period. This example and its mate exhibit a partially finished bottom and do have the central push ups.

78. Table Candlestick, American (made by Roswell Gleason of Dorchester, Massachusetts), late Neoclassical style, pewter, circa 1820-1845. H: 8-⅜ in. Diam. 4-⅝ in. Courtesy Herbert Schiffer Antiques, West Chester, Pennsylvania.

This extremely handsome candlestick is another fairly typical form of pewter candlestick made by Anglo-Americans from around 1825 to 1845. The plain, circular stepped base is seen on other known candlesticks made by Gleason and other pewterers.

79. Two Pairs of Table Candlesticks, American (shorter outside pair made by Rufus Dunham of Westbrook, Maine), pewter, circa 1837-1860, H: 6-⅛ in.; taller pair unmarked, circa 1820-1865, H: 6-¼ in. American Empire style, pewter. Courtesy Christie's, New York.

The favored general shape of American pewter candlesticks made from the late eighteenth century through the 1860s consists of a circular base joined to a baluster-type stem. After the 1860s, pewter candlesticks were seldom made and pewter fell into disfavor as a material for manufacturing household utensils until the Colonial Revival was well established during the 'teens of the twentieth century.

The two pairs of candlesticks seen here both have the domical bases and heavy baluster stems associated with American pewter made from about 1820 to 1865.

80. Hogscraper Candlestick, English or American, sheet metal, circa 1830-1850. H: 4-¼ in. Diam. of base: 3-¾ in. Courtesy Magnolia Mound Plantation, Recreation and Park Commission, Baton Rouge, Louisiana. Photo by Prather Warren.

The base and shaft of this candlestick look very much like the wooden handled, sheet metal devices used for scraping the bristles from hogs, hence the name for this form of candleholder. This example customarily has a side pushup for the ejection of candle stubs. Most hogscraper candlesticks also have a hook that projects from the lip of the bobeche. This hook was used to attach the candlestick to the back of slat-back chairs or the crest of a windsor chair to get the light at the right height for close work or reading. Frequently these hooks are broken off. This example carries the stamped impression "BATEN_____/1850" on the face of its pushup.

Hogscraper candlesticks were made in great numbers, and while they are associated with colonial America, the majority of them were probably made in Great Britain during the first half of the nineteenth century. Unpublished material gathered by Joe Ruggio of the Rushlight Club indicates that Birmingham, England, was a primary place of this model's manufacture.

81. Pair of Candlesticks, English or American, folk or traditional style, tin and pewter, circa 1840-1860. H: 9-¼ in. Diam. 6-⅛ in. Courtesy of Herbert Schiffer Antiques, West Chester, Pennsylvania.

The trumpet feet and mid drip pans of these candlesticks are almost abstractions of some seventeenth-century candlesticks. Seventeenth-century pieces did not have bobeches at the terminal ends of their stems as is seen here. Both are painted a brownish-black color that is seen on other inexpensive Victorian goods. The one pretense of elegance in these candlesticks is provided by the trefoil-shaped pewter side pushup handles.

82. Candlestick, English, late Neoclassical style, cast iron and brass, circa 1825-1840. H: 9-¾ in. Diam: 4-⅜ in. Courtesy James E. Guercio Antiques, Natchez, Mississippi.

This candlestick and others similar to it imitate in cheaper materials some of the high style forms made in silver, patinated bronze and ormolu. These would have been made for a lower middle-class clientele and the styles might be somewhat *retardataire*. These would have been made for the same people who bought cast iron door knockers for their row houses rather than brass. It is impossible to achieve in iron the refinement of casting that can be had with the more expensive base and precious metals. The casting of the acanthus leaf borders on the circular base and on the lower part of the baluster shaft as well as of the fluting on the stem therefore show imperfections. The same can be said for the vase-formed candle cup's reeded decoration. Interest has been added with the moulded necking of thin brass placed between the candle cup and the stem. The necking between the base and stem has been improperly regilded with radiator paint sometime during this century. The original finish would have been a deep bronze or black paint to simulate patinated bronze and a cheap gilding to convey the idea of ormolu. This type of candlestick does not survive in great numbers and it can be assumed that there were more which perhaps were destroyed during the massive scrap drives of the world wars of the twentieth century.

83. Pair of Candlesticks, English or American, early Victorian style, painted sheet metal, gilt brass and glass, circa 1845. H: 12 in. W: 4-⁹/₁₆ in. D: 4-⁹/₁₆ in. Collection of Mr. and Mrs. Raymond St. Germain.

These candlesticks combine the angularity of the English Regency style with the more florid rococo revival style. The sheet metal elements—square base, cylindrical plinth and columnar stem—are all painted black. Both of the plain cylinders are enriched with gilt bands. This contrasts with the rococo revival style of the foliate bobeches on the gilt brass candle cups. The downturned-leaf type of gilt brass prism ring is also rococo revival and this sort of dished prism ring is seen on Boston-made girandoles as well as English pieces. In a more classical vein are the egg and dart borders seen in the gilt brass borders of the plinth.

84. Pair of Candlesticks, English or American, core cast brass, William IV, circa 1830-1860. H: 7-⁵/₁₆ in W: 3-¾ in. D: 3-¾ in. Collection of Anglo-American Art Museum, Louisiana State University, Baton Rouge. Gift of the Family of the late Professor Charles Coates.

These candlesticks with their well defined beehive elements on the stems are early examples of the use of that decorative motif in brass candlesticks. The squat campana-shaped candle cups are another clue that this pair could date back to 1830. The stepped octagonal base is a form used before the American Civil War. Another sign of the early date for this pair is the relative smoothness of the sand casting seen on the base and the fact that some lathe work was done on the inside of the plinth. Natural silica sand was used until late in the nineteenth century, which provides a smoother casting not possible with the coarse synthetic sand that has been used since that time.

85. Candlestick, English or American, William IV-early Victorian style, core cast brass, circa 1830-1860. H: 10-½ in. W: 4-⅜ in. D: 3-⁷/7 in. Collection of Emily S. Jones. Photo by Jim Zietz.

Literally hundreds of thousands of candlesticks in this model and with slight variations were made from the second quarter through the third quarter of the nineteenth century. The higher foot and bolder shapes of the shaft date this piece possibly as early as the 1830s, as does the rather more careful lathing away of excess brass on the inside of the plinth. The undecorated conical element in the shaft in other models has turnings to suggest a beehive. Later examples invert the cone and are cast with reeds to more effectively convey the beehive concept.

86. Pair of Candlesticks, English or American, William IV-early Victorian style, core cast brass, circa 1830-1860. H: 10-¼ in. W: 4-½ in. D: 4-¹/16 in. Collection of Emily S. Jones. Photo by Jim Zietz.

This model and numerous variations on the pattern began to appear during the William IV period with the advent of larger, more commercial foundries which provided inexpensive goods for the rising English, American and British colonial middle classes. Candlesticks such as these featuring spool elements in their shafts and rising on fairly high stepped bases originated during the second quarter of the nineteenth century. The bolder forms of the overall configuration as well as bases whose undersides exhibit fewer sand casting marks differentiate these from later models and twentieth century reproductions. This pair survives with their original drawn wire candle ejectors which have brass push up buttons in the bases and brass dishes for the candle hidden by the candle cups.

87. Pair of Candlesticks, English, William IV-early Victorian style, core cast brass, circa 1845-1865 H: 10 in. W: 4-¾ in. D: 3-⅞ in. Collection of Emily S. Jones. Photo by Jim Zietz.

Candlesticks employing the inverted beehives and diamond faceted knops as decorative devices in their shafts seem to have debuted during the early Victorian period. The robust, high stepped base and the overall strength of design distinguish this as one of the earlier models employing the beehive and faceted diamond motives. This pair also exhibits less roughness in the finishing of the underside of the base which is also indicative of an early date. Both candlesticks survive with their original central pushups.

88. Three Candlesticks, English or possibly American, William IV-Victorian style, core cast brass, circa 1830-1870. Dimensions L to R: (1) H: 10-¾ in. W: 4-½ in. D: 3-½ in. (2) H: 10 in. W and D: 3-½ in. (3) H: 9 in. W and D: 3-¼ in. Collection of Frederick Lee Lawson.

This is a grouping of the common nineteenth century candlesticks which were used domestically in the tertiary rooms of the upper classes, in secondary rooms of the middle classes and the best rooms of the lower classes as well as in commercial establishments. The extreme left-hand example with its high, moulded octagonal base and bold, bulbous baluster stem with the spool turnings on the upper stem is the earliest of the group. It would date circa 1830-1850. The other two with their tall, narrow candle cups and lower, plainer octagonal bases would date circa 1840-1870.

89. Set of Four Candlesticks, English, William IV-early Victorian style, core cast brass and iron, circa 1830-1860. H: 11-½ in. W. and D: 4-⅜ in. Collection of Anglo-American Art Museum, Louisiana State University, Baton Rouge.

   This handsome set of tall candlesticks is one of the better models dating from the 1830-1860 period. The proportions and relationships of the parts composing these candleholders are excellent. Particularly, the flaring baluster is gracefully handled. The underside of the base of the one candlestick which is turned on its side reveals the rougher core casting and the limited amount of lathe work done on these pre-Civil War-made candleholders. The tangs used to join the shaft to the base are evident, as is the drawn iron rod central candle ejector with its circular iron pushup plate. These ejector rods were frequently run through corks so that they would be stable and not rattle.

90. Two Common Candlesticks (one of each from pairs), English, Victorian style, core cast brass, circa 1840-1870. Left H: 9-¾ in. W and D: 3-⅞ in. Right H: 8-⁹⁄₁₆ in. W: 3-¾ in D: 3-½ in. Collection of Eugene D. Cizek, Ph.D. and Lloyd L. Sensat, Sun Oak House, New Orleans.

Hundreds of thousands of candlesticks in patterns like and similar to these were turned out by foundries in Birmingham, Manchester and other English industrial centers for distribution throughout the British Empire, the United States and Latin America. These were manufactured largely for use by the middle and lower classes in both domestic and commercial situations. The most common base was the plain octagonal or chamfered cornered form seen in both of these examples. The stems come in an array of minor variations on the basic baluster with knops and the beehive pattern. The examples made prior to the American Civil War usually have a slightly higher base and the sand casting is not as rough as those dating from the late 1860s forward.

91. Pair of Candlesticks, American (made in Philadelphia by Cornelius and Baker), sheet brass and iron, circa 1855. H: 12-⅓ in. Diam. 5 in. Courtesy Museum of Rural Life, Louisiana State University, Baton Rouge. Photo by Prather Warren.

These candleholders have coiled iron springs within their sheet brass shafts to force each candle upward to the aperture. The aperture cover known as a candle "saver" helps protect the flame from drafts and keeps the candle from dripping. While the pair at hand bears the applied cast plate of Cornelius and Baker of Philadelphia, the idea of the spring action candleholder originated in England. All the principles seen in this pair are to be seen in the English Palmer patent candle lamps which date back to the early 1840s. This technique of forcing the candle by a coiled spring to a small protected aperture was still in use at the end of the nineteenth century as is seen later in this chapter in the advertisement from the New York firm of Edward Rorke and Company.

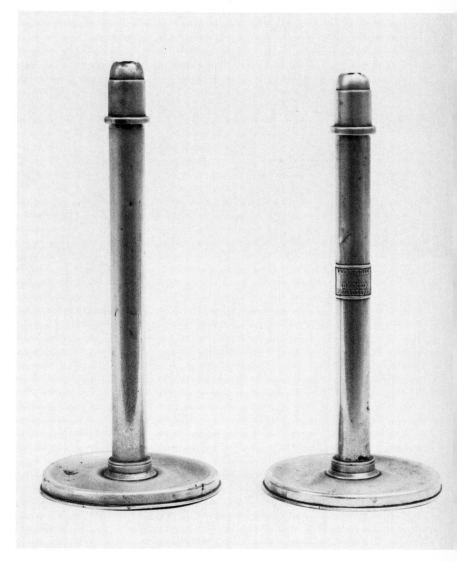

92. Pair of Candlesticks, English, core cast brass, traditional style, circa 1840-1880. H: 8-⅝ in. W: 4-14/ in. D: 4 in. Collection of Eugene D. Cizek, Ph.D. and Lloyd L. Sensat, Sun Oak House, New Orleans.

These candlesticks have the simple straight forward lines that the twentieth century mind associates with the word "Georgian." The heavy core construction and unfinished bases as well as the slightly crude casting of the incised lines of the base point to the Victorian period as the time of this pair's manufacture. Additionally, brass tangs that are a part of the lower shaft join the stems to the bases—a nineteenth century constructional technique. A good number of this model of candlestick have been seen both in Britain and America. The crudeness of the casting is mainly associated with the revival of eighteenth century English and American style, which began about 1870.

93. Three Candlesticks, English, Victorian style, core cast brass, L to R: (1) circa 1840-1860, H: 9-⅝ in. W: 4-¼ in. D: 3-½ in. (2) circa 1883-1900, H: 9-½ in. W and D: 3-½ in. (3) circa 1870-1900, H: 10 in. W and D: 3-¾ in. Collection of Frederick Lee Lawson.

Probably more of the "beehive" model candlesticks have been made than any other pattern in the history of brass founding. The model on the right made before the American Civil War has the bolder proportions and more generous base. On it the beehive on the stem tapers downward. In the second and third examples the beehives taper upward, the overall proportions are more attenuated and the octagonal bases are low. The middle example bears the marks "ENGLAND- /RD2235____" on the face of the foot. The United States Congress required after 1883 that goods imported into the country had to be clearly marked with their place of manufacture. Registry marks appear on English-made goods as early as 1842. This signified that a pattern had been registered with the government and could not be copied. The third candlestick was apparently first used by a Jewish family for religious observances in the home. Its underside is engraved with both the Star of David and an inscription in Hebrew. Let the collector never be deceived into believing that the latter two models shown here were made before 1860. They were terribly common and were used mainly by the middle and lower classes. They are, nonetheless, a pleasant design and are still being made in England, the United States and in India for the Anglo-American market.

94. Three Pairs of Candlesticks, English, late Victorian style, core cast brass, circa 1875-1900. Left pair: "THE/DIAMOND/PRINCESS" H: 10-¾ in. W: 3-⅞ in. D: 4 in.; Center pair: "THE QUEEN of/ DIAMONDS" H: 11-½ in. W: 4-½ in. D: 4-½ in.; Right pair: "THE KING of/DIAMONDS" H: 12-½ in. W: 4-⅝ in. D: 4-⅝ in. Courtesy M. S. Rau Antiques, New Orleans.

Among the most pleasing forms to emerge from the second half of the nineteenth century in English brass candlesticks are the "Diamond" models. "The Diamond Princess" model bears the stamped inscription, "ENGLISH/Rd 38—56" which would indicate that the piece was made after 1883[10] when the United States required that the name of country of manufacture appear on objects imported into that country. The registry number was poorly struck and is therefore incomplete. Registration numbers were, after January 1884, issued to protect particular designs from piracy through registration of the pattern with the London Patent Office. This replaced the system of registration marks used from 1842 through 1883. These candlesticks survive with most of their centrally located, concealed, drawn wire pushups or candle ejectors. Most of these candlesticks have steel pushup buttons and steel candle supports. This change from brass to steel for those internal elements is another characteristic of later models.

95a. Candlestick, English, Georgian Revival style, core cast brass, circa 1870-1900. H: 10-½ in. W and D: 5 in. Courtesy Goudeau Antiques, Baton Rouge, Louisiana. Photo by Prather Warren.

This attractive candlestick falls most properly under the heading of reproduction. Inspired by the Georgian originals in silver, brass or paktong dating from the 1765-1785 period, this model does not possess the seamed stem of the originals and lacks the lathe finishing of the underside of the base. Although the design is excellent, when compared with the eighteenth century-made examples, it will be immediately apparent that this model is both attenuated and more angular than those made in the earlier period. Quite a few of these candlesticks have been seen masquerading as eighteenth century in antique shops both in Britain and America. They are handsome and valuable, but the buyer should not have to pay the price of an eighteenth century example for second period goods.

95b. Underside of Base of Georgian Revival Candlestick

Immediately apparent in this picture are the missing lathe turnings used to finish eighteenth century examples. Note that the original tangs to hold the shaft and base of this candleholder together have been replaced by a modern threaded sleeve. This was done to accommodate wiring when this lighting device was converted to electricity circa 1920.

80

96. Lustre, Anglo-Irish, William IV to early Victorian style, circa 1830-1845. H: 6-¼ in. Diam. 4-¼ in. Collection of Frederick Lee Lawson.

This lustre emerges from the earlier Regency style and indeed its faceted, circular foot and prism ring are no different than those of the Regency. The heavy multi-spool-shaped shaft, however, clearly registers as a design from the William IV or early Victorian periods. The tear drop prisms are hardly different from those of the Regency period.

97. Pair of Candlesticks, American (Pittsburg), late American Empire style, mould blown glass with pewter, circa 1850. H: 9-¾ in. Diam: 5 in. Collection of Craig Littlewood and Craig Maue, Palmyra, New Jersey.

While numerous candlesticks similar to these survive, very few have come down with their original pewter candle sockets. Removable pewter sockets were quite practical for cleaning purposes. The house cleaner did not want to unnecessarily scratch fragile glass with a sharp instrument to remove wax. In the days before hot and cold running water, pouring hot water over wax-covered glass candlesticks might break the glass rather than accomplish the cleaning purpose.

These candlesticks are heavy three-mould blown pieces on circular feet and have hexagonal-shaped domes above, used with six-sided stems and candle cups.

98. Pair of Lustres, probably American with English (?) shades, Victorian style, clear, colored and painted glass and brass, circa 1855. H: 20-⅜ in. Diam. of lip of shade: 5-½ in. Collection of Frederick Lee Lawson.

The hexagonal lobed feet and stems, the lobed prism ring in clear and red stained glass as well as the painted polychrome vignettes, bouquets and gilding appear to originate in eastern Europe. The coffin-shaped prisms are possibly original and are certainly the right scale for the lustres. Coffin-shaped prisms are made even today in Czechoslovakia for the American market. These lustres could well have been made for the Anglo-American market. The shades and their repoussed brass sockets appear contemporary with the candleholders and give every indication of having been together since the 1850s. In design they register as English. Certainly the British made more shades of this type for use throughout the tropical regions of their vast Empire. These candleholders and shades, if this hypothesis is correct, are first-rate examples of an intentional, contemporary assembly of the products of two countries.

99. Pair of Lustres, American or English, early Victorian style, clear glass, circa 1855. H: 9-½ in. Diam. at lip: 4-⅝ in. Collection of the Anglo-American Art Museum, Louisiana State University, Baton Rouge.

Clear flint glass lustres were made in Britain and America. This pair has domical bases with thumb mould borders and moulded baluster-shaped stems. Each lustre has a bowl-shaped bobeche/prism ring which has a scalloped border with diamond overlay pattern on the outside. The prisms are "back-cut Alberts."

Opposite page:

100. Pair of Lustres, probably American, mixture of styles, clear glass, standards date circa 1900-1920, prisms date circa 1855-1870. H: 8-⅝ in. Diam. 5-⅛ in. Collection of the Anglo-American Art Museum, Louisiana State University, Baton Rouge.

These candleholders are a mixture of Regency and Victorian styles as interpreted during the 1900-1920 period. They copy no specific example from the early period and have the flat, attenuated appearance seen in much Edwardian furniture which was inspired by eighteenth and early nineteenth-century examples. In addition to their attenuated appearance, they are very angular. Each base is flat and all of the cut work on the bases, stems and bobeche-prism rings is too sharp. Additionally, there are no wear marks to speak of on the undersides of the bases. The "back-cut Albert" prisms do exhibit some signs of age and appear to be Victorian-made of the 1850 to 1870 period.

83

101. Candlestick, English, Victorian style, marbled pottery, circa 1840-1860. H: 8-½ in. Diam. 4-⅛ in. Courtesy Herbert Schiffer Antiques, West Chester, Pennsylvania.

In the United States almost any pottery that is in a high glaze tobacco juice brown with yellow marbling is called Bennington after the Vermont town which had two potteries specializing in the manufacture of wares in those colors. It was made in great numbers in factories primarily located in the Midwest. Its origin, however, is the Rockingham Works in Yorkshire. The same sort of glazes were produced at the potteries in Leeds and Staffordshire. This candlestick is an unmarked example from one of those northern English potteries. The design is simplicity itself. There is a heavy circular foot with a flared bell-type plinth. A substantial convex knop is the transitional element between the plinth and the upwardly tapering stem. The cylindrical candle cup has an attached rolled bobeche.

102. Four Candlesticks, Chinese Export, porcelain, (left to right - 1) Rose Medallion pattern, circa 1840-1870, H: 6-¼ in. Diam. 3-⅝ in.;2) Pair of blue and white Canton, circa 1820-1840. H: 6-½ in. Diam. 3-¼ in.;3) single blue and white Canton, circa 1820-1840, H: 7-⅞ in. Diam. 4-¼ in.) Courtesy Herbert Schiffer Antiques, West Chester, Pennsylvania.

Among the numerous things made from the earliest period of the China Trade with the West were candleholders. The United States did not enter this trade until the late eighteenth century. The candlesticks made during the nineteenth century whether in blue and white or the newer polychrome rose medallion pattern are usually a variant on a basic trumpet shape. The blue and white Canton examples are usually crudely but charmingly painted with Chinese architecture, willow trees, rocks and the sea or a pond.

104. Pair of Candleholders, American (made by Henry N. Hooper and Co., Boston), plain lacquered brass and glass, circa 1850-1868. H: 10-½ in. W: 5-¾ in. Collection of Craig Littlewood and J. Craig Maue, Palmyra, New Jersey.

This is a most important pair of candleholders because they are labeled in an arc, "HENRY N. HOOPER & CO." They document the Boston manufacture of candle cups that resemble a partially opened bud and prism rings having the downturned leaf which alternates with the downturned grape cluster. The sumptuous foliate and triangular base in the highest of rococo revival taste suggests the 1850s or 1860s for the date of their manufacture. Henry Hooper and Company was in business under that name and style from 1833 through 1868 and manufactured all sorts of lighting devices and bells. The company were also copper dealers. While not illustrated in the 1858 Hooper catalogue as candleholders, the foot and plinth are shown as a lamp.

103. Candlestick, English, Renaissance Revival style, stoneware, circa 1870-1890. H: 8-¼ in. Diam: 3-⅞ in. Courtesy James E. Guercio Antiques, Natchez, Mississippi.

This is a good example of the kind of simple columnar candlesticks that the English potteries were producing and which utilized decorative patterns borrowed from the renaissance. This is especially true of the trailing rinceaux and shamrock bands seen on this candlestick. The two quatrefoil borders in tan, red and black express the delight continually taken by the English in the Gothic style. The beige ground of this candlestick provides an interesting foil for bluish shamrocks on black grounds and gilded rinceaux.

105. Two Candlesticks, both probably American, Rococo Revival style, (left cast iron and brass, H: 11-¼ in. W: 5-¼ in. D: 5-¼ in.; right pot metal, H: 10-⅞ in. W: 5-⅓ in. D: 5-¼ in.) circa 1855-1870. Courtesy James E. Guercio Antiques, Natchez, Mississippi.

These models are extremely rococo revival in design and within the capacity of American mid-nineteenth century iron and zinc foundries to produce. Both have pierced triangular plinths raised on three scrolling feet. The cast iron example features the face of a bearded man set against a striated ground and framed with "S" scrolls. There is a brass necking between the base and the separately cast stem. The stem is a baluster with foliate devices at the bottom and upper portions. The downturned foliate wax pan is a separate casting, as is the hexagonal candle cup. The candle cup's six panels frame a rosette and some foliage per panel. The piece terminates with a detachable, serrated leaf bobeche in brass.

The pot metal or zinc candlestick shows traces of its original patinated bronze finish. Grape leaves, grape clusters and vines form just about everything on this candlestick. Zinc has a low melting point, making it much easier to cast. While in the florid rococo style favored by Henry N. Hooper and Co. of Boston, this could have been made by a foundry such as the J. W. Fiske firm in New York. Fiske made castings in both iron and zinc. The candlestick is missing its bobeche which also would have reflected the vintage theme of the piece.

106. Candlestick, American or European, Rococo Revival style, gilded pot metal (zinc) and gilt brass, circa 1860-1870. H: 9 in. W: 5-½ in. D: 5-¼ in. Courtesy Dornsife Collection.

Without makers' marks it is almost impossible to tell whether a candlestick such as this one was made in Britain, France or the United States. This piece was probably a part of a larger garniture set. The use of pot metal in the fabrication of high-quality goods was a well accepted practice, particularly in the United States. That material was always gilded or bronzed on high-style pieces such as this one. The three-sided base is pierced and is raised on three scrolling feet which contain a shield. Swirling "C" scrolls and shells set against a horizontally striated ground and terminated by a beaded border complete the plinth. This supports the stem composed of a young boy in eighteenth-century garb set in bocage with cabbage roses. The rest of the stem is a scrolling "T" shape which rises from the boy's back. The candle cup is actually cylindrical with leafage projecting from its lower edge, while the sides are decorated with asymmetrical shields. The bobeche is cast brass and has a foliate border.

107. Two Pairs of Candlesticks, probably American, Renaissance Revival style, brass, circa 1875-1895. L to R dimensions: H: 6-5/8 in. W: 5 in. D: 4 in.; H: 5-7/8 in. W: 3-1/4 in. D: 3 in. Courtesy Lambdin Collection.

The first pair which features female busts wearing helmets would probably have been regarded as "Neo Grec" in style at the time of manufacture. Aside from the busts and the anthemion borders on the sides of the candle cups, the rest of each fixture is eclectic. The flattish scrolling element that serves each piece as a stem is renaissance revival with rococo revival overtones. The base with its "C" scrolls is definitely in the rococo revival fashion.

More purely renaissance revival in pattern are the other pair which feature superbly cast griffins as the base for each piece. A console-shaped stem rises from each griffin's head to support a scalloped wax pan and an urn-form candle cup having a foliate border. The undecorated bobeches are detachable.

108. Candlestick, probably American, Renaissance Revival style, bronze, late nineteenth century. H: 7-7/8 in. W: 2-3/4 in. D: 6-1/4 in. Collection of Frederick Lee Lawson.

This is a simpler, less well articulated model of the griffin candleholder. The casting is not as sharp as the previous model. Nor does this piece have the elegance of design or the commanding presence of the previous pair. This candleholder is rather straightforward. An undecorated stem rises from the griffin's head to support a wax pan bordered with cabochons and an urn-shaped candle cup. The candle cup is missing its bobeche.

109. Pair of Piano Candlesticks, American, Renaissance Revival style, brass and lead, circa 1880-1900. H: 5 in. W: 8-¾ in. Diam. of base: 5 in. Collection of Mr. and Mrs. John Callon, Melrose, Natchez, Mississippi.

Grand scrolling branches decorated in the foliate and gouge work of the period spring from circular bases with six paneled plinths. The bases are weighted with lead. The wax pans have a "C" scroll border and the candle cups have acanthus leaf borders in high relief and plain detachable bobeches.

110. Pair of Candlesticks, English or American, Renaissance Revival style, core cast and spun sheet brass, circa 1865-1910. H: 11-¼ in. Diam. at base: 4-¹³/₁₆ in. Collection of Emily S. Jones. Photo by Jim Zietz.

Rather light-weight candlesticks featuring domical bases with cylinder-like shafts accentuated with central bold knops have been popular for use in the church ever since the mid-nineteenth century. This pair, however, was intended for domestic use. The campana-shaped candle cups rise from broad bobeches which were originally fitted with glass shades.

Polished Brass Candlesticks.

No. 5478.
Height, 7 inches.

No. 5479.
Height, 6¼ inches.

No. 5480.
Height, 5¾ inches.

No. 5481.
Height, 6 inches.

No. 5482.
Height, 6¼ inches.

No. 5483.
Height, 7¾ inches.

No. 5484.
Height, 9 inches.

No. 5035.
6, 7, 8 and 10 inches.

No. 5278.
SPRING CANDLESTICK.

No. 5485.
COMBINATION
SPRING CANDLESTICK
AND SHADE HOLDER.
Spring in Tube raises Candle.
Height, 9½ inches.

No. 5034.
Height, 12 inches.

No. 5277.
SUN CANDLESTICK

111. Page from the Catalogue of Edward Rorke and Co. of New York, circa 1890. Courtesy The Athenaeum of Philadelphia's Dornsife Collection, Philadelphia, Pennsylvania.

    All of the candlesticks seen on this page can be found throughout the United States. Those on the upper row are made of heavy core cast brass, while the second and third rows are made for the most part in sheet brass. Rarely used in the latter part of the twentieth century, but most popular up through the mid-1930s, were the combination spring-action candlestick and shade holder. No. 5485 illustrates the model made by Rorke and Company. The shades for these devices are usually pierced and frequently have fringes. They are perhaps seen more often in plated silver rather than plain brass.

112. Chamberstick, English, Neoclassical style, pewter, circa 1780-1800. H: 2-¾ in. W: 6-¾ in. Diam. 5-⅝ in. Courtesy Herbert Schiffer Antiques, West Chester, Pennsylvania.

Since this unmarked chamberstick was acquired in Britain, British manufacture is suggested. It is austere in the cleanness of its lines. The only decoration is the beaded border of the low dish which supports the vase-shaped candle cup and the simple loop-type handle. The handle has a socket for a now-missing snuffer.

113. Two Pan Handle Chambersticks, English or Dutch, traditional or folk style, sheet brass, copper and wire, circa 1800. Dimensions: (circular base) H: 3-¼ in. Diam. 7 in. D: 12 in.; (oval base) H: 1-⁹⁄₁₆ in. W: 7-¾ in. D: 10-¾ in. Courtesy Herbert Schiffer Antiques, West Chester, Pennsylvania.

A considerable number of these sheet brass chambersticks have been found in northern Europe and Britain. Both of these candlesticks have pierced galleries whose upper edge is rolled over an iron wire. Each has a fairly thin pan-type handle with a decorative pierced finial which could also be used for hanging the fixtures out of the way when not in use. The round-based chamberstick has an engraved scalloped line on its inside which is seen on English and Dutch waiters of the 1760-1810 period. The thinness of the brass and the use of the wire support ring indicate that these chambersticks date from the end of the eighteenth or early nineteenth century.

114. Two Chambersticks, L to R 1) English, Neoclassical style, core cast brass, circa 1790-1825, H: 4-¾ in. W: 6-¾ in. Diam. 6-¼ in.; 2) possibly American, Victorian style, sheet brass, circa 1860-1880. H: 2 in. Diam. 4-½ in. Courtesy Lambdin Collection.

The earlier fixture has a plain dish to which is riveted and soldered a handsome flying handle complete with a thumb piece and a detachable conical snuffer. The shaft is baluster shaped and has a knop handle for its side pushup candle ejector.

The Victorian candlestick is made of thin sheet brass. It has a pronounced dome in the center of its dish which supports a short cylindrical stem candle cup. The loop handle is made from brass stamped in an ornate Victorian foliate pattern. Even with the advent of oil fixtures and later gas fixtures during the nineteenth century, the use of candles was not entirely abandoned, especially in rural areas and in more modest town houses.

115. Chamberstick (one of a pair) English (made in London by W.S., probably William Stroud), Neoclassical style, sterling silver, 1807. H: 3-½ in. Courtesy Christie's, New York.

Chambersticks like most candlesticks were made in materials ranging from the basest of materials to silver. In large multi-storied houses, there would frequently be a small table at the foot of the staircase holding several chambersticks for use in guiding both residents and guests to their rooms. This is an especially pleasing model having a shaped circular base enriched with a gadrooned border and an engraved coat of arms. A scroll handle with a foliate thumbpiece rises from the base and holds a conical detachable extinguisher which is gadrooned. The candle cup is vase-shaped and decorated with reeds. The detachable bobeche is gadrooned.

116. Pair of Chambersticks, American (made by Obadiah Rich of Boston), American Empire style, coin silver, circa 1832. H: 2-⅝ in. Courtesy Christie's, New York.

Pre-Civil War chambersticks are uncommon in American-made silver, making this pair doubly rare. These bear the mark of their maker, "O. RICH BOSTON" on the underside of their bases. They are engraved with the contemporary presentation inscription, "Abbie from Danforth." The dished, circular bases are scalloped and support spool and knop-type shafts and vase-shaped candle cups.

117. Pair of Chambersticks, English (marked on underside "GRIFFITH'S PATENT"), folk or traditional style, tin and brass, circa 1800-1830. H: 4-¾ in. Diam: 5-¼ in. D: 5-⅝ in. Courtesy Herbert Schiffer Antiques, West Chester, Pennsylvania.

Many North Americans tend to forget that simple objects fashioned in tin are not unique to the New World. Britain, the founder of the Industrial Revolution, was busy producing inexpensive goods for home use and export to its colonies, former colonies and the world at large. These plain chambersticks with their shallow dishes and domical plinths are given character through the limited use of polished brass. The brass components are the knob handles of the side pushup candle ejectors and the loop handles which pierce the side of each dish before being riveted to each dish. The right fixture has a socket soldered to its side to receive a now-missing snuffer.

118. Chamberstick, English (marked on underside "LOVERIDGE & Co./H.W. HAMPTON") folk or tradition style, tin, wire and pewter, circa 1840-1860. H: 5 in. Diam: 8-¼ in. Courtesy Herbert Schiffer Antiques, West Chester, Pennsylvania.

This pleasant lighting device, with its deep dish, loop handle, conical snuffer on chain and shell-shaped pewter side push up, is painted black. American tinsmiths rarely combined pewter with tin and the very English-sounding name of the company and its location assure an English origin for this chamberstick.

119. Chamberstick, American, folk or traditional style, tin, circa 1840. H: 4-¾ in. D: 5-¼ in. Diam. 5-⅛ in. Courtesy of Herbert Schiffer Antiques, West Chester, Pennsylvania.

This unpainted tin chamberstick with its low dish, very simple loop handle applied to the dish's side and the tin handle for the candle ejector appears to be the work of an American tinsmith.

120. Chamberstick, American, folk or traditional style, tin, circa 1820-1860. H: 3-¼ in. W: 5 in. Diam. 4-¼ in. Courtesy Herbert Schiffer, West Chester, Pennsylvania.

This ordinary candlestick was modeled on finer examples in brass dating back to the mid-eighteenth century. The deep bases of the earlier models have removable dish tops which provided access to the flint, steel and tinder. Here the tin cylindrical base with its pair of concave decorative bands only supports a cylindrical candle cup decorated with three of the same type of bands. A loop handle completes the piece.

121. Pair of Traveling Chambersticks, English (made by W.W. and F.D. of London), Victorian style, sterling silver, 1871. Extended H: 4-⅛ in. W: 3-½ in. Courtesy Christie's, New York.

This pair is perhaps the ultimate word in silver traveling chambersticks. Housed in a rectangular box with ovolo corners are two hinged thumbpieces and hinged lower shafts. The cylindrical principal parts of the shafts are detachable and contain spring actions to force the candles to the small protected apertures.

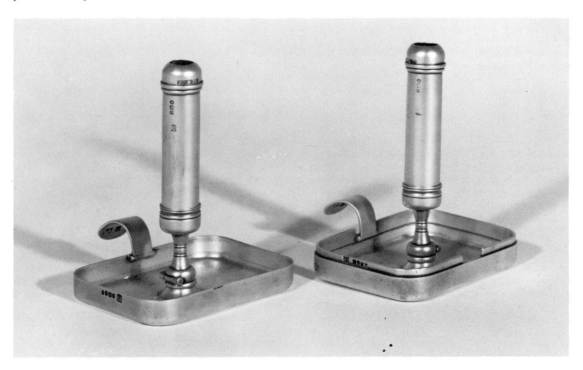

122. Pair of Extinguishers and Snuffer-on-Tray, English, Neoclassical style, painted tin, circa 1800-1825. H: 3-½ in. W: 6-½ in. D: 3-¼ in. Courtesy Herbert Schiffer Antiques, West Chester, Pennsylvania.

Trimming the wicks of tallow candles was essential in order to keep them from guttering. In the eighteenth and early nineteenth centuries, the scissor-like devices were called snuffers and were intended to trim the wicks, not extinguish the candles. The conical devices with ring handles were the extinguishers. In modern parlance, all of these devices are referred to as snuffers.

This set with a pair of extinguishers and a special sleeve mounted on the tray for the snuffer is uncommon. The survival of most of the original black enamel, gilded pin stripes and the attractive vermicelli border make this example all the more desirable.

124. Wax Jack, English (Sheffield), Neoclassical style, silverplate on copper, circa 1795-1820. H: 5 in. W: 4-½ in. D: 3 in. Courtesy Lambdin Collection.

This fine example of Sheffield plated work has a shaped harp with screw to hold the coiled wax taper. The harp's edge and the rectangular burner element are reeded. The rectangular base has ovolo corners and its edge is gadrooned.

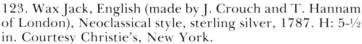

123. Wax Jack, English (made by J. Crouch and T. Hannam of London), Neoclassical style, sterling silver, 1787. H: 5-½ in. Courtesy Christie's, New York.

Wax jacks were made in silver as early as the late seventeenth century. They are also made in brass and in silverplate on copper. Made primarily for use on desks, more wax jacks made during the late eighteenth to early nineteenth century are seen. The wax jack is actually a wax taper coiled around a spindle. The taper, passing through a cylindrical box in this case, made controlling the flame easier. In addition to the control of the flame provided by this system, considerably less wax had to be used than in regular candlesticks.

The example shown here has a circular dish with a reeded border supporting a reeded harp-like element which is also reeded. That component holds the reeded drum through which the wax taper passes for burning. This piece also possesses a handsome cast scroll handle decorated with an acanthus leaf and the handle holds a conical snuffer which is chained to a ring applied to the harp.

126. Wax Jack, English, William IV to early Victorian style, cast and stamped sheet brass, circa 1830-1845. H: 6-5/8 in. W. to handle: 4-3/4 in. Diam. of base: 3-5/8 in. Courtesy James E. Guercio Antiques, Natchez, Mississippi.

This example is a slightly newer variation on the previous model. The photograph does not do justice to the vignettes featuring a paddle wheel ocean-going steamship, a railway locomotive and farming symbols framed in oval cartouches. The styles of the steamship and locomotive are not of the earliest type and provide evidence that wax jacks were being made as late as the opening of the Victorian era. The vignettes alternate with intertwined cornucopias. These masculine themes would indicate that this lighting device was originally intended for use in a commercial office or on the desk of a gentleman's library.

125. Wax Jack, English, Regency style, brass, circa 1810. H: 4-3/4 in. W. to handle: 3-5/8 in. Diam. of base: 3-1/4 in. Courtesy Herbert Schiffer Antiques, West Chester, Pennsylvania.

The simplicity of the principle of the wax jack is readily apparent in this example which does not have a wax taper coiled on its shaft. A wishbone-like device holds the conically-shaped burner and both of these elements are placed horizontally. The base and thumb handle are of heavy stamped brass. The base is dished and bordered with a trailing design composed of a cabbage rose on a foliate stem alternating with lilies of the valley. Other foliate devices enrich the handle. The urn-shaped screw cap finial holding the wishbone element to the stem has the refinement of a cabled border on its knop.

127. Pair of Three Light Candelabra, French, Louis XVI style, patinated bronze, ormolu, alabaster, and colored marble, circa 1785. Courtesy Nesle, Inc., New York. Photo by Helga Photo Studio.

Made near the end of the reign of Louis XVI, this pair of candelabra represents the apogee of the restrained elegance that characterizes the style. Each candelabrum rests on a square colored marble base. This provides the perfect contrast for the alabaster drum decorated with the beaded and milled ormolu as well as the chains and tassles arranged in swags. The rich bronze god and goddess of love are posed in graceful complimentary positions to support horn-pattern shafts out of which the attenuated branches issue. A proper amount of foliage and swags of chains, however, provide a horizontal foil for the overall verticality of the piece. The economy of decoration, which occurs in the *Directoire* period that follows, frequently allows the attenuated verticality to dominate the composition in a not entirely pleasant way.

128. Pair of Three Light Candelabra, French, Consular style, patinated bronze and ormolu, circa 1800. Courtesy Nesle, Inc., New York. Photo by G. Barrows.

The delicacy of the classically scrolled branches with bell flower pendents and the attenuated campana-shaped urn from which the branches grow harken back to the styles of Louis XVI and the *Directoire* as does the overall attenuated nature of the piece. The spread eagle is a precursor of the sumptuous imperial eagle to come. The inventive minds and hands of French metalsmiths, even during those unstable days, are apparent in the charming way in which each figure of a vestal virgin both supports an urn on her head and maintains the urn's balance with patinated sashes which are tied to each handle. That effective contrast of materials continues on the patinated bronze drum-shaped podium which is decorated with an applied ormolu frieze of neoclassical figures and the whole drum is raised on a square base of ormolu.

130. Pair of Four Light Candelabra, French, First Empire style, patinated bronze and ormolu, circa 1805-1810. Courtesy Nesle, Inc., New York. Photo by Helga Photo Studio.

This exuberant pair of candelabra exhibits several decorative devices preferred by the French of this period. Here fully clothed winged figures of Nike in patinated bronze perch lightly on ormolu spheres. Each figure holds two pair of ormolu cornucopia-shaped branches. One pair terminates in a flame device which is capped by a flat, octagonal bobeche while others have the more usual circular candle cups decorated with palmettes. The patinated bronze plinth is decorated with ormolu cupids reaching for stars, anthemia and dragons, all raised on winged griffin legs. The conforming hexagonal base with concave sides was widely used in the First Empire and Charles X periods. The figures here are based on designs made by Pierre-Philippe Thomire (1751-1843), the famed Parisian bronze founder.

129. Pair of Five Light Candelabra, French, First Empire style, patinated bronze and ormolu, circa 1805-1810. Courtesy Nesle, Inc., New York. Photo by Helga Photo Studio.

Art was used extensively to legitimatize the empire of Napoleon I largely through relating early nineteenth century France to Imperial Rome. Nowhere is this better seen than in the metalwork. These candelabra exceed in grandeur and quality much of the fine metalwork done during the *ancien regime*. Here the goddess Minerva bears most of her attributes as a goddess of war. The patinated bronze figures wear ormolu helmets and carry ormolu laurel wreaths to crown the victors. The elegantly crafted ormolu shafts held by each figure do not terminate in spearheads, but are crowned with anthemia-decorated, cornucopia-shaped branches. The podium bases bear military trophies, helmets and masks, as well as a somewhat more difficult to interpret scene on the face of each plinth. Both plinths display the winged horse Pegasus, but each horse is ridden by a putto rather than a man. One putto holds aloft the caduceus of Mercury while the other brandishes a weapon aloft.

131. Six Light Candelabrum (one of a pair), French, First Empire style (based on a model by Pierre Philippe Thomire), patinated bronze and ormolu, circa 1810. H: 37-¾ in. W: 14-½ in. Courtesy New Orleans Museum of Art. Photo by Sidney Liswood.

This candelabrum and its mate carry forth the theme of the triumphant Nike acting as the main shaft for the fixture. Standing on tip toes, on a sphere, and wearing one of the thin neoclassical gowns favored during the Empire period, she raises aloft a bowl of ormolu fruit. From apertures in the fruit, five cornucopia-type branches and one central foliate trumpet rise. The candle cups are cylindrical. There is a double stepped square foot which supports the drum-shaped plinth of patinated bronze. Against that background an ormolu band consisting of winged female figures holding garlands has been placed, the perfect compliment to the Nike figure. This candelabrum also makes a statement about New Orleans collecting taste during the late nineteenth and early twentieth centuries. This candelabrum and its mate were collected by the New Orleans Museum of Art's first benefactor, Isaac Delgado. There was an Empire Revival during the last forty years of the nineteenth century in France and this interest was reflected in New Orleans, perhaps America's most Francophile city. Mr. Delgado gave the pair of candelabra to the Museum in 1912.

133. Pair of Two Branch Candelabra, French, First Empire (Egyptian Revival), patinated bronze and ormolu, circa 1800-1810. H: 20 in. W: 5 in. Courtesy Nesle, Inc., New York. Photo by Helga Photo Studio.

These First Empire candelabra featuring Nubian black-amoors as standards offer a vivid contrast between the new Napoleonic style and the more delicate neoclassicism of the Louis XVI clock of circa 1780. The blackamoors in pati-nated bronze are accentuated with ormolu eyes, necklaces and especially wonderful kilts having betasseled ropes. The dark bronze plinth is spool-shaped and its middle is bright-ened with an ormolu gouge work band. A tripod of ormolu lion feet supports the circular base. Each Nubian holds two of the ormolu pattern branches with spiral fluting.

Opposite page:
132. Three Light Candelabrum (of a set of four), French, First Empire style, patinated bronze and ormolu, circa 1810. H: 23-½ in. W: 9-¾ in. D: 6-½ in. Courtesy Hermann-Grima House, New Orleans.

This exciting set of fixtures raises female figures on taper-ing hexagonal plinths—the principal faces of which are dec-orated with applied ormolu amphorae framed in classical fo-liage. The female fixture with her skirt pinned up holds a pair of scrolling, horn-like branches which are connected to her lips. A central ormolu shaft with a candle cup rises from her head.

134. Clock with Campanion Four Light Candelabra, French, First Empire, patinated bronze and ormolu, circa 1805-1815. Courtesy Nesle, Inc., New York. Photo by Helga Photo Studio.

The concept of having mantel and commode garnitures composed of a clock flanked by candleholders or cassolettes dates from the 1760s and could have originated either with Robert Adam in England or in Louis XVI's France. It is, however, in the nineteenth century that the garniture reaches its apogee in all western countries.

Here the round-faced Paris-made clock is suspended from the litter bearing a seated Empire-attired couple and their dog executed in ormolu. The litter is carried on the shoulders of patinated bronze blackamoors who wear elegant skirts of ormolu palmettes. The flanking candelabra feature bare-breasted female Nubians raised on cylindrical plinths in patinated bronze which are enriched with an applied ormolu anthemion. Each caryatid supports a single candle cup in the shape of a neoclassical urn. From the urn springs the rather Egyptianesque patinated bronze branches with their lotus-like candle cups.

Opposite page:

135. One of a Pair of Ten Branch Candelabra, French, First Empire style, ormolu, circa 1810-1815. H: 21 in. Courtesy Nesle, Inc., New York. Photo by Helga Photo Studio.

This exquisitely cast model was intended for use on a mantel or on a pier table or anywhere that it would not be seen in the round. There are no arms on the back. The stepped base and square plinth embellished with laurel wreaths, egg and dart and bead and reel act as the support for the reeded column which terminates in a Corinthian capital. The lower section of the capital is embellished in the best First Empire manner with various types of palmettes and a band of rosettes. Graduated cornucopia form branches in two tiers which complete the piece. The lower branches are embellished with foliate scrolls.

136. One of a Pair of Eight Light Candelabra, French, First Empire style, patinated bronze and ormolu, circa 1805-1810. Courtesy Nesle, Inc., New York. Photo by Helga Photo Studio.

Late eighteenth and early nineteenth century Europe, especially France and Britain, experienced a limited revival of the Egyptian style in architecture and the decorative arts. The candelabrum illustrated basically veneers a little detail of what a Napoleonic bronze founder thought Egyptian on the usual classical forms. The semi-nude figure is really based on Greco-Roman models but her hair and necklace have been done in the Egyptian style. The principal identifiable Egyptian inspired element, however, is the frontal that drops from below her breasts to the hem of her gown and is embellished with pseudo-hieroglyphics. In two of the upper four branches there is one more subtle nod to Egypt in the pair of hawks, presumed to represent the god Horus. The arrangement of all the ormolu branches is in a fine graduated neoclassical manner. The patinated bronze plinth has applied ormolu masks and the corners are supported by ormolu griffins. The rectangular plinth has an octagonal bronze base whose principal sides are concave and whose corners are chamfered. The base is raised on four ormolu bun feet of a type frequently seen on French clocks of the First Empire and later periods.

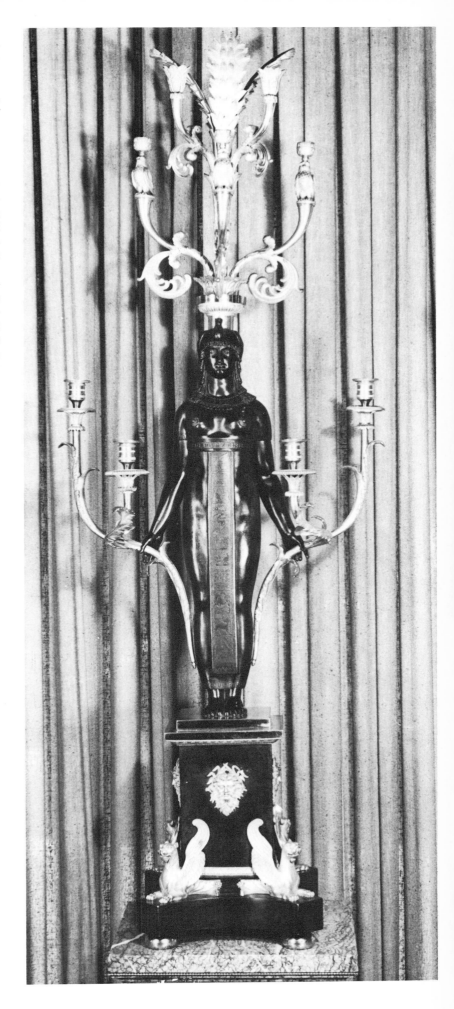

137. Pair of Five Light Candelabra, French, First Empire style, patinated bronze and ormolu, circa 1810-1815. Courtesy Nesle, Inc., New York. Photo by Helga Photo Studio.

The full vocabulary of the First Empire style is employed in this handsome set of mantel or pier table candelabra. The concave, hexagonal feet are embellished with beribboned laurel wreathes and trophies featuring arrows. Each triangular plinth is supported by three Assyrian winged lions, while the bas reliefs on the sides depict Cupid. The upper corners of the plinth feature neoclassical rams' heads. The tapered, patinated column rises from an interesting three-footed support with acanthus leaves. Three sets of two classical females in bas relief ormolu each hold laurel wreathes and intertwine their other arms to hold up a torch in a band around the middle of the column. Two graduated tiers of horn-shaped branches spring from the upper part of the column. The lower ones are enriched with masks of First Empire ladies wearing double chokers of pearls and upturned foliage which goes down two branches from their necks. Each of the candelabra has a neoclassical flame finial.

138. Two Pairs and One Single Candelabra, French, Outer pair First Empire style, circa 1805-1815; Center single, Charles X, circa 1820-1830; Smaller pair, Louis Philippe style, circa 1840-1850, patinated bronze and ormolu. Courtesy Nesle, Inc., New York. Photo by Helga Photo Studio.

These examples provide a study in the evolution of style in French candelabra from the opening of the nineteenth century to midcentury. The earliest set represents the best in First Empire taste. Here the patinated bronze figure of Nike standing with her toes on an ormolu sphere which originated with Pierre-Philippe Thomire is combined with the basket of ormolu fruit from which the branches rise. The basket of fruit design can be credited to Jean-Demosthene Dugoure (1749-1825)[12] on the basis of a watercolor attributed to him in the collection of the Musee des Arts Decoratifs, Paris. The typical horn type of branch is employed for the five horizontal arms, each of which terminates in cylindrical candle cups decorated with a diapered band. The central vertical branch is like a palm tree and is crowned with a foliate candle cup. The patinated bronze, drum-shaped plinth has applied ormolu swags running from neoclassical tripod stands to bas relief Nikes. The diaphanous quality achieved by the founder in the sculptures of Nike in the round and in the bas reliefs on the drum are high watermarks of the First Empire.

A little heavier in feeling, but crisply cast, is the Charles X five branch candelabrum which rests on a hexagonal base with concave sides. The patinated bronze and ormolu base is the springboard for the tripod of lion's legs that functions as the support for a foliate plinth and a tapered, fluted column. The column has a triple capital—the first one of vertical ormolu palmettes. The second is made of patinated bronze rosettes and leaves. The third capital is crowned by a stylized ormolu Corinthian model. From that capital the five patinated bronze horn-shaped branches rise, each having an anthemion pendent and terminating in a cylindrical ormolu candle cup. The central vertical branch is crowned by a larger ormolu candle cup composed of splayed palmettes.

The smaller pair of three branch candelabra complete the stylistic survey. While in idea they are very similar to the First Empire pair, in execution, however, they fall far short of the standards of excellence established by the earlier pair. The Nikes' dresses lack the articulation seen in the earlier works and the figures themselves do not have the grace and poise of balance on their spheres. The octagonal plinth is basically classical and has Roman torches set in niches on the chamfered corners. The pseudo-eighteenth century figure in bas relief on the facade of each plinth bears a relationship to the torches on the Nikes. The branches present a highly inventive aspect of these fixtures, but one that is not complimentary to the rest of the design. Scrolling branches which terminate in eagle head support floral candle cups are beyond rococo revival and are real proto art nouveau. These candelabra are an example of nineteenth century eclecticism that is not totally successful.

139. Plateau with Three Four Light Candelabra, French, First Empire style, ormolu and St. Louis cut glass, circa 1805-1810. Courtesy Nesle, Inc., New York. Photo by Helga Photo Studio.

The dining table plateau is a form that can be credited to eighteenth-century France. This example is a tour de force of design, combination of materials and craftsmanship. Each candelabrum rises from a rectilinear podium-type plinth whose face is embellished by an applied lyre with supports. Baluster-shaped shafts of diaper pattern cut glass rise from each plinth and combine with ormolu neckings decorated with palmettes and bead and reel motives. The cornucopia-type branches issue from an ormolu capital at the head of each cut glass baluster. A central element also rises from the capital and terminates in a faceted ovoid glass finial. The bezel holding the circular mirror base has a decorative band of overlapping rosettes—a device originating in First Empire France. The gallery is perhaps the most spectacular feature of this grand piece. Antefix-shaped pieces of St. Louis cut glass alternate with circular faceted "jewels" of glass framed in cast ormolu borders of rosettes.

140. Two Light Candelabrum (one of a pair), French *Restauration* style, clear glass, amber glass and ormolu, circa 1820. H: 23-½ in. W: 15 in. D: 6 in. Collection of Rosedown Plantation and Gardens, St. Francisville, Louisiana.

John W. Keefe, the Curator of Decorative Arts at the New Orleans Museum of Art which owns the well-known Billups Glass Collection, suggests that the clear glass is likely to have been made at the St. Louis Glass House. In his opinion the amber colored prisms could very likely have been made in Bohemia for the French market. Both the glass and metalwork of this fixture and its mate are spectacular. They represent a curious blending of the Apollo and sunburst symbol of royal Bourbon France with the neo-classical lyre and griffins more associated with Napoleon's Empire. Spiral twists are seen in the bobeche which is a part of the candle cup and on the sides of the candle cup proper and on the principal prism rings. The circular base and the edges of both the prism rings and bobeches are serrated. The secondary sunburst composed of amber prisms fanning out behind the ormolu sunburst is one of the most notable features of this striking pair of candleholders.

141. Pair of Six Light Candelabra, French, First Empire style, Vieux Paris porcelain and ormolu, circa 1810. H: 28 in. W: 12 in. Courtesy Nesle, Inc., New York. Photo by Helga Photo Studio.

This pair of candelabra has been turned for the purposes of this photograph to show the central candle socket; but in use on a mantel or pier table, the set would have faced the other way. With the exception of the candle branches and cups, which are made entirely of ormolu, the rest of the candelabrum alternates between ormolu and porcelain. From the square ormolu base a drum-shaped porcelain plinth rises and is framed by palmette-decorated ormolu bezels. All the gilt paint decoration is in the First Empire taste. The painted floral bouquets set within the oval reserves and other bouquets appearing on a band of the shaft recall the style of Louis XVI and even Louis XV. The baluster-shaped shafts have a band of ormolu with gouge work at the thickest part of the baluster. Swan heads appear as finials on the lyres which are painted on porcelain. The swan theme is repeated as whole birds and comprises five of the six branches. Curiously, the flying swans' bodies, after joining the shaft, each terminate in a loop and fish tail. Rising from each swan's head is a secondary bobeche with gadrooning to which an inverted bell-shaped candle cup is screwed. The sides of each of these candle cups are decorated in spiral beading which is another form of decoration that appears to be peculiar to the French.

142. Pair of Thirteen Light Candelabra, French, *Restauration* style, patinated bronze and ormolu, circa 1820. Courtesy Nesle, Inc., New York. Photo by Helga Photo Studio.

These pieces could date from as early as the late First Empire period, but the bas relief on the face of the plinth features a lady dressed in medieval costume. The blending of the neoclassical females as the standards with the busts of the medieval ladies points to these candelabra having been manufactured in the more romantic and eclectic period of Charles X. The figural supports were inspired by those originating with the Parisian designer Claude-Michel, known as Clodion (1738-1814).[13] The heaviness and sumptuousness of the cornucopia-pattern branches suggest the slightly later date for this highly successful pair.

144. Pair of Six Light Candelabra, French, *Restauration* style, patinated bronze and ormolu, circa 1825-1835. Courtesy Nesle, Inc., New York. Photo by Helga Photo Studio.

Of pre-Victorian candelabra this pair has to be among the most lavish and ingenious. The massive nature of these pieces requires the double-strap rectangular plinths with tops and double palmette borders in ormolu all raised on Charles X-style feet composed of scrolled acanthus leaves with rosette supports. From the less than amiable bronze swans, like a giant tail, a vertical scroll springs decorated with acanthus leaves and other foliage. The upper scroll supports an ormolu cornucopia-like component from which five heavy scrolling bronze branches and one central branch in ormolu rise. Each candle cup is made of ormolu and has a band in the form of foliate guilloche. The oil lamp then hangs jointly from each fixture's "S" scroll and the cornucopia may at first blush seem bizarre; however, the lamps add visual balance as well as help keep the candelabra from being top-heavy.

143. Four Light Candelabrum (one of a pair), French, First Empire-*Restauration* style, patinated bronze and ormolu, circa 1810-1830. H: 20-¾ in. W: 9-¼ in. D: 7-½ in. Courtesy Hermann-Grima House, New Orleans.

This is a fine example of a type of candelabrum developed late during the First Empire period. The Corinthian column with its ovolo base is a favorite form of the French. Here the principal columnar stem and baluster-shaped shaft of the central light are fluted and executed in patinated bronze. The upper surface of the circular base is domical and is enriched with classical torches and foliate motives. The ormolu branches are in the simpler cornucopia shape.

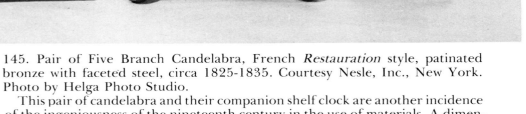

145. Pair of Five Branch Candelabra, French *Restauration* style, patinated bronze with faceted steel, circa 1825-1835. Courtesy Nesle, Inc., New York. Photo by Helga Photo Studio.

This pair of candelabra and their companion shelf clock are another incidence of the ingeniousness of the nineteenth century in the use of materials. A dimension is added to a basically First Empire format for candelabra in the use of polished steel rather than ormolu against patinated bronze. A jewel-like quality in the beading runs up the reed of each column. The foliate steel arabesques applied to the plinth, as well as the reticulated anthemion applied to the lower part of each column, are truly filigree work. The heavy drum-shape knop at the head of the column and the almost spherical candle cups are another indication of these pieces having originated in the Charles X period.

146. Four Light Candelabrum (one of a pair), French, *Restauration* style, patinated bronze and ormolu, circa 1835. H: 21-1/16 in. W: 8-1/4 in. Depth of base: 6 in. Courtesy Stanton Hall, The Pilgrimage Garden Club, Natchez, Mississippi.

More purely horn-form branches are supported on a patinated bronze column having a stylized ormolu Corinthian capital and foliate base. The typical six-sided plinth has a first step in ormolu with an egg and dart border and a plain patinated bronze second step. The tripod plinth is not the usual animal leg and paw variety, but is composed of three scrolling ormolu water leaves.

147. Two Pairs of Candelabra, French (middle pair Second Empire style—circa 1860; outer pair *Consular* style—circa 1800), patinated bronze and ormolu. Courtesy Nesle, Inc., New York. Photo by Helga Photo Studio.

The outer pair of candelabra represent the timid beginnings of what will soon evolve into the First Empire style. The rectilinear characteristics of the late eighteenth century *Directoire* style are seen in the attenuated figural standards as well as in the almost chaste branches and candle cups. The fold of the vestal virgins' drapery is so nearly symmetrical that it adds to the static nature of the pieces.

The other pair represents the other end of the spectrum, the time when Louis Napoleon was trying to revive the imperial grandeur of Napoleon I. Several features immediately announce the Second Empire style. The figural standards are modeled on the dancing girls of Pompeii which were discovered long after the reign of Napoleon I. Additionally, the faces of those females are precisely the same as those seen in sentimental Victorian portraits. The tapered hexagonal, patinated bronze and ormolu plinth has precedent in the First Empire period; however, the bas relief ormolu Nike figures are more crudely cast. The four branches very much resemble First Empire examples but the scrolls of the flame pattern candle cups are the florid rococo revival style.

148. Seven Light Candelabrum (one of a pair), French (made by E. Hugo of Paris), Rococo Revival style, sterling silver, circa 1850. H: 24-½ in. Courtesy Christie's, New York.

Many candelabra were made during the 1840s, 1850s, 1860s and early 1870s in France, Britain and the United States employing a configuration much like this pair. Silver is the usual material used for setting a style and was soon copied in bronze, brass and even potmetal which was bronzed.

The base is a rounded triangle and is raised on three scroll and rocaille feet with pierced scrolls and shells running between the feet as an apron. The plinth consists of "C" scrolls which frame diapering and a central cartouche. The principal element of the stem is one of the favorite rococo revival decorative motives—the putto. The putto holds a naturalistic branch which supports a foliate dish and baluster from which the foliate, scrolling arms flow. The chased vase-form candle cups have their original detachable bobeches. The central light has a decorative flame finial attached to a bobeche.

149. Pair of Six Light Candelabra, French, Rococo Revival style, ormolu, circa 1850-1860. H: 23-½ in. W: 13-½ in. Courtesy New Orleans Museum of Art. Photo by Sidney Liswood. Gift of John G. Agar in memory of his father, William Agar.

These cast, chased and gilded bronze candelabra epitomize the rococo revival style. This style was referred to as the "French Antique" in English-speaking countries during the period. The base is composed of pierced "C" scrolls, shells and foliate devices. Each candelabrum's foot flows into a highly asymmetrical foliate plinth. The principal element in each stem is a seated child—the one on the left a female and the one on the right a male. The children face each other and the male is raised on a rock-like plinth while the female is situated on a foliate stump. Each figure holds a spirally foliate branch embellished with one rosette. Each of the elements of the stem terminates in a lily-like device. From the lily, seven exotic, twisting foliate branches rise. Six of the branches terminate in foliate wax pans and highly foliate candle cups. The central or seventh arm terminates in the wax pan and is missing either a candle cup or finial. It is quite likely that the candle cups originally possessed detachable bobeches. Practically every motif of the delicate eighteenth-century rococo vocabulary has been brought forward and reinterpreted in a less frolicsome and more substantial nineteenth-century manner.

150. Pair of Three Branch Candelabra, French, Second Empire style, ormolu, patinated bronze, marble and feldspar, circa 1860-1870. Courtesy Nesle, Inc., New York. Photo by Helga Photo Studio.

This handsome set revives the First Empire style quite effectively, but provides new innovations of the Napoleon III period. The modestly clad young female figures, while posed in the same manner, are not a pair in either dress or facial expression. The faces are the hyper-sentimental ones of the Victorian era. The ormolu candle branches have *Directoire* to First Empire antecedents; however, the inventive use of blue feldspar in combination with ormolu in the reel-shaped finials is Victorian.

110

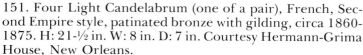

151. Four Light Candelabrum (one of a pair), French, Second Empire style, patinated bronze with gilding, circa 1860-1875. H: 21-½ in. W: 8 in. D: 7 in. Courtesy Hermann-Grima House, New Orleans.

This candelabrum and its mate present a curious blend of revival First Empire design, coupled with rococo revival and renaissance revival forms. The overall configuration harkens back to the First Empire with its hexagonal base and tripod plinth arrangement and the employment of cornucopia-type branches. The scrolling feet and heavy foliate ornaments on the branches relate to the rococo revival. The shaft which tapers upward and is decorated with gilded beading and stylized foliate devices is renaissance revival. The central light holds a gilded flame which is heavy and cumbersome when compared with those from the early period. A cheap gilding has been used rather than the finer gilding of earlier periods.

152. Seven Light Candelabrum (one of a pair), French, Louis XIV Revival, ormolu, circa 1860-1870. H: 32-¾ in. W: 19 in. D: 15 in. Courtesy Dornsife Collection.

The coffer-like plinth raised on turnip-shaped feet harkens back to the early eighteenth-century designs of Andre-Charles Boulle. The putto with tambourine has the massive quality of sculpture of the Louis XIV period. A standard rises behind the putto to hold a vase having "S"-shaped handles embellished with foliage and rosettes. Emerging from the vase is a rich bouquet of lilies, roses and foliage. The branches from which the flowers and foliage grow terminate in candle cups, some of which are lily shaped and others rose shaped. All of the sumptuousness for which the nineteenth century is noted is reflected in the grandeur of this candelabrum.

153. Pair of Four-Light Candelabra, French, Renaissance Revival, patinated bronze and ormolu, circa 1875. H: 19-½ in. W: 8-½ in. D: 7-¼ in. Courtesy Goudeau Antiques, Baton Rouge, Louisiana. Photo by Prather Warren.

The patinated bronze figures represent the Renaissance Revival interpretation of a seventeenth century cavalier and his lady. During the highly eclectic second half of the nineteenth century, numerous decorative arts in the Louis XIV through Louis XVI revival styles and combinations of those styles were made. The more angular lines of the 1870s and 1880s are apparent here. Note particularly the flattened consoles with gougework used as an element on the upper shaft of each candelabrum. The separately cast and applied high relief masks seen on the plinths are another characteristic of the period. The bold lion's masks, cartouches, and scrolling feet of the bases are in the Louis XIV revival taste. The gilded areas of these candelabra have recently been regilded by the electroplating process. These pieces would not be nearly so dramatic if they lacked that extreme contrast in color between the gilding and the patinated bronze.

155. Three Light Candelabrum, Scandinavian (probably Swedish), Neoclassical style, ormolu, marble and glass, circa 1810-1825. H: 30-½ in Diam.: 12-⅜ in. Courtesy Bernard and S. Dean Levy, Inc., New York.

The three candle cups on this delicate yet sizeable candelabrum indicate that it was once one of a pair intended for use on a mantel or console table. The use of the ormolu wire sprays as prism supports is in the Russo-Scandinavian taste. The restraint of the design and use of prisms seems not to be effusive enough for Russian work and therefore suggests Scandinavia and Sweden in particular as the fixture's place of origin. Several refinements are to be noted in the candelabrum. Color contrasts are provided by the white square marble foot and the drum-shaped plinth which is made of cobalt blue glass. All of this plays against the ormolu mounts and clear faceted glass. The casting of the cabled and moulded mounts for the glass drum are crisp and clear and are the heaviest on the piece. The candle cups and bobeches, large prism ring and scrolling branches which support both the candle cups and the prism ring are thinly cast. Screwed into the center of the shaft is a multi-faceted glass obelisk which rises to support the necking that holds the upper spray of prisms and an ormolu spherical finial.

154. One of a Pair of Three Light Candelabra, French, Louis XVI Revival style, ormolu, white marble, porcelain, circa 1880. H: 20 in. W: 12-½ in. D: 11 in. Courtesy Nesle, Inc., New York. Photo by Helga Photo Studio.

Intended as mantel or commode garniture this candelabrum and its mate really mix the vocabulary of the neoclassical Louis XVI style with that of the rococo. The Louis XVI Revival urn is of white porcelain with ormolu cockhead handles, swags, acanthus decorated neck and octagonal foot. This rises on a square white marble base with a beaded ormolu border and ormolu foliate chain—all supported on four ormolu sabots. The foliate branches which are embellished with white porcelain flowers, however, are rococo revival in their heaviness. In the case of both urn and branches the casting, while good, lacks the crispness associated with the 1770-1790 period. The candle cups in particular are good examples of the more florid and sentimental tastes of the Victorians.

156. Pair of Three Light Candelabra, Russian, Alexander I-Nicholas I style, malachite, porphyry, slate and ormolu, circa 1820-1830. Courtesy Nesle, Inc., New York. Photo by Helga Photo Studio.

Sumptuous is the only way to describe these candleholders which employ a variety of semi-precious stones, slate and ormolu in a distinctly Russian interpretation of the French First Empire-Charles X styles. The color pattern of the stone heightens the exotic effect desired in these neo-Egyptian taste candelabra. Placed against a square malachite column in bookend fashion are pairs of neo-Egyptian female figures whose heads abut capitals that evoke the Egyptian style. The horn-shaped branches, which are more angular and heavier than French models, blend the use of the Egyptian lotus petals seen in the candle cups with classical rosettes, water leaves and anthemia. The shaft is raised on an oval porphyry plinth, which in turn sits on a rectangular piece of slate. The stepped base is made of malachite and is enriched with a large bead and reel ormolu border.

157. Three Light Candelabrum (one of a pair), French or possibly German or Scandinavian, First Empire style, ormolu, circa 1810-1825. H: 14-⅜ in. W: 4-¾ in. D: 7-¾ in. Courtesy Rosedown Plantation and Gardens, St. Francisville, Louisiana.

The circular foot decorated with anthemia, the fluted, tapered shaft with the cojoining feet and the masks decorating the upper part of the shaft are certainly in the French taste. The rectilinear, console-shaped branches, however, are more commonly seen in the Germanic countries. The Germanic countries tend to be somewhat *retardataire* in matters of style and if this pair were made in Germany or Scandinavia, they might date as late as 1825. Regardless of origin, this candelabrum and its mate are splendid examples of early nineteenth century continental design and casting.

158. Three Branch Candelabrum, German or Austrian in the French First Empire style, ormolu, circa 1810-1825. H: 14-½ in. W: 10 in. Courtesy Nesle, Inc., New York. Photo by Helga Photo Studio.

While the Germanic countries were very much influenced by the fashions of Paris, as they had been since the reign of Louis XIV, there is a distinct Germanic character to all the decorative arts produced in the various German states and Austria. The main Germanic hallmark in this candelabrum is the shape of the branches. Made in the form of classical consoles, a flat upper surface is left holding inverted bell-shaped candle cups. The fact that the candle cups appear a little large in proportion to the branches is typical. At the end of each console a finely cast classical mask is seen. The standard itself is a slightly heavier edition of a French round based candleholder of the late Louis XVI period.

159. Two Light Candelabrum (one of a pair), German (made by H. B. in Augsburg), Neoclassical style, silver, 1823. H: 19-¾ in. Courtesy Christie's, New York.

This candelabrum and its mate are splendid examples of the Germanic conception of the neoclassical style. While certainly inspired by earlier French work, the German use of neoclassical motives and their idea of proportions differ considerably from that of the French or the English. The shaft which is devoid of ornament except for two vertical acanthus leaves (one seen here) tapers to a very narrow spool-like necking before it joins the base—very much in the French manner. The high circular foot with the severe dome is a preference that is especially Germanic. The base is enriched with four applied Medusa masks set within oval frames. Also in the Germanic tradition is the upper part of the shaft where two graduated neoclassical urns complete the stem. Both urns are decorated with applied oval plaques containing anthemia. An additional casting applied to the upper urn is the pair of rams' heads. Springing from the top of each ram's head is a thin rather angular hexagonal branch. Each branch terminates in a plain circular drip pan and a cylindrical candle cup. These short, angular branches are seen in Germanic and Scandinavian work, but not elsewhere. The rather delicate detachable floral and foliage spray finial comes from that same tradition and certainly relates to some of the decorations on chandeliers from that region.

160. Three Light Candelabrum (one of a pair), German (made by W. P. of Berlin), early Rococo Revival, silver, circa 1835. H: 24-⅜ in. Courtesy Christie's, New York.

Immediately apparent in this candelabrum is the German penchant for attenuated proportions and arms that are somewhat shorter than those seen on candelabra of this size made elsewhere. Each lighting device rises on a shaped octagonal base which is decorated with shells and foliage. The two-part octagonal plinth is composed of one element having gougework and an upper plain spool component. The partially fluted baluster stem rises from a bell-shaped dome chased with acanthus leaves and terminates in a stylized Corinthian capital. Fitted into the capital is a coronet from which issue the two detachable open-worked, scrolling foliate branches and a central straight branch with foliate console supports. Each branch terminates in a fluted vase-shaped candle cup having detachable bobeches and matching wax pans.

161. Two Branch Candelabrum, Russian, Louis XVI Revival style, patinated bronze, ormolu, marble and slate, circa 1860-1875. Courtesy Nesle, Inc., New York. Photo by Helga Photo Studio.

The heavy proportion of the candle cups and foliate and floral branches of this piece point to this piece being in the Louis XVI Revival style, as well as having been made in Russia. The dichotomy in the quality of the casting is explained by the possibility of combining the works of two foundries in one piece. Certainly the cabling and beading on the foot, the beading and chains decorating the urn and the ormolu necking of the urn with its cabled and beaded motives are of excellent quality. This contrasts with the rough casting of the palmettes supporting the urn and the gouge work decorated spool-shaped shaft. Also, the cabling, beading and palmette motives enriching the candle cups do not compare in quality to those of the urn proper. The rosettes rising on ormolu vines from the branches are clumsily cast. These criticisms should not be taken as a general commentary on the quality of Russian work of the second half of the nineteenth century. In 1870 the twenty-four year old Carl Faberge took over his father's jewelry business and was soon to be directing the creation of the finest quality gold, silver and enamel and jeweled presentation pieces ever made.

162. Six Light Candelabrum (one of a pair), Austrian (made by L. K. of Vienna ?), late Rococo Revival style, silver, circa 1875. H: 29-¼ in. Courtesy Christie's, New York.

Perhaps no part of the world enjoyed the styles of the rococo and rococo revival periods as much as south Germany and Austria. Each candelabrum rests on a shaped circular base with a domed center which is decorated with three repousse and chased cartouches depicting classical gods and goddesses. The lower part of the shaft is flanked by three dancing putti, while the upper part has chased scroll panels. There are two tiers of branches composed of "C" scrolls and other foliate scrolls terminating in cherub's busts which support foliate wax pans and chased, foliate candle cups. There is a putto finial at the head of the central shaft.

163. Two Light Candelabrum and Single Cassolette, English (probably the Soho Factory of Matthew Boulton near Birmingham), Derby Blue John feldspar, alabaster and ormolu, circa 1780-1795. Courtesy Nesle, Inc., New York. Photo by Helga Photo Studio.

The stunning beauty of fluor feldspar mined at two sites in the Derbyshire mountains interested Matthew Boulton as early as 1768.[14] Rarely thicker than four inches, the pieces from which the ovoid element of the candelabrum and the baluster of the cassolette were carved must have been at least seven inches thick. The candelabrum has a square base of alabaster framed by a guilloche bordered ormolu element. An urn is formed which focuses on the Blue John center and its scrolling handles which issue from ram's head mounts. Beribboned swags adorn the two other sides of the urn. Ormolu, scrolling and foliate branches rise from the top of the urn and terminate in candle cups, which are decorated with gouge work and palmettes and which sit on delicate bobeches composed of palmettes.

The cassolette which is shown here to be used as a candleholder unquestionably had a now missing lid. Its baluster-shaped shaft is in the brownish colored feldspar. The ormolu is magnificently cast, having a classical urn decorated with reeding and a Greek key at its apex. The round base is the most appropriate form for the baluster and is handsomely ornamented with water leaves, egg and dart motives, and a superb guilloche border—each part of the chain framing a bold rosette.

164. Pair of Adjustable Two Light Candelabra, English, Neoclassical style, core cast brass, circa 1780-1810. H: 14-½ in. Courtesy Herbert Schiffer Antiques, West Chester, Pennsylvania.

The quest for comfort which was renewed by Europeans during the Renaissance saw some improvements made in adjustable table fixtures in Flanders. Interestingly enough, the idea of the adjustable candelabra was not popularized or spread around Europe at that time. It is not until the latter part of the eighteenth century that the concept comes into general use. The candelabra seen here have purely neoclassical shafts capped by urn finials coupled with scrolling branches in the rococo taste. These lighting devices would be particularly suitable for use on a large desk or more especially for use on either a harpsichord or pianoforte.

165. Four Light Candelabrum (one of a pair), Adam style, Anglo-Irish, patinated bronze and glass, circa 1790. Courtesy Bernard and S. Dean Levy, Inc., New York.

This handsome neoclassical example is yet another exhibiting the extraordinary heights reached by the Anglo-Irish glass blowers and cutters. The circular base is distinguished by borders of beading flanking gouge work. The cut glass plinth is a cylinder with shoulders which have been cut with three graduated bands of elongated diamonds. On the upper side of the glass plinth another patinated bronze cylinder with dome supports a bowl-like element in bronze. The bowl is the support for both the four scrolling arms and a faceted obelisk which rises from the center of the bowl. The Van Dyke-type candle cups are used here with upturned star-shaped prism rings. Graduated pyriform prisms drop from these rings and in threes from the canopy crowning the obelisk. The finial for the canopy is an hexagonal faceted urn.

166. Two Light Candelabrum (one of a pair), English, Adam style, glass and ormolu, circa 1780-1795. H: 31 in. W: 19 in. Courtesy Nesle, Inc., New York. Photo by Helga Photo Studio.

This is the classic model of Adam cut glass candelabrum. Its simplicity suggests that it probably dates from the 1780s. The piece begins with a square, stepped base which flows into a slightly flared podium plinth. A faceted baluster rises from the head of the podium to support a hemispherical branch dish. The dish provides sockets for two plain but graciously scrolling arms which move to the side first, then forward and finally upward. The Van Dyke candle cups and star-shaped prism rings with graduated pyriform drops are key ingredients in the formula. A third decorative branch comes straight forward and is fitted with a canopy having graduated pear-shaped prisms. This canopy has a crescent finial occasionally seen in Adam-type fixtures. Emerging from the center of the branch dish is a tall triangular spear whose edges are cut with crescent borders. The upper canopy is fitted over an ormolu cap which provides a threaded socket for the neoclassical urn which is cut with a diminutive diaper pattern border. Graduated, pear-shaped prisms hang straight from all but one of the points on the canopy. On the facade, however, after having two drops fall from the canopy, there is a patera and from there two chains of prisms swag—one to the left and the other to the right prism ring. Coming straight down from the paterae are three graduated pyriform prisms.

Opposite page:

167. Pair of Three Light Candelabra, English, Adam style, glass and ormolu, circa 1790. H: 31 in. W: 18 in. Courtesy Nesle, Inc., New York. Photo by Helga Photo Studio.

There are a number of variations on the general theme for these cut glass candelabra which were intended for use originally on large neoclassical mantels and pier tables. This pair has a square base with a stepped octagonal plinth and a faceted knop surmounted by a canopy which has pyriform prisms. Above that canopy the faceted glass and ormolu half-ovoid dish for branches is attached. Five faceted, scrolling branches rise from the dish. Three have Van Dyke candle cups, star-shaped prism rings and pear-shaped drops while the two arms to the rear hold decorative canopies with graduated prisms and tall finials. These finials have graduated, faceted knops, each of which terminates in a spearhead. From the back side of each branch dish, a tall beautifully cut triangle rises. Another canopy with pyriform prisms fits over the top; and an ormolu fitting covers the top of each triangle so that an ormolu rod can be screwed to it, which in turn upholds the cut glass finial. The finial in this case is a very interesting urn which is cut all over in a diaper pattern and crowned with a stylized fleur-de-lis. The usual swags of prisms fall both from the upper canopy and the prism rings.

169. Pair of Two Light Candelabra, English, Adam style, glass and silvered brass, circa 1790. Courtesy Nesle, Inc., New York. Photo by Helga Photo Studio.

This model has in essence the same type of base as the previous model, but the notching on the plinths of each candleholder is more pronounced. The pair of decorative branches has especially florid palmette finials. Each great, faceted, triangular central spear rises to a canopy which is capped by an appealing eleven-pointed sunburst.

Opposite page:

168. Pair of Two Light Candelabra, English, Adam style, glass and ormolu, circa 1790. Courtesy Nesle, Inc., New York. Photo by Helga Photo Studio.

Each fixture in this handsome set begins with a variation on that most typical of the Adam-type supports—a square stepped base with a podium plinth. The plinths are made more architectonic by the notches on the terminal corners which give the illusion of quoins. The air bubble blown into each podium is another superior decorative touch. The branch dish provides sockets for four arms. The lower ones have the Van Dyke candle cups, star-shaped prism rings and pyriform prisms. The upper two branches have canopies and prisms with magnificent faceted ball and triangle finials screwed into the arms and rising through the center of each canopy. That same motif is repeated in the spire that rises out of the branch dish. It is capped with a large canopy having graduated pyriform prisms. The finials which hold each canopy in place are spirally fluted neoclassical urns.

121

170. Pair of Two Light Candelabra, English, Adam style, ormolu, clear cut glass and gilded blue glass, circa 1790. Courtesy Nesle, Inc., New York. Photo by Helga Photo Studio.

Here the drum-type of plinth which is evocative of Louis XVI's France is interpreted in an English neoclassical manner. Each Bristol blue glass cylinder is enhanced with gilt bell flower borders and an oval reserve is formed on the face with a gilt chain. Each reserve (only one seen here) frames a neoclassical fishing lady which was probably drawn from the needlework theme so much in vogue during the period. The bell-shaped ormolu element above the glass plinth is also in the Louis XVI taste. The rest of the candelabra's decorative devices are of fine quality and typical of the period, save one. Rather than the Van Dyke or shaped candle sockets, the cups are plain cylinders with star-shaped bobeche/prism rings fitted over them.

171. Pair of Two Light Candelabra, English, Adam style, clear cut glass, gilded blue glass, and ormolu, circa 1780-1795. Courtesy Nesle, Inc., New York. Photo by Helga Photo Studio.

This pair is amongst that highly select group of very fine fixtures which employ to great effect colored glass, cut clear flint glass and ormolu. Each ormolu base is octagonal and raised on four flattened ball feet. The principal sides of the stepped bases are concave. The blue glass plinths are flared and each is framed at the bottom with a thin ormolu gallery whose terminal corners are embellished with ram's heads. The corners above the ram's heads are notched. Each elevation of both fixtures are copper wheel engraved with either a tear-drop or a swag and an oval ormolu boss is applied to the head of each of those decorations. Aside from the uppermost spirally decorated urns which have ormolu handles, the rest of these fixtures are the standard Adam form.

173. Two Light Candelabrum (one of a pair), English or Scandinavian, Neoclassical style, ormolu, porcelain, and glass, circa 1790 H: 28 in. W: 17 in. Courtesy Bernard and S. Dean Levy, Inc., New York.

172. Two Light Candelabrum (one of a pair), English, Adam style, clear cut glass, gilded blue glass and ormolu, circa 1780-1795. H: 13-½ in. W: 13-½ in. Courtesy Nesle, Inc., New York. Photo by Helga Photo Studio.

Simpler and less effusive than the previous example, this model has a very similar base. The square base with concave sides raised on beaded ball feet is the same. The flared Bristol blue plinth has gilded notched corners, ormolu, ram's heads and an ormolu patera with gilded swags much like the foregoing model. The gallery with interlocking circles is not ormolu, but gilt paint in the present case. The scrolling branches have Van Dyke candle cups and star prism rings with a modicum of graduated pyriform prisms. Scrolling decorative snake branches support more pear-shaped drops. The tall faceted spear has the usual canopy with prisms and a faceted, pineapple-type finial.

The initial reaction to this piece is that it is absolutely of English manufacture. The spindly nature of the fixture's superstructure suggests that this piece might be at least in part of Scandinavian manufacture. The lumbering industry of Scandinavia had made that region of continental Europe strong trading partners with Britain, whose Royal Navy was very much dependent on others for its naval stores. English taste in the decorative arts had a great deal of influence on Scandinavian and north German designs throughout the eighteenth century, but especially during the neoclassical period at the end of the eighteenth and beginning of the nineteenth centuries. It is indeed quite likely that parts of this piece could have been made in England and shipped to Scandinavia. The Wedgwood factory is known to have exported plaques of its jasper wares which were incorporated into objects made in Europe and even in America.

174. Two Light Candelabrum (one of a pair), English, Neo-classical style, glass, bronze, and enamel, circa 1790. H: 23-¼ in. W: 15-½ in. D: 6-½ in. Collection of Rosedown Plantation and Gardens, St. Francisville, Louisiana.

French influence is very apparent in this example with its circular bronze foot and matching upper frame for the enameled cylindrical plinth. The quality of gilding and other paint work is so sophisticated that it is highly likely that the enameled plinths were imported into England from France. The rest of this pair of fixtures is in the English taste. Scrolling, cut branches support star-shaped prism rings and Van Dyke candle cups. Pear-shaped prisms are used as drops and swags. A domical canopy having a star-shaped base crowns a triangular shaft of glass whose terminal edges are serrated. A seven pointed star in faceted glass is the finial for each piece's canopy.

175. Pair of Two Light Candelabra, English, Adam style, ormolu and glass, circa 1800. Courtesy Nesle, Inc., New York. Photo by Helga Photo Studio.

This model is simple, but exciting in its imaginative design and use of materials. The bases and plinths are in the form of a neoclassical garden temple. Four cut glass Tuscan columns and a semi-concealed central ormolu rod form each device's plinth and each is raised on a circular ormolu base which is embellished with cast borders in a guilloche pattern as well as smaller beaded and reeded borders. The "roof" of the temple is a lobed glass dome set in an ormolu bezel which has a guilloche border. The temple's dome has a fluted ormolu finial which provides the socket for the faceted branch dish. Two scrolling arms flow from each dish to star-shaped prism rings holding graduated pyriform prisms. The Van Dyke candle cups are unusual in that they too have graduated pear-shaped prisms. The multi-sided shaft that rises from the center of each branch dish is unusual as well. Each is capped with a tall ormolu pinnacle from which short, arched, ormolu prism branches spring. These frond-like devices originated on the continent and were not seen in English work until about the turn of the century. The finial of each of the ormolu pinnacles is a finely cut glass pineapple.

Below

176. Pair of Two Light Candelabra, English, George III style, patinated bronze and cut glass, circa 1790-1810. Courtesy Nesle, Inc., New York. Photo by Helga Photo Studio.

The British who led the world in the Industrial Revolution did not have to live in the shadow of the French with regard to producing stylish lighting devices in metals and cut glass. Here attractively posed putti in patinated bronze are raised on stepped circular bases which are embellished with checkerboard-pattern engine turnings, cast beading and cable work. Each putto holds a spirally twisted cabriole branch in ormolu. The candle cups with the crenellated rims were in the "Van Dyke"-shape according to eighteenth and early nineteenth-century terminology. The star-shaped prism rings hold graduated faceted headers and terminate in pyriform faceted prisms.

177. Two Light Candelabrum (one of a pair), English (made by H. Hopper of London), Regency style, giltwood, marble, patinated bronze and glass, dated April 10, 1809. H: 17-¼ in. W: 11-¾ in. D: 7-½ in. Courtesy Rosedown Plantation and Gardens, St. Francisville, Louisiana.

It is fortunate that this pair of candelabra bear the script legend on the plinths, "Apr' 10, 1809 H. Hopper London." H. Hopper is probably the Humphrey Hopper who was a sculptor in London and exhibited at the Royal Academy in 1799 and 1834.[15]

Each lighting fixture is composed of a square white marble base, a plain circular plinth of giltwood and an exquisitely carved winged neoclassical female figure as the standard. The figure holds a reeded vase-shaped giltwood device directly in front of her. From the center of the vase, a turned baluster in bronze rises and terminates in a cut glass artichoke finial. This device partially conceals the scrolling heavy wire branches that issue from the body of each of the female standards. In the best Regency manner there is a crenellated prism ring from which a series of faceted circular buttons in groups of four drop before terminating in a pear-shaped prism. Each urn-shaped candle cup is cut in a diaper pattern on its bulbous lower section while each bobeche has a serrated edge.

125

178. Candelabrum (one of a pair), English (made by Matthew Boulton and Matthew Boulton and Plate Co., Birmingham), Neoclassical style, candlestick is sterling, branches are plated, 1805. H: 20-⅝ in. Courtesy Christie's, New York.

Typical of the high style of English-made candelabra, this candelabrum features a tall circular base with gadrooning and reeding. The stem, unlike French and continental-made examples, does not taper to a very narrow juncture between the base and shaft, nor does extreme narrowness occur between the head of the stem and the candle cup. In both cases, generous spool-shaped devices act as the transitional elements. The swirling, reeded silverplated branches have gadrooned wax pans and the entire branch component is literally socketed into the sterling candlestick's candle cup. The candle cups are vase forms whose lower halves are gadrooned. A unicorn crest is engraved on the base and the central candle socket.

179. Candelabrum with Plated Branches (one of a pair), English (made by Matthew Boulton of Birmingham), Regency style, sterling silver and silverplate on copper, circa 1810. H: 21-¼ in. Courtesy Christie's, New York.

Each of these candelabrum bears a engraved royal crest and crown and shows that even members of the British royal family did not reject the mixture of sterling silver and plated silver. The use of the more stable copper with silverplate for the broad and rather delicate scrolling branches is simply more pragmatic —especially in the case of these gigantic candelabra. Each circular base is lobed and has a plain center surmounted by a gadrooned knop. Each tapering stem's lower section is decorated with alternating flutes and reeds, while at the head of each stem appears a knop with a bold guilloche border. The plated, scrolling branches are reeded and terminate in vase-shaped candle cups and detachable bobeches. There are also separate drip pans below the branch sockets.

180. Pair of Two Light Candelabra, English, Regency style, glass and ormolu, circa 1810. Courtesy Nesle, Inc., New York. Photo by Helga Photo Studio.

Regency pieces tend to be more rectilinear and bulky than the pieces made in the earlier taste of the Adam brothers. A bold circular foot having a sawtooth border and a series of graduated steps serve as the support for an egg-shaped plinth decorated with deeply cut diapering in each candelabrum. A short cylindrical ormolu shaft rises from the plinth to uphold an extraordinarily broad oval cut glass prism ring. Two faceted headers hang above each faceted tear-drop prism. The ormolu branches express the Regency period's interest in the exotic. Two roaring leopard heads appear tied together and a scrolling water leaf emerges from the neck of each beast's head. The upper side of the terminal of each branch is capped by an ormolu ball upon which a Van Dyke candle cup rests. These candle cups are heavier and more deeply cut than those from the Adam period. Screwed into a socket at the back of each pair of leopard heads is an ormolu sabot which holds a tapering, spirally twisted shaft. This decorative shaft has a spool-like capital from which a short, spirally-turned ormolu shaft rises to uphold a circular ormolu bezel. Each bezel frames a large faceted glass disk and the outer part of each bezel has thirteen prisms cut to resemble rays, thus creating a sunburst effect.

181. Four Light Candelabrum (one of a pair), English, Regency style, silverplated, circa 1810. H: 26-¼ in. Courtesy Christie's, New York.

Even during the height of hostilities between Napoleon's French Empire on the continent and the far flung British Empire, there were constant interchanges of ideas in the fashion of clothing and the decorative arts. Both countries left behind the delicate designs of the Louis XVI period and Robert Adam and moved toward a more scholarly interpretation of ancient Roman materials. As usual there are certain British preferences that differ from the French. Here the double incurved octagonal base raised on four lion's masks, double paw and foliage feet contrasts with the usual French predilection for incurved hexagonal bases. In essence the French will usually select a more triangular format for their massive candelabra and the British will more often choose a more four-square configuration. The secondary base has a neoclassical mask canted at each corner that supports a shaped square from whose foliate center the shaft rises. Each columnar shaft begins with a reeded border followed by a plain band and vertical out-turned palmettes. That entire element is separately cast and serves as the socket for the plain column. Each column is terminated with a separately cast capital composed of two rows of the same out-turned palmettes seen at the base of each column. The central light and the three swirling reeded branches spring from a gadrooned socket. Each candle cup is vase-shaped and reeded and has a gadrooned detachable bobeche, as well as a separate drip pan with gadrooning. A full coat of arms is engraved on each base.

182. Six Light Candelabrum-Centerpiece, English (made by Paul Storr of London), Regency style, silver-gilt, 1813. H: 23-½ in. Courtesy Christie's, New York.

The piece is a superior example of Paul Storr's best work and it was sold through the firm of Rundell, Bridge and Rundell and bears their stamped Latin signature on both the exterior and interior of the base. Bold in conception and magnificently executed, this piece is the type of silverware that fits into the decorating schemes of the most advanced of the Regency period designers. As a single center piece, the two-tiered, incurved triangular base resting on three shell and palm foliage feet makes better aesthetic sense than a four-square format. Running as an apron between the feet is a border composed of pierced anthemia and scrolling foliage. At the top of the lower base there is a heavily cast border of acanthus leaves. The second tier of the base is supported by three splendid couchant lions with acanthus leaves and rosettes as hindquarter supports. The principal shaft is composed of palm foliage which rises from an acanthus calix. Situated directly at the apex of the stem is a shallow bowl which is partially fluted and has a cast down-turned acanthus leaf border. The six reeded branches that spring from the palm shaft each have foliate mounts and terminate in low candle cups having separate, fluted drip pans with acanthus leaf borders.

183. Five Light Candelabrum, English (made by Edward Cornelius Farrell of London), Regency style, silver-gilt, 1819. H: 30 in. Courtesy Christie's, New York.

This is an extraordinarily sophisticated device and harkens back to the renaissance and early baroque continental tradition of the great princes having treasure rooms of marvelous and exotic works of artistic and scientific curiosity. All of this would have been fostered in Britain by George, Prince of Wales. Indeed, a candelabrum matching this one was in the possession of his kinsman, the Duke of York during the 1820s.

On a domed rockwork base, cast and applied with corals, shells, fish and sea monsters, the shaft is formed as the figure of Neptune astride a sea horse. Neptune supports with his right hand a shell with four scrolling branches terminating as the heads of a hydra. Each branch has a detachable bobeche in simulated coral-work and there is a similar central light missing its bobeche.

185. Pair of Five Light Candelabra, English, Regency style, ormolu and glass, circa 1810. Courtesy Nesle, Inc., New York. Photo by Helga Photo Studio.

This magnificent pair of candleholders can perhaps be regarded as the quintessence of the Regency style of candelabra. Everything about them is sumptuous. The hexagonal patinated bronze base is raised on ormolu dragons' feet. Upturned chinoiserie foliage provides a plinth in each device for the cut glass and ormolu shaft. The cylindrical ormolu and diaper cut shafts are largely concealed by surrounding bobeches, prisms and graduated canopies from which up to five faceted, circular headers are strung up each shaft. Out of each dish foliate, spirally-twisted branches scroll downward and then rise to support Regency-type Van Dyke candle cups which have button drops. The bobeche/prism rings are true dishes with elegantly cross-hatched lobes alternating with clear ones in the same manner as the canopies on the central shafts. The matching finials of the shafts are urns of glass which have been spirally cut in such a way to appear like flames.

186. Pair of Five Light Candelabra, English, Regency style, glass and ormolu, circa 1805-1815. Courtesy Nesle, Inc., New York. Photo by Helga Photo Studio.

This pair, which is slightly less elaborate than the previous model, displays shafts composed of a graduated series of four drums having alternating plain and cross-hatched vertical panels. The lowest drum of each device is separated from the domical plinth by a narrow ormolu ring. The circular part of the plinth has a double row of boldly cut squares which are cross-hatched. Four ormolu lion's paw feet resting on a circular base support each lighting device. To the reeded ormolu neckings between each drum on the shafts of both devices, pairs of reeded ormolu branches are socketed. These branches support an interesting, graduated double tiered prism ring. Plain, multi-faceted prisms are suspended from octagonal headers on each of the lobed bobeches. The fifth candle socket is atop the central shaft and has a similar two-tiered arrangement of bobeches and prisms.

184. Two Light Candelabrum (one of a pair), English, Regency style, glass and ormolu, circa 1810-1820. H: 20-½ in. W: 16 in. Diam. of base: 7 in. Collection of Rosedown Plantation and Gardens, St. Francisville, Louisiana.

Heavier in feeling than the delicate Adam style candelabra, the Regency style models such as this one display a sumptuous quality of their own. The low, domed foot, the center of the baluster-shaped shaft and the prism rings are all deeply cut with bands of strawberry and diamond pattern. An ormolu element continues the stem above the glass baluster and provides the supports for the richly cast, scrolling branches. Two secondary branches are cast as a part of each main arm. One of the branches scrolls downward to support a single prism. The candle cups are vase shaped but they flare broadly at the top to form a broad bobeche with serrated edges. Rising from the center of the juncture of the two branches is a series of flower-like ormolu elements which provide support for two graduated tiers of "J"-form prism sprays. Unlike the Scandinavian and Russian sprays, which are fashioned from round wire, these sprays are created from flattened sheets of metal.

187. Pair of Two Light Candelabra, English, Regency style, glass and ormolu, circa 1810-1820. Courtesy Nesle, Inc., New York. Photo by Helga Photo Studio.

The Regency penchant for double tiers of bobeches makes these and other similar candelabra appear more complex. Each of these fixtures rises from a lobed circular foot directly into a plinth in the form of a flared vase which is deeply cut with diapering. Resting at the head of the vase a domical ormolu flange supports both a large prism ring and the ormolu shaft from which the two ormolu branches spring. From the crenellated and diaper cut prism ring and the double bobeches, graduated plain, multi-faceted prisms with ovolo tips fall. Octagonal headers are used in pairs, singles or not at all as the tiers move higher. The central ormolu shaft continues to rise in a fluted taper until it terminates in an artichoke finial.

188. Three Light Candelabrum, English, George IV-early Victorian style, silverplated copper and etched glass, circa 1825-1845. H: 27-³/₁₆ in. W: 19-¾ in. Diam. of lip of shades: 6-¼ in. Lambdin Collection.

A shaped circular base with a foliate and floral repoussé border supports a plain tapered stem which has the same foliate and floral decoration repeated in graduated sizes as knops at the base and head of the stem. By the large ventilated, cylindrical shade holder/candle cup above the shade, it is apparent that this fixture has interchangeable parts. It can be used as a single candlestick with the shade or the three-branch device can be plugged into the central socket. A pair of reeded, looping and scrolling arms with foliate and floral connectors spring from the side of the attachment while another central light rises from the center of the secondary stem. The repoussé foliage and floral decoration seen on the candlestick proper are repeated atop the pseudo-wax pans of the side branches. The shades are full, inverted, waisted bell-shaped ones with flaring lips which have been etched with trailing foliage in a late neoclassical manner.

189. Six Light Candelabrum-Centerpiece, English (made by Paul Storr in London), early Rococo Revival style, silver-gilt, 1835. H: 28-¾ in. Courtesy Christie's, New York.

By the 1830s, the rococo revival was about to overtake neoclassicism in British silver design. The voluptuous forms that were present during most of the Victorian period are present here. The base is a shaped triangle resting on three scrolling acanthus leaf feet. Three vignettes are framed on the sides of the base by heavy scrolling acanthus leaves and shells. The three cast vignettes include two featuring a seated figure of Britannia and the other depicts Neptune and a reclining Indian warrior. The acanthus foliage stem is flanked by a figure of a bacchanal playing cymbals and two dancing nymphs. The scrolling acanthus branches are bifurcated having shaped flower and scroll wax pans, vase-shaped candle cups and detachable bobeches. The central finial element is composed of a bouquet of flowers.

190. Pair of Seven Light Candelabra, American (possibly made by Henry N. Hooper and Co., Boston), American Empire style, matte and bright gilded bronze, circa 1845. H: 27 in. W: 11-⅝ in. Base: 6 in. square. Collection of Garrison Grey Kingsley, Greenville, Delaware.

The style of this superb pair of candelabra was obviously derived from French *Restauration* models. The matte and bright gilded finish, as well as the slightly less sophisticated quality of the female figures serving as stems are executed in the American manner. The treatment of the rectangular plinths are in the Anglo-American taste. Especially interesting are the niches, each of which contains a separately cast classical urn raised on a fluted plinth which is supported by a plain, hexagonal foot. The matte finished urns themselves are decorated with bright gilt vertical bands and palmettes. The fully dressed female figures have their flowing gowns embellished with floral bouquets. Each figure holds a cornucopia-like shaft which terminates in a vase-shaped element from which the scrolling branches and one central branch spring. The upturned foliate drip pans and the urn-shaped candle cups are decorated with palmettes.

The candle cups are certainly in the Boston style. They are seen in Hooper's 1858 catalogue on rococo style pieces. It is too bad that at this writing no Hooper catalogue earlier than the 1858 edition has surfaced to help identify that firm's work in the more classical taste of the 1830s and early 1840s. Other Boston manufacturers could have been using this same candle cup. Even more troublesome is the fact that the finish is most like that seen on the work of the Cornelius firm. Unfortunately, there is no known Cornelius catalogue that antedates the Civil War.

192. Five Branch Candelabrum (one of a pair), English, gilded bronze and glass, circa 1830-1845. H: 19-¾ in W: 16-¾ in. D: 10 in. Collection of the Pilgrimage Garden Club, Natchez, Mississippi.

This splendid pair of candelabra exhibits the finest of crisp casting and rich gilding and best relates to the work seen on the finest of English-made lamps and chandeliers. Another thing that divorces these candleholders from American work is the use of cut glass prism rings. I know of no American lighting devices of the period employing such components. Attribution to a Birmingham or London manufacturer is therefore logical. There is a missing set of elements on these fixtures—the headers or buttons on the lowest set of prism rings. The bud-like candle cups could have served as inspiration for some models used by the Boston firm of Henry N. Hooper.

191. Twelve Light Candelabrum-Centerpiece, English (centerpiece made by Robert Garrard of London in 1863; branches made by Robert Hennell, Jr. of London in 1872), Rococo Revival style, sterling silver. H: 39 in. Courtesy Christie's, New York.

The elaborate candelabrum-centerpiece provides one of the rare examples of an earlier piece having been added to at a later date and the resulting "marriage" being happy. The shaped oval plinth is raised on four scroll feet—two having cartouches. The feet and plinth have applied thistles and roses and the plinth has a cartouche on each of its two long sides which is engraved with a cypher and coronet. The scrolling open-worked stem is flanked by two semi-nude figures—one holding a bouquet and the other a staff. Between the dual stems there is an ornamented fountain resting on dolphin feet. From the center of the foliate bordered bowl, an infant bacchanal rises on one foot atop a sphere. The double stems join in a foliate dish from which two tiers of scrolling branches spring. The candle cups are embellished with lobes or cabochons and there are ornate, supporting foliate bobeches. A standing female figure finial presides from a central perch above the branches.

193. Five Light Candelabrum (one of a pair), Three Light Wall Bracket and Two Light Candelabra, American (all attributed to Henry N. Hooper and Co., Boston), Rococo Revival style, matte and bright gilded brass, circa 1850-1868. Dimensions for Five Light Candelabrum - H: 22-½ in. W: 16 in. D: 10 in. Collection of Craig Littlewood and Craig Maue, Palmyra, New Jersey.

The three-tiered candelabrum is shown here with its prisms removed. While this exact model is not shown in the 1858 catalogue, several models having lower swivel branches are shown. All the elements composing the candelabrum appear on some fixture in that catalogue. Note that the foot and stem are in the same pattern as Illustration 195. Here, however, there are three graduated balusters decorated with iris-like foliage and stylized foliage. The scrolling, highly foliate branches and grape cluster and leaf prism rings are exactly the same as a three-tiered model illustrated as number 519 in the catalogue. The candle cups on model 519 are the same as the ones shown above except a plain bobeche has been substituted for the scalloped one.

The three-branch sconce or bracket with the very foliate arms again resembles several of the Hooper models shown in the 1858 catalogue. The candle cups with palmette decorated sides and foliate bordered lips are typical of that foundry's work. The two-light candelabrum with its tripartite foliate stem is the most floridly rococo of the lot. Again, the branches and base are seen in the Hooper catalogue. The scalloped, detachable bobeche is another refinement on this elegant piece.

135

195. Five Light Candelabrum, American (made by Henry N. Hooper and Co., Boston), Rococo Revival style, matte and bright gilded brass, circa 1855-1868. H: 21 in. W: 13 in. Collection of Garrison Grey Kingsley, Greenville, Delaware.

While this precise model does not appear in the 1858 Hooper catalogue, each element appears on some lighting device in the catalogue. Parts are obviously interchangeable. This exact pattern could have appeared in an earlier or later Hooper catalogue or it may have been put together as a special order. The casting and double gilding are of the first order. The ornate base, shaft branches and wax pans provide yet more evidence that the Hooper firm produced the highest style rococo revival designs of the foundries manufacturing lighting devices in the United States. The base is composed of three scrolling feet with foliate "C" scrolls and cartouches and three separately cast and applied asymmetrical floral bouquets and foliage. The baluster-shaped stem blends naturalistic iris-type foliage with stylized flowers. Atop the baluster, a large foliate cup serves as a support for the four scrolling branches and one central branch. Unlike the typical Philadelphia and New York examples, the Hooper branches' flowers are intermixed with the foliage of the branches. The scalloped, vase-shaped candle cups are seen on many Hooper pieces.

194. Two Light Bouquet-Candelabrum (one of a pair), American (made by Henry N. Hooper and Co., Boston), Rococo Revival style, matte and bright gilded brass and amethyst glass, circa 1845-1868. H: 22 in. W: 17-½ in. Collection of Garrison Grey Kingsley, Greenville, Delaware.

All of the elements composing this interesting fixture and its mate are illustrated as parts of various candleholders, lamp bases and bouquets in the 1858 Hooper catalogue. The massive tripod base is raised on flattened bun or button feet. The hexagonal, baluster-shaped stem is especially rich with its original finish of a matte ground combined with bright gilding on the terminal edges. A broad palmette-decorated candle-cup-like element is atop the baluster to support a circular component which holds both the scrolling and foliate branches in its sockets. These are combined with the grape cluster and leaf pattern prism rings. The cylindrical candle cups have fluted sides. The typical Hooper pierced cone decorated with masks and foliage serves as the frame for the amethyst glass bouquet holder whose lip is broad and folded over. The piece is not shown with a full complement of prisms, but those displayed are in the tapered spear pattern favored by Boston manufacturers.

196. Five Light Candelabrum, American (attributed to Henry N. Hooper and Co., Boston), gilded brass and glass, circa 1850-1865). Collection of the Mississippi Governor's Mansion, Department of Archives and History, Jackson.

In Hooper's 1858 catalogue no less than three different models of girandoles and gas table lamps are illustrated having pierced grape clusters, vines and foliage wrapped around the larger scrolling grape vines which function as the arms of the candelabra. The vintage pattern shaft, grape cluster and leaf prism rings and the campana-shaped foliate candle cups are all to be seen in Hooper's catalogue. The very ornate tripod base raised on striated bun feet is similar to other examples from Hooper. Note that only three of the five prism rings are punctured to receive prisms. The faceted teardrop prisms are neither old nor of the proper style for this candelabrum.

The Hooper firm's designs appear to be the most rococo of all the known American manufacturers of lighting devices. This candelabrum can be regarded as a quintessential example of that statement.

197. Four Light Candelabrum- Bouquet, American (probably made by Henry N. Hooper and Co., Boston), Rococo Revival style, ormolu, marble, blue glass and mirrored glass, circa 1845-1860. H: 23-¼ in. Collection of Russell B. Wilkes. Photo courtesy Neal Alford Company, New Orleans.

A piece similar to this candleholder having a reverse painting on glass in place of the mirrored panel is to be seen in the 1858 Henry N. Hooper and Co. catalogue. The large four-light candelabrum illustrated here is an uncommon form in lighting devices. A light blue bouquet with a crenellated lip is held by a pierced ormolu frame decorated with masks and foliage as seen in the Hooper catalogue. It acts as a finial for the elaborate mirror frame which is composed of interlocking "C" scrolls which have been embellished with rosettes, lilies and a rose. The four candle arms almost grow organically from the frame. The scrolling, foliate branches terminate in fluted campana-shaped candle cups with downturned leaf wax pans. The entire standard is raised on a moulded, rectangular block of white marble.

198. Five Light Candelabrum, American (Boston), Rococo Revival style, matte and bright gilded brass and white marble, circa 1855. Collection of the Mississippi Governor's Mansion. Photo courtesy the Department of Archives and History, Jackson.

The foliate candle cups and the rich, deep golden finish suggest Boston as a place of origin for this stunning example. The downturned leaf and palmette pattern drip pan is designed like a prism ring but has no holes for the prism pins. The arms are foliate and scrolled. The foliate plinth is very much like those seen on the "Blake Patent" girandole. Unusual and quite handsome is the large, rectangular white marble base which is carved as a triple step.

199. Pair of Two Branch Candelabra (Buck and Doe model) probably American (Boston), Rococo Revival style, patinated bronze and marble, circa 1845-1865. Buck: H: 10-¾ in. W: 8-⅛ in. D: 4-⅛ in. Doe: H: 10-½ in. W: 8 in. D: 3-¹³/₁₆ in. Collection of Anglo-American Art Museum, Louisiana State University, Baton Rouge, Given in memory of Dennis Thetford.

If this pair of candelabra had prisms, they would have to be called girandoles by the definition used in this book. Each candelabrum has grape vines with foliage and grape clusters rising as the central stem from a rectangular white marble plinth. The branches are also grape vines with foliage. The lower drip pans consist of short downturned palmettes while the scalloped-edge candle cups are also cast with vintage decorations. The detachable bobeches are scalloped. Separately cast and affixed to the marble plinth in front of each candelabrum is a recumbent deer—a buck on one and a doe on the other. The animals, though somewhat naive in concept, are beautifully cast with great attention having been given to the sculpture of the animals' coats, hooves and antlers. The rather two-dimensional quality of the grape vine and grape cluster elements and the naive appearance of the deer suggest an American attribution. The extreme rococo revival nature of the style points to Boston as their place of manufacture.

200. Two Light Candelabrum, American (Boston), Rococo Revival style, gilt brass and marble, circa 1855. Private collection.

If this example had prisms, it would be a girandole under the definition used in this book. It certainly has a white marble base and the stem is a trellis embellished with cabbage roses and two other morning glory-like flowers. The naturalistic branches spring from the trellis and have the morning glory vine growing around them until they abut the floridly rococo revival, foliate wax pans. The vase-formed candle cups' sides are decorated with a border of large and small vertically placed leaves. This fixture quite possibly originally had detachable bobeches.

The rich, deep gold gilding of the metal parts and the extreme rococo nature of the design points to Boston as its place of origin. The pattern of the stem, branches, wax pans and candle cups are not like any shown in the Henry N. Hooper catalogue of 1858. This fixture is of good quality and certainly was well within the manufacturing capabilities of the Hooper firm and several other Boston makers. The two-dimensional quality of the stem seems to preclude a European origin of the piece.

201. Three Light Candelabrum, American (made by Henry N. Hooper and Co., Boston), Rococo Revival style, gilded brass, circa 1850-1868. H: 18-½ in. W: 16-½ in. Collection of Garrison Grey Kingsley, Greenville, Delaware.

While not quite so florid as the following vintage pattern candleholder, this candelabrum with its twisting vines, grape clusters, and broad leaves does exhibit the high rococo taste of Boston. Here again, an identical model to this example does not appear in the 1858 Hooper catalogue. All of the elements do appear on other similar fixtures in that catalogue. The square, pierced base is largely composed of big grape leaves. The stem is composed of two graduated balusters decorated with stylized foliage. There is a double beaded spool serving as the transitional element between the base and the large baluster, but it is cast as a part of the baluster. The spool-type necking between the lower and upper baluster holds the candle branches and is cast as a part of the upper baluster. The candle cups, as with several Hooper models, are vase shaped and decorated with grape leaves. The bobeches are in a grape leaf and grape cluster pattern.

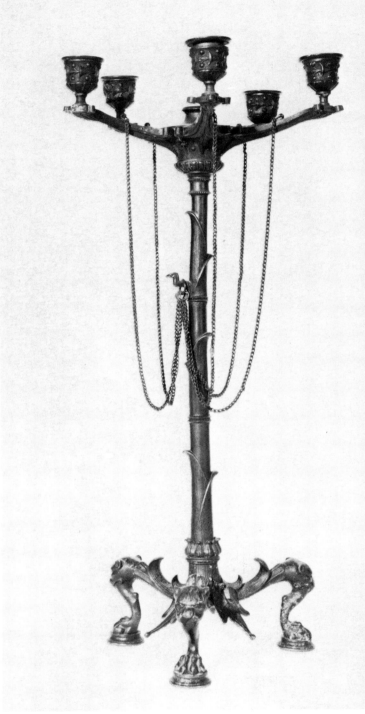

202. Five Light Candelabrum, American, (made by Henry N. Hooper and Co., Boston), gilded brass and marble, circa 1858-1868. H: 23 in. W: 16-½ in. Collection of Garrison Grey Kingsley, Greenville, Delaware.

This is probably the ultimate example of a vintage pattern in an American candleholder. Fortunately, this piece is documented by the 1858 Hooper catalogue as a product of that foundry. The exact five-light model is illustrated as number 580 and the catalogue states that the same pattern can be bought as a three-light fixture as number 581. The foliage, grape clusters and vines are so dense that it is difficult to tell that this is a three-tiered candleholder. The owner of this fixture has placed a handsome etched glass and brass spirit lamp of American manufacture in the uppermost candle socket. Peg lamps were interchangeable with candles in many fixtures during the rococo revival period.

203. Five Light Candelabrum (one of a pair), English or French, Renaissance Revival style, circa 1860-1875. H; 20 in. D. and W. 9-¾ in. Courtesy Hermann-Grima House, New Orleans.

Handsome candelabra in this pattern are seen in Britain, France and the United States. The tripod of bold cabriole legs actually has a griffin head at each knee supported on a monopod lion's leg and claw foot. The shaft is not unlike a palm tree rising to hold the flattened five branches. A chain falls from each branch and joins a ring which is looped over a duckhead projecting from the side of the shaft.

140

204. Three Light Candelabrum (one of a pair), French, late Rococo Revival style, cast and stamped gilded brass and iron, circa 1875-1910. H: 14-⅜ in. W: 14-¼ in. D: 6 in. Courtesy Goudeau Antiques, Baton Rouge, Louisiana.

There are several variations on this model which employ lilies and lily fronds. This example is one of the smaller sizes of this pattern which can range well over forty inches tall. A short threaded iron rod joins the base to the separately cast spool-shaped shaft which is capped with a foliate device. The threaded iron rod then joins the cluster of three brass rods which turns into the three principal stems of the plant-like candelabrum. The foliage made of stamped brass has an effective natural texture. The same is true of the lilies which are made in the same manner and which center on brass stamen to which pistils have been soldered.

The gilding on the "lily" pattern candelabra was usually inexpensive and has not held up well. These were not regarded as fine objects when they were new, but they were popular, appealing to the late rococo revival aesthetics as well as those of the art nouveau.

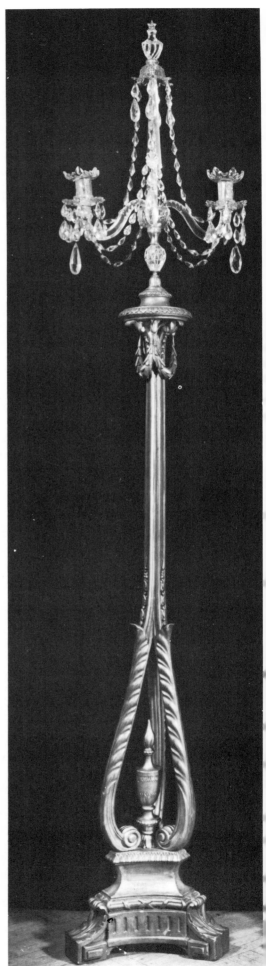

Far left:
205. Pair of Three Branch Torcheres, English, Adam style, gessoed, painted and gilded wood, ormolu, iron, plaster and glass, circa 1790. Courtesy Nesle, Inc., New York. Photo by Helga Photo Studio.

Pavement lights became increasingly popular during the neoclassical period. Robert Adam himself, other architects and furniture designers produced many designs for sets of these lights to be used in specific locations. This pair is painted pale green with gilt trim to harmonize with the color scheme of the room for which the pieces were originally designed. The hexagonal plinths raised on flattened ball feet support tripod secondary legs which in turn uphold the reeded shafts which terminate in circular, reeded platforms holding the candelabra. The candelabra have bases of turned wood which have been gessoed, painted and gilded in the same manner as the stands. The branches, however, are gilded iron and uphold star-shaped prism rings and prisms and ormolu candle cups whose cylindrical sides are embellished with cast rosettes.

Left:
206. Two Light Torchere (one of a pair), English, Adam style, giltwood, ormolu and glass, circa 1790. Courtesy Nesle, Inc., New York. Photo by Helga Photo Studio.

This robust torchere and its mate are splendid examples in the most refined neoclassical taste. The six-sided base has fluted concave sides and rectilinear consoles act as feet. The hexagonal plinth is embellished with more neoclassical motives—fasces and egg and dart borders. The plinth supports a shaft whose lower half is composed of a tripod of inverted consoles which turn into a reeded column decorated with carved wheat husks and bell flowers. The column terminates with foliate scrolls from which laurel swags are suspended. The circular platform above the column is decorated with a foliate border and serves as the base for the candelabrum. The shaft of the candelabrum is an inverted pyriform-shaped piece of cut glass with ormolu neckings. Typical scrolling branches, swags of chains, star-shaped prism rings and pyriform prisms compose the candelabrum. The finial of the candelabrum is an urn with spiral cuttings which is capped with a small star. The glass urn relates to the giltwood urn with the flame finial which is situated between the three consoles that comprise the lower part of the shaft of the torchere.

Right:
207. Twelve Light Torchere, French, First Empire style, giltwood and ormolu, circa 1805. H: 76 in. Courtesy Nesle, Inc., New York. Photo by Helga Photo Studio.

Pavement lights which had been popular in classical antiquity had a great revival after the middle of the eighteenth century with the neoclassical designs of Robert Adam. Large torcheres in sets were used in the early nineteenth century especially in galleries and dining rooms. The two-tiered fixture illustrated here has a flat hexagonal base with concave sides which is used to support the tripod of massive lion's paw feet. The knees of the legs have a shell-like cap composed of acanthus leaves. Rising from a nest of acanthus leaves is a spirally fluted column which terminates in a stylized Corinthian capital. The column bears a double dish. Eight ormolu cornucopia-shaped branches spring from the lip of the lower dish, while from the center of the larger second dish a palm-like shaft grows which supports four smaller arms and a flame finial. The English made almost the identical shape of torchere save for the fact that polychrome floral decoration seen on the large dish was not used, nor did the English aesthetics prefer the diaper and rosette decorations seen on the lower dish.

208. Eight Light Figural Standard (one of a set of four), American, Rococo Revival, wired plaster, brass and glass, circa 1865. H: 55 in. W: 20 in. D: 19 in. Courtesy Dornsife Collection.

Fueled by the Civil War, the United States reached its full potential as an industrial giant during the 1860s. Many great fortunes were created during this period and the mansions of these new captains of industry rose in unparalleled numbers in the East, Midwest and to a lesser extent the West. The baronial piles demanded the creation of furnishings in scale with the immense rooms and suited to convey that sense of splendor and awe desired by the owners.

Sets of standards to be used in the corners of entrance halls, dining rooms and drawing rooms were fashioned to a large extent out of plaster set on wire frames. Modestly clad female figures reflecting the classical antique were popular models for the standards. Here the figure in her carefully draped gown and sandals holds a brass candelabrum aloft with her left hand. The cornucopia-shaped branches in the *Restauration* style emerge from an armature. They terminate in scalloped cut glass bobeches which are missing their prisms. These standards could be either made for candles or gas. This example could have easily been piped for gas.

209. Two Light Candle Lamp, French, Louis XVI style, ormolu and tole, circa 1780-1785. Courtesy Nesle, Inc., New York. Photo by Helga Photo Studio.

Candle lamps in ormolu with tole shades were another type of lighting device which originated with the French. Several models have been reproduced in the twentieth century ranging in quality from very poor to excellent. The present example combines the use of a high-style circular candlestick base having gadrooning, reeds and foliate motives with a plain, square shaft terminating in a carrying ring. The branches are straight and reeded and are joined to a movable rachet. Each cylindrical candle cup has a beaded bobeche with an artichoke pendent drop. The shade, too, can rise and descend on the shaft and it is composed of two sheets of slightly curved pieces of bright brass which have been painted black on the outside.

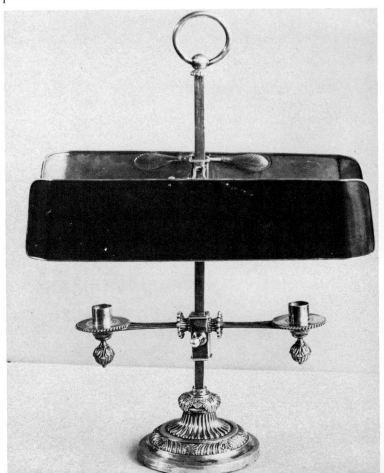

210. Three Light Bouillotte Candle Lamp, French, transitional style from Louis XVI, First Empire, ormolu, wrought iron and tole, circa 1785-1800. Courtesy Nesle, Inc., New York. Photo by Helga Photo Studio.

The ormolu wire-work basket base raised on the circular beaded base is in the Louis XVI taste, as are the three sabot-shaped candle cups. The branches, however, which are basically Louis XVI in style, provide a hint of the forthcoming Napoleonic fashion in the bas relief profiles of a helmeted Roman soldier which embellish each arm. An iron rod which bears the candle sockets and the tole shade rises from a reeded Louis XVI column. The iron rod is adjusted with an ormolu handle placed at the candle cup level. The shade is adjusted with a similar rachet attached to a movable ormolu sleeve which fits over the square rod and is also joined to the shade. The sheet metal shade itself is flared and painted dark green with foliate borders painted in gilt.

211. Candle Lamp, English (made by Greenhill and Co., Bury Street, Saint James, London), Neoclassical style, gilded and painted brass, circa 1800. H: 17-⅛ in. W: 7 in. Courtesy of the Henry Francis duPont Winterthur Museum, Winterthur, Delaware.

The style of this single candle adjustable lamp was doubtless influenced by the larger, multi-candle French-made lamps. There are a number of subtle refinements to be seen in this piece. The dish-type base has a continuous border of anthemia as well as a loop thumb piece to facilitate the carrying and balancing of the lamp. It would be used in conjunction with the carrying handle at the head of the square stem. The adjustable rachet supports a bracketed arm with a fluted vase-shaped candle cup. That same rachet has a socket for the candle snuffer. The brass shade whose exterior is painted black is also on its own adjustable rachet.

212a. Palmer Patent Lamp, English, William IV style, gilded brass, iron and etched glass, circa 1830-1840. H: 31-¼ in. Diam. of shade: 9-¾ in. Courtesy Dornsife Collection.

Patented in 1830 by William Palmer, the Palmer patent lamp had a large columnar shaft which was fitted with a brass cylindrical sleeve and a coil spring. Large candles were especially made with three wicks composed of woven wire and cotton. These triple-wick candles did burn brighter and put out more light.

This lamp is an example of the earlier type of standard. There is a square, stepped foot and a square plinth in matte gilded brass which supports a bright gilded brass column having a lotus-like capital. The etched, domed shade with squatty vase-shaped secondary element is the most frequently encountered type of shade seen on Palmer patent lamps. According to the present owner, this lamp came to the United States in 1840 and was in New England until he acquired it.

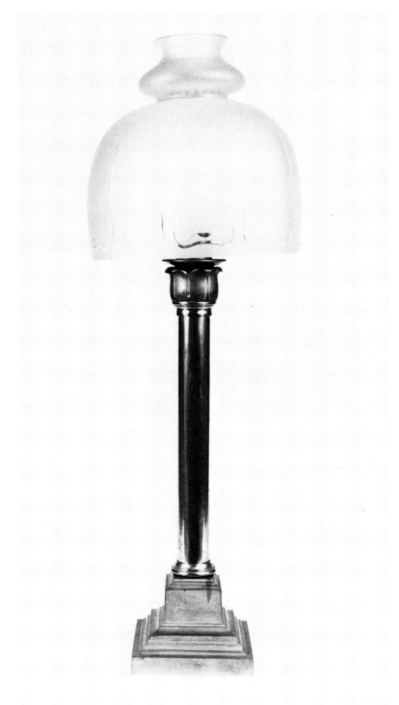

212b. Detail of label, candleholder, chimney support and shade ring of William IV style Palmer patent lamp. Courtesy Dornsife Collection.

While this lamp has been electrified, it shows the appearance of the early Palmer shade and chimney holders. Note that the shade stand and ring support for the chimney are brass, while the pierced shade holder is made of iron. An applied octagonal brass plaque, bearing the legend "PALMER & Co" "PATENT" with a pseudo-royal coat of arms between the two words, is affixed to the side of the cap on the casing for the candle. This format and style of label appears on all Palmer patent lamps.

146

213a. Palmer Patent Lamp, English, Rococo Revival style, ormolu, enameled brass, etched glass, circa 1845-1855. H: 37-⅞ in. W. and D. of base: 7 in. Diam. of shade: 9-½ in. Courtesy Dornsife Collection.

This could well be the Palmer patent lamp that best survives in original condition in the world. Everything remains including one of the three wicked candles and a snuffer. The ornate four-square base is raised on button or bun feet whose sides are decorated with cabochons. Cabochons are placed regularly in amongst the scrolls and foliate motives that comprise the base and plinth. The columnar stem is enameled a rich blue color. It is terminated with a capital of ormolu which echoes the forms of the base and plinth.

It is important to note that the Palmer patent candle lamp is the only fixture of its kind illustrated in the catalogue of the Crystal Palace Exhibition held in London in 1851. Two of the lamps with quite exotic standards are shown—one has elephant heads in its base and the other employs lions' legs and masks. These are shown by Mr. Potts of Birmingham, but had to have been made under license from William Palmer. Palmer renewed his patent in 1852.

213b. Detail of circa 1845-1855 Palmer Patent Lamp. Courtesy Dornsife Collection.

With the shade removed the improved model of shade and chimney support can be seen. The shade holder is composed of three vertical brass struts which are bowed at the bottom. These struts are soldered to rings at both terminal points. The upper ring is made like a bezel with a rabbet to hold the shade in place. A separate hook which serves as a hanger for the snuffer is soldered to the lower ring. Additionally, three cabriole struts are soldered to that lower ring and they support the chimney. The chimney is raised up to emit more air. This arrangement copies the early argand lamps whose chimneys were raised in this manner to increase the turbulence.

214a. Palmer Patent Lamp, English, William IV-early Victorian style, ormolu, gilt brass, enamel and etched glass, circa 1840-1851. H: 32 in. W. and D. of base: 7-½ in. Diam. of shade: 10 in. Collection of Anglo-American Art Museum, Louisiana State University, Baton Rouge.

Regretfully the enameling done in imitation of damasked work on the stem of this handsome lamp is much rubbed and because it is black, it is difficult to capture the overall diaper pattern in a photograph. The hexagonal base with its concave sides supports a scrolling foliate and floral plinth which stylistically could date back to William IV's reign. The patterned damasked stem, however, points to a date of manufacture in the 1840s and 1850s. This lamp has a swirling foliate and floral capital which partially conceals the drip pan. The domed shade of etched glass has a similar vase-form secondary element. It also has the same continuous border composed of modified "U" shapes, each of which contains a secondary serpentine line.

214b. Detail of marks and struts of the William IV-early Victorian style Palmer Patent Lamp. Collection of Anglo-American Art Museum, Louisiana State University, Baton Rouge.

A plaque identical to the one seen on the earliest Palmer Patent lamp shown in this chapter appears here. On one of the struts, a second mark, the impressed or cold struck legend, "PALMER & Co/PATENT," appears. The supports for the chimney are small projections on the struts of the shade holder.

Stand, simple in construction, with much of the character of the antique. Following this is

body of the vase; the subject is a youthful sylvan, "Pan," kneeling at the altar of Hymen, where he is crowned by Flora: it is termed by

a CANDLE LAMP, the pedestal composed of elephants' heads, very skilfully wrought. Across

the maker, "A Festival in honour of Spring." The other engraving is from a CANDLE LAMP:

is judiciously applied, and executed with much spirit. There are few objects of manufacturing art which have exhibited, during some years past, more manifest improvements than the table candle-lamp in all of its many varieties of form.

215. Illustration from the Crystal Palace Exhibition, London, 1851 of two candle lamps made by the Potts firm of Birmingham, England. Courtesy Dover Publications, Inc., New York and from their unabridged reissue of The Art-Journal Special Issue, p. 24.

Potts was one of two Birmingham firms manufacturing candle lamps under license from Palmer and exhibiting at the Crystal Palace Exhibition. The two lamps illustrated here are certainly amongst the most sumptuous examples known. The example employing elephants' heads as a part of the plinth is particularly spectacular. Note that the shade is slightly flared and scalloped at the bottom and is etched with a tassel pattern. The other lamp's shade is in the conventional Palmer shape but is etched with a pattern of stylized anthemia set within arches.

The commentator on the works in the exhibition states:

"Mr. Potts, of Birmingham, has long been distinguished as a manufacturer of LAMPS, CLOCKSTANDS, CANDELABRA, and articles of virtu, displaying pure taste in design and refined skill in manufacture. It is not perhaps, too much to say, that his abilities and exertion have done much to elevate the character of the Birmingham bronze and brass works. The whole of his numerous contributions are entirely the work of English hands; we select, we believe, the best."[17]

Messrs. BLEWS & SONS, of Birmingham
nd London, are extensive manufacturers of
rass candle and ship lamps, candlesticks,
ells, imperial weights and measures, &c.

Ve engrave on this and the succeeding
olumn four examples of their CANDLE-
.AMPs: the first is called the "armorial

mp;" the second, termed the "vine-
wreath foot," shows that graceful plant
imbing up the shaft and over the shade;
he leaves and fruit being coloured. In the

third example the convolvulus forms the p
cipal ornament at the base. The fourth h
a very elegant pedestal of leaves, dogs' hea

and birds; the pillar is of richly-cut ruby gla
with centre groups of flowers. The glass, it

sufficient to say, is from the factory of Messr
Richardson, of Stourbridge; the bronze an
brass castings are exceedingly sharp and brillian

216. Illustration from the Crystal Palace Exhibition, London, 1851 of four candle lamps made by Messers. Blews and Sons of Birmingham and London with shades made by Richardson of Stourbridge. Courtesy Dover Publications Inc., New York and from their unabridged reissue of The Art-Journal Special Issue, pp. 216-217.

Much valuable information is imparted by these illustrations and the commentary from the Crystal Palace Exhibition catalogue. Beyond the illustrations of four more patterns of candle lamps made by another manufacturer, the accompanying commentary provides the name of the glass house which fabricated the shades and the name of the lamp patterns. The text written about the lamps by the anonymous commentator therefore bears quoting.

"Messers. BLEWS & SONS, of Birmingham and London, are extensive manufacturers of brass candle and ship lamps, candlesticks, bells, imperial weights and measures &c. We engrave on this and the succeeding column four examples of their CANDLELAMPS: the first is called the "armorial lamp;" the second, termed the "vine-wreath foot," shows the graceful plant climbing up the shaft and over the shade; the leaves and fruit being colored. In the third example, the convolvulus forms the principal ornament at the base. The fourth has a very elegant pedestal of leaves, dogs' heads, and birds; the pillar is of richly-cut ruby glass, with centre groups of flowers. The glass, it is sufficient to say, is from the factory of Messers. Richardson, of Stourbridge, the bronze and brass casting are exceedingly sharp and brilliant."[18]

In the case of each of these lamps, the shades are bell-shaped, but each is etched with a different pattern. The two lamps illustrated at the top of each page also have shades with spool-like secondary elements rather than the usual vase shape.

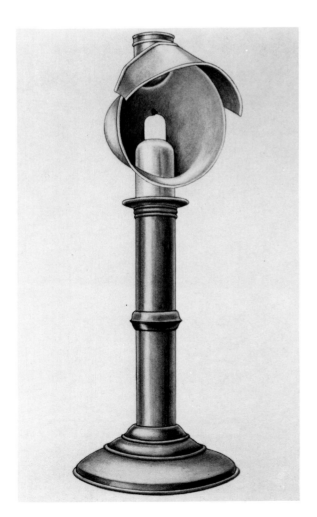

217. Candle Lamp, American, Victorian, sheet brass and iron, circa 1840-1865. Photograph by permission of Index of American Design, National Gallery of Art, Washington, D.C.

This is just about the same candleholder as the spring action pair (vide p. 77, ill. 91) with the exception of being fitted with a brass reflector shade. These were indeed used as pulpit candlesticks in the church. They certainly could be used to great effect in counting houses and other commerical enterprises, as well as for doing close work such as sewing or reading in the home.

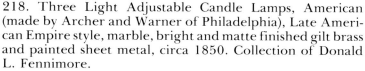

218. Three Light Adjustable Candle Lamps, American (made by Archer and Warner of Philadelphia), Late American Empire style, marble, bright and matte finished gilt brass and painted sheet metal, circa 1850. Collection of Donald L. Fennimore.

The Archer and Warner firm is fairly well-known for its manufacture of girandoles and gas lighting devices. This lamp applying the spring action principles of the Palmer patent lamp is the only known example by the Philadelphia firm. The oval label of applied brass reads "ARCHER & WARNER/MAKERS/ PHILADELPHIA." The bright and matte finish of the plinth and the candle cylinders survive in excellent condition and the color of the gold is the same as seen on Philadelphia-made girandoles and oil lamps. The arrangement of the three candle cylinders in cojoining brass rings on an adjustable rachet is another unusual feature of this rare lamp. A loop carrying handle serves as a finial at the top of the stem. The black painted, sheet metal shade is also adjustable.

219. Two Light Adjustable Candle Lamp, English, late Neoclassical style, core cast and sheet brass, circa 1840-1870. H: 29 in. W: 6-¼ in. D: 9 in. Courtesy Herbert Schiffer Antiques, West Chester, Pennsylvania.

The simplicity of this candle lamp's design would initially suggest an early nineteenth-century design. The round rod used as a stem rather than a square one almost precludes this piece having been made in the early part of the century. The standard is not too different from those seen on post-Civil War student lamps. The composition of the lamp is very pleasing with its circular dish-type base and the graduated urns on the lower part of the stem. The carrying handle is a nicely cast inverted stirrup and the rachet for adjusting the candles has a well-made baluster handle. The oval dish and plain cylindrical candle cups are almost too crude for the rest of the fixture.

220. Three Light Bouillotte Lamp, American (made by Baker, Arnold and Co. of Philadelphia), Louis XVI Revival style, brass and painted sheet metal, circa 1871-1878.[19] H: 26 in. Diam. of base: 5-¼ in. Diam. of shade: 16-¾ in. Courtesy of the Henry Frances duPont Winterthur Museum, Winterthur, Delaware.

Published several times as having been made in the United States between 1800-1820, this bouillotte lamp is one of those things that is too good to be true. Even the most discerning and discriminating of collectors and curators have been guilty of ignoring technological evidence and of not thoroughly searching commercial records to document an object that, if made at an early time, is a great rarity. This piece bears the legend "BAKER, ARNOLD & CO/PHILADELPHIA." This firm was a brief partnership formed after the dissolution of the Cornelius and Baker firm. The 1875 Directory lists, "Baker, Arnold & Co. (William C. Baker, Crawford Arnold & Robert C. Baker) gas fixtures, 710 Chesnut & N. 12th c. Brown." The firm was founded by 1871 according to the Directory for that year and lasted until 1878.

Even without the maker's mark, the technology employed in the piece's fabrication provides the necessary proof of its late manufacture. The dish-shaped base is made of spun brass, a technique not used in the United States until 1850. The shank or stem to which the adjustable branches and shade are affixed is round rather than the square standards seen on the eighteenth and nineteenth century French and English candle lamps. The stem is the same type of tubing that was used for gas pipes. The foliate projections are long and seem to have as their design inspiration the rococo revival rather than the neoclassical period.

The piece is important as an early example of the Louis XVI-Empire Revival occurring in the United States. In style it is sympathetic enough to the earlier pieces to have convinced that great collector of Americana, Henry Francis duPont, that the piece dated from the early nineteenth century. The decorative detail work includes bands of stars that in the illustration appear to be beading. They are located on the thick lower shaft, as well as on the bobeches and wax pans. Reeding appears on the lower part of each candle cup and on the side of the central flange to which each branch is attached. This is probably as sophisticated a reproduction of a bouillotte lamp as was being made in France or Britain at the time.

1. O'Dea, William T. The Social History of Lighting (Routledge and Kegan Paul, London: 1958) p. 3.

2. The New Encyclopaedia Britannica Macropaedia (Encyclopaedia Britannica, Chicago: 1985) Vol 23, p. 30.

3. O'Dea, William T. The Social History of Lighting, p. 54.

4. Ibid.

5. The New Encyclopaedia Britannica Macropaedia (Encyclopaedia Britannica, Chicago: 1985) Vol p. 798.

6. O'Dea, William T. The Social History of Lighting p. 54.

7. Thuro, Catherine M.V. Oil Lamps: The Kerosene Era in North America (Wallace-Homestead, DesMoines: 1976) p. 15.

8. A fine illustrated essay on eighteenth and early nineteenth century casting techniques is to be found in Peter, Nancy and Herbert Schiffer's The Brass Book (Schiffer, Exton, Pa.: 1978) pp. 24-32.

9. Gentle, Rupert and Feild, Rachael, English Domestic Brass 1680-1810 and the History of Its Origins (E. P. Dutton, New York: 1975) p. 127, fig. 62a.

10. Fisher, S. W. English Pottery and Porcelain Marks (Wallace-Homestead, DesMoines: 1970) pp. 68-69.

11. I am indebted to John W. Keefe, Curator of Decorative Arts at the New Orleans Museum of Art, for calling my attention to the fact that these figures are a known Thomire model.

12. Keefe, John W. Selected Works of Eighteenth Century French Art in the Collections of the Art Institute of Chicago (Art Institute, Chicago: 1976) p. 155.

13. Ibid.

14. Delieb, Eric and Roberts, Michael The Great Silver Manufactory: Matthew Boulton and the Birmingham Silversmiths: 1760-1790 (Studio Vista, London: 1971) pp. 106-107.

15. Benezit, E. Dictionnaire de Paintres, Sculpteurs, Dessinateurs et Graveurs (Libraire Grund, Paris: 1961) Vol. 4, p. 758.

16. Gloag, John (introduction) The Crystal Palace Exhibition Illustrated Catalogue·London 1851 (Dover, New York: 1970) p. 24 and pp. 216-217. The Dover Pictorial Archive Series has reproduced an unabridged edition of the original Art Journal Illustrated Catalogue.

17. Ibid, p. 23.

18. Ibid, pp. 216-217.

19. For a brief history of Baker, Arnold and Co., see Denys, Peter Myers Gaslighting in America: A Guide for Historic Preservation (U.S. Department of the Interior, Washington: 1978) p. 157.

20. I am grateful to Donald L. Fennimore, Curator of Metals at the Henry Francis duPont Winterthur Museum, for telling, in detail, about the construction of this fixture.

Girandoles

Paradoxically it is not the lighting devices demonstrating the nineteenth century's latest technological advances that most evoke an image of that century in late twentieth-century American minds. Girandoles, those marble-based candleholders having gilded bronze or brass shafts and branches and multi-faceted glass prisms suspended from ornate prism rings, are the fixtures most symbolic of lighting during the last century in the United States.

Unlike the various oil lamps of the late eighteenth and early nineteenth centuries, whose forms are neo-classical, and the majority of the later oil and gas fixtures so effusively decorated with floral and foliate motives, the girandoles' pictorial shafts alone convey the hyper-romanticism and sentimentality of the century. Romantic literary themes such as Saint-Pierre's Paul et Virginie and Washington Irving's Rip van Winkle served as models for Rococo Revival-style girandoles. An actual historical event such as the American Revolutionary War capture of Major Andre or historical personages such as George Washington and Benjamin Franklin provided the inspiration for other designs. Architecture, particularly in the Gothic Revival taste, was the source for patterns having chapels or castles as their decorative shafts. Amusing stags, friendly spaniels and other animals appear decoratively on other girandoles. There was no paucity of imagination on the part of the pattern makers for the girandole manufacturers, and indeed, no hesitation in that eclectic period to blend Rococo, Gothic and Classical Revival elements in one object.

Girandoles were made in vast numbers and because of their decorative nature and portability, they are to be found all over the United States in private houses, historic house museums and in the decorative arts departments of the art museums. Whether of the expensive, limited-production models or of the cheaper, mass-produced patterns, girandoles with their gilded metalwork and glistening prisms connoted elegance atop the gilded pier tables of the wealthy or as garniture on a middle class mantel. Girandoles, with their usual two-dimensional shafts, did not lend themselves to piping for gas or wiring for conversion to electricity. They have therefore not suffered from the generally unsympathetic conversions to electricity undergone by the vast majority of surviving oil and gas fixtures. While the definition of the word "girandole" employed here would be commonly understood by most English-speaking Americans, both of the nineteenth and twentieth centuries, the term has had other meanings in the past and does have some dual meanings even today. These should be delved into before continuing the examination of this particular form of lighting device. The origin of the word is the Italian, "girandola"—"A kind of revolving firework; a discharge of rockets, etc. from a revolving wheel."[1]

The word becomes "girandole" in French and entered the English language by the mid-eighteenth century when Thomas Chippendale illustrated ornate Rococo-style giltwood mirrored wall sconces as "gerandoles" in his Gentleman and Cabinet-Maker's Director (both in the second edition of 1754 as plate CXL and in the 1762 edition as plates CLXXVII and CLXXVIII). In the London "Public Advertiser" for 10 June 1769, there is mention of glass sconces and girandoles.[2] In a 1804 "Sporting Magazine"[3] a bill of sale for sofas, pier glasses and girandoles appears. In the third chapter of the first book of his 1844 novel, Coningsby, Benjamin Disraeli in describing Monmouth House, a fictionalized Palladian palace says, "It led into a vestibule, . . . hung with Venetian girandoles . . . "[4] Quite obviously Disraeli had cut glass sconces in mind in this description. Convex looking glasses, either embellished with candle branches or not, have long been referred to as girandole looking glasses.

The third definition of girandole in the Oxford English Dictionary sums up the British interpretation of the word. "A branched support for candles or other lights, either in the form of a candlestick for placing on a table etc. or more commonly as a bracket projecting from a wall."[5] American interpretation is even looser and less confining, "An ornamented branched candle holder."[6] Illustrations in surviving American commercial lighting device catalogues from the 1850-1860 period, such as Starr, Fellows and Company and Dietz and Company of New York City feature precisely the type of device defined in the opening paragraph of this essay. There can, therefore, be no question as to what the word meant in the United States.

While the most typical surviving girandole sets consist of a central three-branch candleholder with flanking single-light girandoles, there are many other variations and permutations. A garniture could at its simplest be a pair of single-light candlesticks, but it could range up to a massive grouping of five girandoles. Apparently only a small number of the large five-light girandoles were made. They were intended to serve as the principal fixture in a grouping but could be used alone.

MANUFACTURER AND PATENTEE OF THE

SOLAR BURNER,
198 WASHINGTON STREET,
Opposite the Marlboro'—eight doors south of Franklin st.

LAMPS, CHANDELIERS, CANDELABRAS, GI-RANDOLES, WICKS AND GLASSES.

The subscriber now offers the LARGEST ASSORTMENT ON THE COUNTRY, at prices much *less* than can be found at any other store or manufactory, and the quality and finish warranted equal to any that can be obtained, or the money will be refunded. Together with the patterns manufactured at this establishment, may be found those of Messrs. Cornelius & Co.; W. Carleton; Gooding & Co.; Hooper & Co, and a good assortment of RICH ENGLISH LAMPS, of entire *new patterns*, among which are some Damask Solars, never before offered for sale in this country; all of which will be sold as above.

Old Lamps repaired, rebronzed or finished in Or Molu. Lamps and Chandeliers of all kinds, altered to Solars with Shaw's improved Patent Shadowless Solar Burner, at $1,50 each, and warranted to burn at 3-4 cent per hour, with *Oil* furnished by me at *fifty-five cents per gall.*

W. F. SHAW.

Best solar heads fitted to old astral pedestals for $2.
198 *Washington street, Boston.*

Plate 6
Advertisement of William F. Shaw from Stimpson's Boston Directory (Charles Stimpson, Boston: 1845) p. 14. Courtesy Middleton Library, Louisiana State University, Baton Rouge.
  Note that the Shaw firm handles girandoles and other lighting devices made by other American manufacturers, as well as English-made lamps and fixtures of his own manufacture.

They are, however, occasionally seen in pairs.

The number of candle branches is just one consideration in the study of what made better and more expensive girandoles. Double marble bases with separate applied, cast, gilt-brass or bronze mouldings between steps added more refinement at greater price per piece. White marble was routinely used to make girandole bases, but occasionally a more exotic, imported black marble with gold chain veining was used.

Another factor affecting the cost of girandoles was the type and quality of their finishes. A well-done gilt finish incorporating matte areas with bright highlights would be more attractive and more expensive than a single finish—usually a matte one. Silvering was less frequently used, but the rarest finishing technique employed on girandoles was that of damasking the metal parts in beautiful blue and pale gold—a finishing process customarily reserved for the finest solar and sinumbra lamps.

The marble, gilt brass or bronze and cut glass girandoles illustrated in this chapter very much depend upon their cut-glass prisms to provide the important accent of brilliance to even the most humble of girandoles. There are various shapes of prisms acceptable for use on the circa 1830-1860 girandoles. They range from the straight, many-sided, "Georgian" models which terminate in multi-faceted tips, to coffin-shaped, to those decorated with floral, vine, star and snowflake motives (See Plates 1-4 for line drawings of prisms.) The majority of the prisms were probably of British or continental Europe manufacture, but some of the Pittsburgh glass houses did advertise coffin-shape prisms of their own manufacture.

No evidence has surfaced to support the use of three-sided prisms that terminate in short, hexagonal spearheads on the girandoles dating from before the Civil War. These prisms and their more decoratively back-cut cousins lack the breadth necessary for the aesthetically pleasing appearance afforded by the various styles of prisms described earlier. Apart from the aesthetic considerations, the only type of prisms shown in the 1856 Starr, Fellows and Company catalogue are those with the star and snowflake motives, while the Dietz and Company catalogue of 1860 illustrates eleven different girandole patterns with that type of prism and one pattern having the coffin-shape type of prisms.

Fragile prisms are the first casualties when girandoles are cleaned or moved. A girandole surviving with original or period prisms is one that will have some chips. There is a shortage in today's market of antique prisms of the kind appropriate for use on girandoles. Dealers will frequently hang the three-sided, spear-tipped prisms on girandoles missing all or a part of their original prisms. The dealer-collector-restorer does have another alternative when faced with the prism replacement predicament. Fine-quality reproductions of the coffin shape and some of the three-sided prisms ornamented with stars and snowflakes are being made in Czechoslovakia and can be found with some effort in the United States. These reproductions can be quite convincing except for the fact that they are usually in perfect condition.

The type of girandole under consideration in this chapter seems to be an American phenomenon with few exceptions. There are three centers of manufacture for girandoles—Philadelphia, New York and Boston. The largest manufacturer of girandoles was the Cornelius firm in Philadelphia. It is apparent that that company under its various names was inconsistent as to whether it labeled a product or not. None the less, this is the manufacturer whose name most commonly is found on girandoles. The maker's marks are usually struck or applied to the backs of the shafts; however, at least one Philadelphia firm, Archer and Warner, placed their label inside the prism ring.

Only a few cautious general statements can be made concerning regional differences between the products of the three American manufacturing centers. Philadelphia and New York are very much alike in the types of candle cups, prism rings and gilt finishes they preferred. This is explained in part by the close proximity of the two cities and because some Philadelphia firms such as Archer and Warner expanded their operation into New York City. At any rate, the stylistic preference in candle cups in both places was for palmette bordered bobeches or spun-brass examples with moulded or moulded and cabled bobeches. The differences in prism rings are far more subtle and there seem to be exceptions to every rule. A delicate ring composed of downturned water leaves appears to have originated in Philadelphia, but was copied in New York. At least one Boston firm, Henry H. Hooper & Co., made a slightly heavier edition of this model. The illustrations and their captions in this chapter I hope will assist in sorting out the nuances of the various prism rings. New York and the Dietz firm in particular made an inexpensive stamped brass prism ring.

If the documented Philadelphia examples surviving with their original gilt finishes are to be relied upon, a soft lemon gold matte finish combined with bright highlights was preferred. Boston on the other hand seems to have leaned toward rich, deep gold finishes to combine with their rather foliate candle cups. There are, however, known New York examples exhibiting both the lighter and darker types of gilding.

At best, the above stylistic preferences are only tentative suggestions demanding further research. The relative rarity of the signed examples makes all the above statements inconclusive. Indeed, at this writing only the girandoles manufactured by two Philadelphia companies, Cornelius and Archer and Warner, are known through signed examples. William Shaw produced the majority of the signed Boston examples seen today. Although rarely signed, many more girandoles can be attributed to the large Boston foundry, Henry N. Hooper and Company. The firm was active under that name from 1833 through 1868. Fortunately a copy of that company's illustrated catalogue of 1858 is preserved at the Essex Institute in Salem, Massachusetts. There are signed examples by Dietz and Company of New York City as well as further evidence of products of their manufacture shown in the 1860 catalogue of that firm. An annotated facsimile of that catalogue by Ulysses G. Dietz appeared in 1982. The work of another important New York firm, Starr, Fellows and Company and its successor Fellows, Hoffman and Company, are

221. Pair of Girandoles (Dolphin model), English or American (Boston), George IV or American Empire style, gilded brass and glass, circa 1825-1840. H: 10 in. W: 6 in. D: 3-⅞ in. Collection of Mr. and Mrs. William McGehee, Dr. Dubs Town House, Natchez, Mississippi.

This pair of short girandoles featuring rather playful dolphins have rectangular bases raised on button feet which are reminiscent of some seen on English-made argand lamps. The scalloped bobeches are similar to some made by the Henry N. Hooper firm. Whether made in George IV's or William IV's England or in Boston during President Andrew Jackson's term of office, they are charming.

known through their respective catalogues dated 1856 and 1858-1859. I have seen no marked Starr, Fellows and Company girandoles, although some of the "Capture of Andre" models bear the impression "PATENT APPLIED FOR."

Caution should be observed in attributing unmarked girandoles to specific cities, much less specific companies. The nineteenth century was rife with the pirating of other firms' designs. Another factor that further confuses the issue is the possiblity that larger firms such as that of Cornelius could have easily sold parts such as prism rings and candle cups to other manufacturers. Also affecting the transfer of styles from one center to another was the fairly rapid rail transport system that had developed along the corridor running between the manufacturing centers of Philadelphia, New York and Boston by the 1840s. The ingenious 1845 city directory advertisement (Plate 6) of William F. Shaw not only reproduces his name in an unusual type face which features lamps as ornaments, but documents the practice of a Boston lamp and girandole maker retailing lighting devices of his competitors far and near.[7] He seems only too pleased to announce that his store handles the wares of his large and famous Philadelphia competitor, Cornelius and Company. Perhaps more surprising are the Boston manufacturers who appear in the same list—William Carleton and Henry N. Hooper and Company. This strengthens the supposition that parts could have been purchased by smaller manufacturers

from the large factories. Additionally, it would help to explain the easy way in which a Boston firm could quickly pick up the latest Philadelphia pattern and alter it slightly if the design were patented. For these various reasons a fairly conservative approach has necessarily been taken in attributing unmarked examples in the captions accompanying the illustrations.

While every effort has been made to include all the known girandole models, there are some regretful omissions of known models for which it was impossible to locate a photographable example. The "Little Eva" and "Robinson Crusoe" patterns are among the few that are not illustrated. Also missing from the illustrations is a rare form of girandole having a colored glass panel fitted into an open reserve in the shaft.

For collectors, girandoles are probably the most underpriced of all nineteenth-century lighting devices. Good quality objects can be found at most auctions, in antique shops and in estate sales around the United States for modest amounts of money. With the current return to favor and vogue for nineteenth-century material culture, the finest and rarest examples of girandoles are increasing in price, as is only to be expected. When one, however, compares the price of girandoles to that of nineteenth-century lamps and chandeliers, much less with eighteenth-century lighting devices, the relative inexpensiveness of girandoles will be readily apparent.

222. Pair of Three-Branch Girandoles (George Washington/Benjamin Franklin model), American (Philadelphia or New York, possibly the Cornelius firm of Philadelphia), late American Empire style, gilded brass, marble and glass, circa 1840-1855. Washington-H: 23-⅞ in W: 16-¼ in Depth at base: 6-½ in. Franklin-H: 23-¾ in W:15-⅝ in. Depth at base: 6-½ in. Collection of Anglo-American Art Museum, Louisiana State University, Baton Rouge. Gift of Mrs. Mamie Henry and Mr. and Mrs. Stephen G. Henry, Jr. in memory of General Stephen G. Henry, Sr.

This is certainly one of the finest surviving sets of girandoles known. Their enormous size and the fact that they have large sculptures in the round of prominent early American figures indicate these girandoles were custom-made or a very limited edition model. This is the only pair that I have seen and I have heard of only one other George Washington example.

These girandoles represent the apogee of American-made examples. They were originally owned by Dean Robinson, the first president of the New York Central Railroad. Stylistically they combine the neo-classically posed figures with Rococo Revival branches and prism rings. The soft, matte and bright finish gilding is superior and is in very good condition. The seventy-two, plain, rectangular prisms are original and in excellent condition with the exception of one badly chipped prism and one replacement button.

The three-dimensional figures were cast from a well-sculpted mould. Additionally iconographical interest is found in the scroll held in the hand of the George Washington statue, which is inscribed in script, "Declaration/of/Independence." The Franklin figure clasps a similar scroll which is inscribed, "The Law/of/Pennsylvania."

The lavish nature of everything about these girandoles points to their having come from a large and experienced firm. The candle cups have bobeches with palmette borders in the Philadelphia-New York style. Both the prism rings and the color of gilding exhibit the taste predilections of those cities. The quality and the style of these girandoles relate to the best documented work of the Cornelius firm, allowing the strongest of attributions to be made in favor of that company.

223. Single Girandole (Jenny Lind model from a garniture set composed of a flanking single socket candleholder and a three-branch centerpiece), American, Rococo Revival style, gilded brass, marble and glass, circa 1852-1865. H: 15-½ in. W: 6-½ in. D: 3-½ in. Courtesy Didier, Inc., New Orleans.

Jenny Lind (1820-1887), the Swedish soprano who was nicknamed "the Swedish Nightingale" was one of the most celebrated concert and operatic singers of the nineteenth century. Her concert tour of the United States in 1850-1852, under the management of P. T. Barnum, was a smashing success which was long remembered. Many souvenirs, both inexpensive and fine, were created as memorabilia of her visit. This girandole and the garniture of which it is a part have a very light gold-colored matte finish with bright highlights which are associated with Philadelphia and New York work. The candle cup with the palmette bordered bobeche is also identified with those centers. The exact figural and supporting foliate, floral and harp elements are illustrated in the 1860 catalogue of the New York firm of Dietz and Company. The prism ring is, however, a rare one which has not at this time been associated with a specific maker or city of manufacture. The design is a border of standing sprigs of flowers which alternate with bull rushes. Also, relatively uncommon are the prisms and their accompanying headers. Cut into each prism and header are two rows of decorative "C" scrolls or crescents.

224. Pair of Girandoles (St. John model), American (made in New York by Dietz, Brother and Company), Rococo Revival style, gilded brass, marble and glass, circa 1859-1860. H: 15-5/16 in. W: 6-5/8 in. D: 3-11/16 in. Collection of Dr. and Mrs. C. C. Coles.

Religious subjects seem to have been the least popular of all the themes used to decorate girandoles. St. John the Baptist, who appears here with exposed legs, partially bare chest, beard and lion skin, is an example not only of a religious figure, but of a semi-nude figure as a part of a girandole. The back of the plinth is cold stamped "DIETZ PATENT 1859." The engraved illustration appearing in the 1860 Dietz catalogue as "31. Girandole, St. John" shows grape cluster, vine pattern prism rings. The stamped brass prism rings as manufactured are actually more inventive in that a winged putto alternates with a foliate device. The candle cups are of spun brass and have a plain moulded bobeche which is a part of the candle cup.

St. John the Baptist's pose is the classic "contrapposto" position with his right arm raised and forefinger pointed upward. His left arm is outstretched to hold a crude cross. The figure is framed by bocages which were doubtless inspired by those seen on Staffordshire pottery figures of the 1840s and 1850s.

The stamped brass parts and the relatively poor casting of this model would indicate that these were less expensive models. These examples have lost their original gilding and have been electroplated.

225. Three Branch Girandole (one of a pair of the Damascene model), American (probably Philadelphia), Rococo Revival style, damasked brass, marble and glass, circa 1840-1861. H: 16-¾ in. W: 17 in. D: 5 in. Collection of Rosedown Plantation, St. Francisville, Louisiana.

The term "Damascene" model is my own and seems an appropriate way to distinguish this pair of candelabra having a finish not usually found on girandoles. Several variations of this pattern having the upward tapering shaft are found in gilt brass.

In addition to the exceptional finish, the piece has a magnificent set of large coffin-shaped prisms and pressed glass secondary bobeches. The glass bobeches were incorrectly installed when these fixtures were electrified. Properly they should rest on the top of the metal candle cups where the broader glass bobeches, which are easier to clean, protect the metal finish from wind-blown dripping wax.

The candleholders were possessions of Daniel and Martha Turnbull, who built "Rosedown" in 1834-1835. Many of the finest furnishings for this house, one of the best of the surviving grand plantation houses of the Deep South, were made in Philadelphia. These girandoles have the palmette bordered bobeches, downturned water leaf prism rings and the damasked finish seen on some of the best quality Philadelphia-made oil lamps.

226a. Pair of Three Branch Girandoles, (Blake's Patent model), American (made by Henry N. Hooper and Co. of Boston), Rococo Revival style, gilded brass, marble and glass, circa 1850-1865. H: 16-⅝ in. W: 14-½ in. D: 4 in. Collection of Anglo-American Art Museum, Louisiana State University, Baton Rouge.

This rare pair of Rococo Revival girandoles is a variation of the lyre models made elsewhere. Both of these girandoles bear the incised block letter legend "BLAKE S PATENT" on the back of the lyre. William Blake and Thomas Richardson were two brass founders who went into partnership with Henry N. Hooper and Company. The girandoles are classic examples of the best work of that Boston firm. This pair is a slightly different version of model number 352 in the Hooper firm's 1858 catalogue. The catalogue model has an octagonal, stepped base made of gilded brass and having an egg and dart decorative moulding. The catalogue model's candle cups are of the four-sided foliate shape that resemble flower buds opening. The candle cups on this set of the Blake's Patent girandoles is a form seen throughout the Hooper catalogue. While the plain bobeches appear to be detachable they are really cast as a part of the candle cups. The matte finish with bright gilded highlights is original and is in the deep gold color favored by the Boston manufacturers.

226b. Maker's Mark for Blake's Patent Model Girandole

227. Three Branch Girandole (one of a pair of the Lyre model), American, Rococo Revival style, gilded brass, marble and glass, circa 1845-1861. H: 18-5/16 in. W: 17-3/4 in. D: 4-1/4 in. Collection of Mr. and Mrs. Raymond St. Germain.

This high Rococo Revival model seems to have found favor with a number of Americans. They survive in both gilded and silvered finishes. "Lyre" is used here as a descriptive term until such time as a period document is discovered revealing its nineteenth-century name. The coffin-shaped prisms, while correct, have been used on the side branches of this pair of girandoles in conjunction with alternating single and double headers above. While this use of double headers is not incorrect in itself, the alternating pattern of single and double headers is not supported by period illustrations. From an aesthetic point of view, the use of double headers make them out of proportion with the metalwork.

228. Pair of Four Branch Girandoles, American, Rococo Revival style, patinated bronze, marble and glass, circa 1835-1855. H: 22-½ in W: 17 in. D: 11 in. Collection of Mr. and Mrs. George Crounse, Jr.

A dark patinated bronze finish is not the one usually preferred for girandoles. Here it is used to good effect on these rather restrained examples which feature as plinths fully sculpted in the round neoclassical urns rising from massive, square, white marble bases. Rather simple rococo revival shafts spring from the urns and likewise the branches coming off the shafts exhibit the same simplicity. The finely cast downturned water leaves of the prism rings and the rather cylindrical candle cups with palmette bordered bobeches indicate that Philadelphia was their place of manufacture. The magnificence of the girandoles' size and the quality of the casting and prisms all suggest the work of a large foundry such as the Cornelius firm.

229. Three Branch Girandole (Vase model), American (Boston), Rococo Revival style, gilded brass, marble and glass, circa 1845-1865. H: 14-⁵/₁₆ in. W: 16 in. D: 4-¾ in. Courtesy Eugene D. Cizek, Ph.D. and Lloyd L. Sensat, Sun Oak House, New Orleans.

A pattern almost identical to this is one of the eleven patterns in the Dietz and Company catalogue of 1860, where it is titled the "Vase" pattern. This example has been stripped of its original gilding but the reeded candle cups with foliate bobeches and the broad, heavy, downturned leaf prism rings permit a Boston attribution for this girandole. Variations on this pattern were probably made in Philadelphia.

230a. Single Girandole (Basket of Flowers model), American (made in Philadelphia by Cornelius and Baker), Rococo Revival style, gilded brass, marble and glass, circa 1851-1861. H: 16-¼ in. W: 6 in. D: 3-¼ in. Collection of Anglo-American Art Museum, Louisiana State University, Baton Rouge.

Without the label "CORNELIUS & BAKER" in raised letters in a rectangle on the lower back of the flower basket, this girandole could be as easily attributed to New York as Philadelphia. The prism ring composed of the flaring grape leaf and grape cluster and the candle cup with the striated sides are associated as much with Starr, Fellows and Company of New York as with any firm.

230b. Label on back of Basket of Flowers Girandole

When Dutch-born Christian Cornelius, the founder of Cornelius firm died in 1851, the style of the company's name changed from Cornelius and Son to Cornelius and Baker. Robert Cornelius, the son of Christian, had joined his father in 1831. Isaac F. Baker was Christian Cornelius' son-in-law who formed the new partnership with Robert Cornelius. The style of the firm's name changed again by 1861 after two sons of Robert Cornelius joined the company. The new name was Cornelius, Baker and Company.

The Cornelius and Baker label and the style of the piece delimits this girandole's manufacture to the ten-year span of 1851 to 1861.

162

231. Pair of Five Branch Girandoles (Urn model), American, Rococo Revival style, patinated bronze and glass, circa 1850-1865. Courtesy Christie's, New York.

The refined casting and the handsome moulded marble bases of this pair point to these girandoles being the product of a major manufacturer. The candle cups with their bobeches having palmette borders in the Philadelphia-New York style point to those two centers of metalware manufacturing. The grape vine and cluster prism rings are not too dissimilar from those seen on the "Stagg" and "Capture of Andre" models associated with Starr, Fellows and Company of New York. Sculptured marble bases occur several times in the 1858 catalogue of Henry N. Hooper of Boston. The candle cup and prism rings and the overall restrained nature of this set most closely resemble New York-Philadelphia work. The set survives with a good part of what appears to be its original set of "star and snowflake" prisms.

232a. Two Branch Girandole (one of a pair of the Cornucopia model), American (attributed to Henry N. Hooper and Company, Boston), Rococo Revival style, gilded brass, marble and glass, circa 1845-1868. H: 12-⅞ in. W: 14 in. D: 4 in. Courtesy Gallier House, New Orleans.

With slightly different candle cups this pattern is illustrated as model number 460 in the one known surviving Hooper catalogue which is dated 1858. That sixty-three page long catalogue preserved in the collections of the Essex Institute in Salem, Massachusetts, provides a wealth of information. The campana-shaped candle cups with fluting on the lower part of the body do not appear on any of the Hooper candleholders in the catalogue; however, the plain bobeche is seen time and again throughout the catalogue. The downturned palmettes of the prism rings are broader and heavier than those that can be documented as having been made by one of the Philadelphia or New York manufacturers. The branches embellished on their upper side with a single rosette are probably unique to Boston and perhaps to the Hooper firm.

The casting is crisp and of the first order—especially the cabbage roses and other flowers that rise from the cornucopia. Easily missed in casual observation is the delightfully Victorian vignette at the base of the cornucopia. Here a reclining putto embraces with affection a couchant hound. Rounding out the picture are the fine faceted prisms that taper upward from the spear-like tips.

232b. Page from the SAMPLE BOOK OF LAMPS, CANDELABRA & LIGHTING FIXTURES FOR GAS AND OIL by Henry N. Hooper & Co., Boston, 1858. Courtesy, Essex Institute, Salem, Massachusetts.

The "cornucopia" model appears in the upper left corner of the page. The other models shown with all their exuberant foliage provide strong evidence of the Hooper firm having been one of the most important of the American manufacturers working in the rococo revival style. The single socket "setter" model on the lower left of the page also shows that the Hooper firm made models having no marble bases.

Opposite page:
233. "Girandoles," Page from the Starr, Fellows and Co. catalogue of 1856. Courtesy Old Sturbridge Village, Photo by Henry E. Peach.

The copy of the Starr, Fellows and Co. catalogue of 1856 combined with the Fellows, Hoffman and Co. catalogue of 1858-1859 together form the only extant catalogue from this important manufacturer of candle, oil and gas lighting devices. Depicted here are the "Capture of Andre" model on a double base and the "Stagg" pattern raised on a single base. The note at the bottom of the page calls attention to the fact that they manufacture some twenty other patterns.

Capture of Andre.

Stagg.

☞ Beside the above, we manufacture some twenty other patterns, and among them are: "Paul and Virginia," "Robinson Crusoe," "Bears and Bees," "Spirit of '76," "Bouquet," "Girl, Dog, and Deer," "Fisher Boy and Girl," "Girl and Boy," &c., &c., with Double or Single Bases.

234a. Complete Girandole Garniture Set (Capture of Andre model), American (made by Starr, Fellows and Co. or Fellows, Hoffman and Co. of New York), Rococo Revival style, gilded brass, marble and glass, circa 1856-1865. Photographs show the central three branch fixture, a detail of the figural group depicting the capture of Major John Andre, one of the pair of single socket flanking girandoles and a detail of the military trophy composing the lower part of its shaft. Courtesy New York State Office of Parks, Recreation and Historic Preservation. Bureau of Historic Sites—Clermont State Historic Site—Taconic Region.

The "Capture of Andre" garniture is probably the finest of the girandoles celebrating a military feat. The story deals with the capture in Tarrytown, New York of British Major John Andre in 1780. Major Andre was hanged as a spy having been captured with General Benedict Arnold's traitorous plans for turning West Point over to the British. Not surprisingly a number of sets of these girandoles are found in the Hudson River Valley near the site of the event. All evidence points to these designs being the exclusive work of Starr, Fellows and Co. or its successor, Fellows, Hoffman and Co., a firm active in New York City under one of the two names from 1854 to 1880. With the exception of the prism ring composed of grape vines and grape clusters, this garniture is exactly like the illustration from the Starr, Fellows and Co. catalogue of 1856. "PATENT APPLIED FOR" in incised block letters appears on the back of the trophy ornamented girandoles as well as inside the prism ring. Thin spun-brass candle cups having attached moulded bobeches appear on the garniture in the company's catalogue in the following "Stagg" pattern girandoles.

234b. Detail of the Capture of Major Andre on three branch piece.

234d. Detail of the military trophies on the Capture of Andre flanking girandoles.

234c. One of a pair of single socket "Trophy" model girandoles made as companions to the Capture of Andre model.

235a. Pair of Girandoles ("Stagg" model), American (attributed to Starr, Fellows and Co. or Fellows, Hoffman and Co. of New York), Rococo Revival style, gilded brass, marble and glass, circa 1854-1865. H: 15-7/8 in. W: 6-5/8 in. D: 3-1/2 in. Collection of Anglo-American Art Museum, Louisiana State University, Baton Rouge.

The same set of "Stagg" pattern girandoles has been illustrated first in the condition when acquired by the Museum and second after the set had been stripped of radiator paint and regilded. Additionally, the ill proportional, Colonial Revival prisms of circa 1920 have been replaced with period "coffin-shaped" prisms. The Museum cannot be faulted for replacing the twentieth century prisms with prisms of a configuration compatible with the girandoles. Open to question, however, is the regilding of the metal work by the modern electrolytic plating process. The new finish is entirely too dazzling and harsh and does not reproduce the low sparkle of the set's original matte finish with bright gilded highlights. Given the curatorial dilemma of choosing between an existing finish of gold radiator paint with no traces of the original finish underneath and a too bright finish that at least evokes the lustre of the original finish, the latter appears to be the more palatable choice. Only a handful of professional metal conservators can come close to replicating the marvelous old double gilded finishes and then only at great expense.

235b. Pair of preceding "Stagg" model girandole, after restoration.

236. Three Branch Girandole (Recumbent Stag model from a garniture composed of this fixture and two flanking single socket examples), American (Boston), Rococo Revival style, gilded brass, marble and glass, circa 1845-1865. H: 16 in. W: 15-⅛ in. D: 6-¼ in. Courtesy Didier, Inc., New Orleans.

Shown on these pages are four variations of the recumbent stag and doe models. The first recumbent stag shown with its prisms removed can be attributed to Boston. The branches are of the twisting vine variety that have been associated with the girandoles and other candelabra from the foundry of Henry N. Hooper and Company. The prism rings which feature cabochon decorated, downturned leaves alternating with similarly positioned fleurs-de-lis are also seen in the Hooper catalogue. Also, the candle cups with the reeded sides, whose design source was probably British, seem to be a form used occasionally in Boston. The plinth on which the stag sits has trailing vines placed against a punchwork ground—all centered on the crudest of rosettes. The rosette looks more like a square with an "X" scratched on its center. This crudeness in the overall casting permits an attribution to Boston, but not to the Hooper firm. The same crudeness is seen in the casting of the "Recumbent Doe" bouquet.

238a. Bouquet (Recumbent Doe model), American (Boston), Rococo Revival style, gilded brass and glass, circa 1850-1865. H: 11-¾ in W: 4-¾ in D: 3-½ in. Collection of Garrison Grey Kingsley, Greenville, Delaware.

It is impossible to divorce the bouquet or vases made in Boston from girandoles. Occasionally a New England glass vase will appear where a candle cup normally would have been on a three or five socket model girandole. In this bouquet it is easy to observe that the pierced gilt brass vase holder has been used in place of a girandole shaft. The neoclassical mask on the side of the holder, plus the deep gold of the gilding and the casting of the trailing vine all relate this piece to Boston work. The vase itself is made of an emerald green glass and has a deeply scalloped border.

237. Three Branch Girandole (one of a pair of Recumbent Stag model), American (Philadelphia or New York), Rococo Revival style, gilded brass, marble or glass, circa 1840-1861. Courtesy New York State Office of Parks, Recreation and Historic Preservation, Bureau of Historic Sites—Clermont State Historic Site—Taconic Region.

This recumbent stag girandole and its mate are located at Clermont—one of the Hudson River Valley estates of the fabled Livingston family, a family prominent in the commercial and political life of America since colonial times. Most of the earlier and later furnishings of Clermont are of New York and Philadelphia origin. With its crisp casting, matte and bright lemon-gold finish, downturned water leaf prism ring and cylindrical candle cups with the palmette border and bobeches, a Philadelphia or New York attribution can be made.

In comparing this model with the girandole and bouquet made in Boston, finer casting is immediately observable. Note the fine detail of the punchwork ground, the trailing vine and the rosette on the plinth supporting the stag. The rococo revival shaft and branches, while rococo revival in style, are much more straight forward than the twisting Boston example.

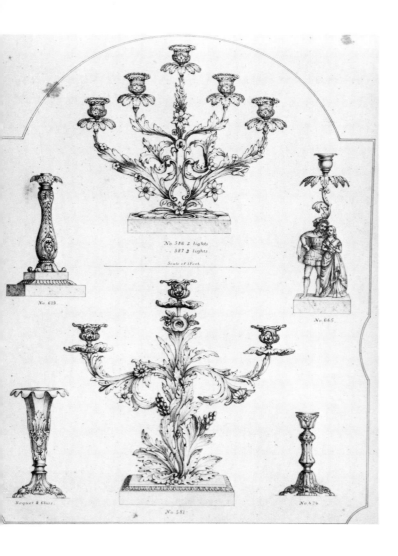

238b. Page from the SAMPLE BOOK OF LAMPS, CANDELABRA & LIGHTING FIXTURES FOR GAS AND OIL by Henry N. Hooper, & Co., Boston 1858. Courtesy, Essex Institute, Salem, Massachusetts.

At the lower left of the page is a gilt brass bouquet holder and glass vase that relates directly to the preceding "Recumbent Doe" model of bouquet. The illustrated bouquet from the Hooper catalogue features a similar mask with leaf crest to that seen in the "Recumbent Doe" bouquet. The paneled glass liner with the scalloped border is precisely the same model. Model No. 665 in the illustration is the Hooper version of the popular "Elizabethan Couple" model.

239. Garniture Set (Three Branch Warrior with Musket model with flanking Recumbent Stag models), American (Boston), Rococo Revival style, patinated brass, marble and glass, circa 1850. Dimensions Warrior - H: 16-¾ in W: 13-¾ in. D: 4-⅛ in; Stags - H: 14-¼ in. D: 3-½ in. Collection of Garrison Grey Kingsley, Greenville, Delaware.

This set which has come down together illustrates how it was possible to assemble a garniture set of one's own choice. Rather than having a three-branch recumbent stag for the center piece, a variant on the "Warrior" model has been chosen. The warrior with musket is the same figure wearing a lion's skin cape seen in the warrior model holding a spear (Ill. 266). The set illustrated here has the dark "antique bronze" finish offered by Hooper and Company of Boston and other founders which make it difficult to see many of the Boston characteristics. All the pieces have candle cups with the small band of palmettes below the bobeche as seen in the pair of Boy and Dog girandoles (Ill. 258). The prism rings are the Boston broader leaf variant of the Philadelphia downturned water leaf ones. The scrolling branches of the three-branch girandoles are also associated with Boston stylistic predilections. The secondary Sandwich glass bobeches are period, but not original to this garniture.

241. Three Branch Girandole (Fierce Lion model), probably American (Boston), Rococo Revival style, gilded brass, marble and glass, circa 1840-1860. H: 16-½ in. W: 14-¼ in. D: 5-¾ in. Collection of Garrison Grey Kingsley, Greenville, Delaware

There will possibly be questions as to whether this pattern is English or American. An American city of manufacture is likely because the piece conforms to the usual American girandole configuration of marble base, two-dimensional figural plinth and the American type of foliate stem and branches. A Boston origin is plausible since this lion does resemble some of the other animal model girandoles known to have been made in that city. The foliate motives of the downturned prism rings are a variant that I have been unable to positively document as used by American manufacturers, but they do relate closest to known Boston examples. All of this evidence is not enough, however, to confirm an American manufacture. Even the lion which is pure folk art does not preclude a British origin for this piece. Such a lion as this with his blared teeth, thick lips and silly mane and tail certainly evokes images of American folk art. Serious study done during the past decade has revealed British nonacademic art that is strikingly American in feeling.

240. Girandole (one of a pair of Birds model), America (Boston), Rococo Revival style, gilt bronze, marble and glass, circa 1850-1865. H: 11-¼ in. W: 5-¼ in. D: 3-⅝ in. Collection of Frederick Lee Lawson.

The 1860 Dietz catalogue depicts a girandole in this pattern with different prism rings and candle cups. This was doubtless a well-liked model produced in several if not all centers of girandole manufacture. The illustrated example has the candle cup with the band of palmettes directly below the bobeche which seems to have been exclusive to Boston. The rather heavy grape cluster and downturned leaf prism ring is also thought to be a Boston characteristic. The three birds in a tree which form the shaft of the girandole are of a generic type.

242. Double Branch Girandole (Couchant Hound model), English (?), rococo revival style, patinated bronze, marble and glass, circa 1840-1850. H: 11 in. W: 8-¼ in. D: 4-¼ in. Collection of Rosemont Plantation, Woodville, Mississippi.

 This rococo revival girandole bears no real relationship in the design of its candle cups and bobeches to any of the known American-made models. While these prism rings are composed of downturned water leaves (the ring on the right has been placed wrongside up), they are much shorter than those seen on Philadelphia or New York examples. As has been observed, three-dimensional figural sculpture is very rare in known American work. The couchant hound with his crossed paws is sculpted in the round and is sleek in his handsome patinated finish. This girandole is probably one of English manufacture. The prisms while of an appropriate scale are not original.

173

Opposite page:

243a./243b. Set of Mantel Garniture (Five Branch Daniel Boone or Leather-stocking model with flanking single socket Colonial Officer model), American (made by Cornelius and Company of Philadelphia), Rococo Revival style, gilded brass, marble and glass, Daniel Boone model patented December 5, 1848 and Colonial Officer patented April 10, 1849. Boone - H: 22-$^{11}/_{16}$ in. W: 16-$^{17}/_{16}$ in. D: 4-¾ in. Colonial Officer - H: 17-⅛ in. W: 6 in. D: 3-½ in. Collection of Anglo-American Art Museum, Louisiana State University, Baton Rouge. Gift of Dr. and Mrs. C. C. Coles.

As of this writing researchers are hampered by there being no known surviving copy of any catalogue from the Cornelius firm dating earlier than circa 1876. What the company under its various corporate names called some models is unknown. The five-branch central fixture of this garniture features a seated male figure in buckskins in the company of a seated and a standing Indian. A similar three-branch model is shown as plate 111 in the Metropolitan Museum of Art's 1970 exhibition catalogue 19th-Century America: Furniture and Other Decorative Arts. The writers of the caption accompanying that illustration suggested the model name, "Daniel Boone," based on costume since Daniel Boone had achieved international celebrity through the 1823 publication of Lord Byron's poem, "Don Juan." Seven stanzas are devoted to Boone. An American literary source provides several possible names. James Fenimore Cooper published a series of five novels between 1823-1841 which dealt with the pioneers and the Indians in New York State. The series became known as the Leather-Stocking Tales because of the leather leg coverings worn by Natty Bumppo, the hero of the novel in the series entitled The Deerslayer. Obviously this model of girandole could have been called the "Natty Bumppo" or "Deerslayer" model as well as "Hawkeye" the hero of another of the Cooper series.

Logically, the flanking figures which usually accompany a central girandole with this theme would be a pair of colonial officers or the colonial officer and his lady. This garniture appears always to have been together because everything matches except for the central lighting device having a double step base. The matte lemon-gold finish with bright highlights is original and in excellent condition. The basically cylindrical candle cups with palmette bordered bobeches and the prism rings composed of a floral band with lovebird finials all typify the best of the Cornelius firm's work.

In order to make a five-branch girandole, a three-branch element is raised above a broader two-branch component whose arms curve forward. With the central fixture stripped of its prisms, the divisions of the castings are apparent, as are the documented shaft and branches from the Cornelius factory.

243c. Detail of the back of the figural section of the "Daniel Boone" or "Leather-stocking" model girandole with the maker's mark in incised block letters, "PATENT/DECEMBER 5/1848" over incised script, "Cornelius & Co."

243d. Detail of the back of the "Colonial Officer" pattern showing the legend in incised script, "Cornelius & Co." over incised block letters, "PATENT./APRIL.10.1849."

Undoubtedly these patterns and the "Colonial Lady" model continued to be made after the company changed its name to Cornelius and Baker in 1851. Baker was the son-in-law of Christian Cornelius, the founder of the firm, and his joining the firm probably did not elicit a need to make a whole new mould in order to reflect the firm's new name style. Placing their name on the back or bottom of all their products was not a policy consistently followed by Cornelius, or most of the American and British metalware manufacturers of that period.

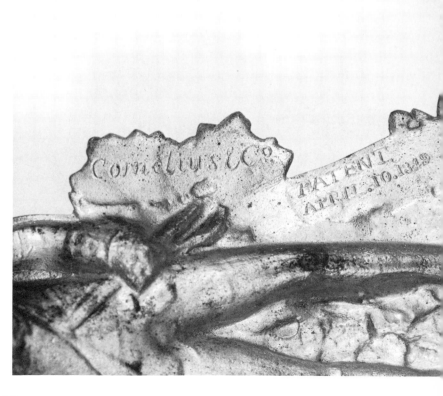

244a. Single Girandole (Colonial Lady model), American (made by Cornelius and Company of Philadelphia), Rococo Revival style, gilded brass, marble and glass, circa 1849-1860s. H: 16-½in W: 5-⅞ in. D: 3-½ in. Collection of Garrison Grey Kingsley, Greenville, Delaware.

This model is frequently seen either in pairs or coupled with the Colonial Officer girandole. The lady's costume is a much looser interpretation of colonial dress than that of her male companion. Adding special lustre to this girandole are the unusual prisms which are a variation on the coffin-shaped model. Here four decorative dots embellish each prism and two adorn each button or header.

1860. H: 16-½ in W: 5-⅞ in. D: 3-½ in. Collection of Garri-

244b. Maker's mark on Colonial Lady Girandole

Appearing on the back of the lady's dress is the incised script legend, "Cornelius & Co" and in mixed incised script and block letters, "Patent/April10/1849." With a long-lived family firm like the Cornelius Company, care must be taken to remember that a model could have been produced for several years before it was patented. By the same token, this popular model of girandole doubtless was made after 1851 when the firm changed to Cornelius and Baker. There would have been no real need to change the lettering on an existing Cornelius and Company mould when in essence the same people were still running the company.

245. Three Branch Girandole (Rip van Winkle model), American (probably Boston), Rococo Revival style, gilded brass, marble and glass, circa 1850-1865. H: 17-⅛ in. W: 16 in. D: 4-½ in. Courtesy M.S. Rau Antiques, New Orleans.

This is a charming scene of the sleeping Rip van Winkle, the setter-type dog and the Victorian lady with her forefinger to her lips in a gesture for quiet. Rip van Winkle is both the title and hero of a tale from Washington Irving's Sketchbook, first published in 1819-1820. This example does not exhibit refinement in casting and was a less expensive piece initially. The design of the prism rings, while not of the quality associated with the Henry Hooper firm of Boston, is similar to those of Boston origin. From a dish-like element embellished with an incised line spring crudely cast leaves which hold the prisms. The cut-glass prisms and headers are correct for the piece.

246. Five Branch Girandole (part of a set composed of this and a pair of single socket flanking pieces in the Paul and Virginia model), American (probably Philadelphia), Rococo Revival style, gilded brass, marble and glass, circa 1840-1861. Five Branch H: 20-⅜ in. W: 16-½ in. D: 8-⅜ in.; Single Socket H: 15-9/16 in. W: 5 in. D: 3 in. Collection of Anglo-American Art Museum, Louisiana State University, Baton Rouge.

There are several variations of girandoles which have the Paul and Virginia story as the theme for their figural subject. This literary source is the French romance Paul et Virginie by Bernardin de Saint-Pierre which was first published in 1787 in volume IV of his Etude de la Nature.[8] This story was translated into many languages and was appreciated as much for its didactic digressions as it was as a romantic tale. Paul and Virginia, two fatherless children, were brought up in poverty and innocence on the tropical island Ile de France (Mauritius). They loved one another from their infancy and were crushed when Virginia was recalled to France by a cruel but wealthy aunt. Virginia was miserable and after two years returned to the Ile de France. Her ship wrecked in front of Paul and she drowned. She could have been saved had she been willing to strip her clothing off and jump into the storm with a naked sailor who tried to rescue her. The story is extremely sentimental and had wide appeal in that very moralistic age.

The melancholy story is well conveyed in this girandole's scene of a barefooted Paul, wearing a sash instead of a belt, and holding the hand of Virginia who is seated with her head bowed. The allusion to a tropical setting is enhanced with the banana plants and palms in the background. In the Deep South this model is occasionally referred to as the Evangeline pattern because of the sad story of the Acadian lovers Evangeline and Gabriel. South Louisiana's subtropical climate and foliage makes this a logical deduction. Longfellow's poem "Evangeline" enjoyed a national popularity but no document for an Evangeline model girandole has surfaced yet. Paul and Virginia are, however, mentioned. This large impressive fixture, having its original matte finish with bright highlights, is in near perfect condition. On the basis of the quality of casting and the lemon-colored golden finish, an attribution to a superior Philadelphia firm is possible.

247. Pair of Girandoles (Sultana model), American, Rococo Revival style, gilded brass or bronze, marble and glass, circa 1845-1861. H: 15-¹/₁₆ in. W: 5 in. D: 4-⅛ in. Collection of Anglo-American Art Museum, Louisiana State University, Baton Rouge.

The nineteenth century, an age of expansion, was captivated by the strange and the unusual and the exotic. China, India and the Middle East had a special fascination for westerners which manifested itself in architecture, painting and the decorative arts. Houses such as the Royal Pavilion at Brighton, England, best exemplify this blending of Eastern-influenced architecture. This type of architecture is the exception to the rule in America; however, some examples such as P.J. Barnum's oriental villa at Bridgeport, Connecticut, and the fabulous octagonal "Longwood" at Natchez, Mississippi, were built. Americans did take delight in decorative furnishings featuring what they regarded as Turkish or Persian subjects.

The "Sultana" model girandole illustrated here and the companion "Sultan" model evidently enjoyed great vogue from the number of surviving examples. The sultana with her turban and shoes with upturned toes none the less gives all the appearance of a western Victorian lady dressed in the costume of the Middle East. For the Victorian mind all that was necessary was an evocation of the Middle East or Far East, not a precise copy.

The model again seems to be the product of Philadelphia and New York manufacturers. The candle cups with the palmette bordered bobeches, downturned water leaf prism rings and light gold matte finish all point to those two cities as its place of origin. The coffin-shaped prisms on this example appear to be original.

248. Five Branch Girandole (Sultan model from a pair), American (New York or Philadelphia), Rococo Revival style, silvered brass or bronze, marble and glass, circa 1845-1861. H: 22-¼ in. W: 18-½ in. D: 10 in. Courtesy Didier, Inc., New Orleans.

Only rarely are pairs of five branch girandoles encountered. Doubtless, they graced a large mantel or serving board originally. Like the related sultana pattern, the sultan model of girandole more resembles a mid-nineteenth century opera singer costumed as an eastern potentate than it does an actual sultan. The figure stands wearing a Persian or Turkish-style beard, turban, dress, overdress and scimitar, while his right hand rests on an oil lamp raised on a pseudo-Eastern-style plinth.

The candle cups with their bright band around the center of the cylindrical cup and their palmette bordered bobeches are in the Philadelphia manner of the Cornelius firm. This is true of the downturned water leaves forming the prism rings. The spear-tipped prisms are old, but improper for the fixture.

249. Three Branch Girandole, (Scottish Dancers model from a garniture composed of this fixture and two single socket models), American, Rococo Revival style, gilded brass, marble and glass, circa 1845-1860. H: 17-½ in. W: 16-¾ in. D: 4 in. Courtesy Didier, Inc., New Orleans.

Scottish tartans and Scottish things in general were in vogue with the Victorians due in large part to the romantic novels of Sir Walter Scott. The dancing couple forming part of this girandole's shaft loosely evokes an eighteenth century couple performing a Highland fling. The set forming this garniture was doubtless expensive when new. Rather than common white marble, black marble with grey and gold chain veining was employed in making each unit's base. The fine spear-shaped prisms having double headers or buttons are another better quality feature. The candle cups are of a type favored in Philadelphia and New York; however, the prism rings and what remains of the original matte and bright gilded finish is of the deeper golden color found desirable by the Boston founders.

250a. Pair of Girandoles (Elizabethan Couple or Romeo and Juliet model), American (made by Dietz, Brother and Company of New York), Rococo Revival style, gilded brass, marble and glass, circa 1840-1855. H: 13-¾ in W: 5-½ in D: 3-⅜ in Collection of Anglo-American Art Museum, Louisiana State University, Baton Rouge. Gift of Dr. and Mrs. David W. Wall.

The Dietz firm, established in 1840, has been in business through the present time under various styles of the firm's name. According to Ulysses G. Dietz, the company ceased producing decorative items in 1870.[9] This piece like the majority of the surviving signed Dietz lighting devices was made during the Dietz, Brother and Company period which lasted from 1840 to 1855. It is marked on the back of the stem in incised block letters, "DIETZ BRO. & CO., N.Y."

The novels of Sir Walter Scott helped to popularize Scottish and Elizabethan themes, as did the plays of William Shakespeare. A name contemporary with their manufacture has not been determined, making the modern descriptive names of "Elizabethan Couple," "Elizabethan Man and Woman" or "Romeo and Juliet" a way of identifying the model.

Ulysses G. Dietz suggests that this "Elizabethan Man and Woman" model is the same as that shown in Henry N. Hooper and Company's 1858 Boston catalogue (vide Hooper model number 665 in the catalogue preserved at the Essex Institute, Salem, Massachusetts). Dietz further states that this model was probably actually manufactured by the Hooper firm and retailed by Dietz, Brother and Company under their own name.[10] This is possible; however, Mr. Dietz says at the same time that his research indicated that " . . . girandole designs seem to remain 'faithful' to their designers, whether they are patented or not."[11] The photographic reproductions of girandoles in this chapter provide adequate evidence that opposite was true—pirating was common. Examine the variants of "Recumbent Stag," the "Boy and Girl" and the "Roman Centurion" models in the illustrations. Not only are the local preferences in candle cups, prism rings and finishes to be noted, but subtle differences in the figural subjects and the quality of the castings are to be seen.

250b. Detail of Dietz Brother and Company label on the Elizabethan Couple girandole.

252. Grouping composed of Bouquet Vase, Three Branch Girandole (Dog model) and Single Socket Girandole (Dirk Platternick model), American, Rococo Revival style, gilded brass, marble and glass, circa 1840-1865. Collections of Craig Littlewood and J. Craig Maue, Palmyra, New Jersey. Photograph by David A. Gentry.

251. Single Girandole (one of a pair of Les Merriles model), American, Rococo Revival style, gilded brass, marble and glass, circa 1840-1860. H: 19-½ in W: 7 in. D: 4 in. Collection of Garrison Grey Kingsley, Greenville, Delaware.

The title of this pair of girandoles, like its companion "Dirk Platternick" model, is a corruption of a fictional character from Sir Walter Scott's novel, Guy Mannering, first published in 1815. Meg Merriles is an old gypsy woman in this story set in the eighteenth century, who helps to restore the hero of the tale to his rightful inheritance. Harry Bertram, the son of the laird of Ellangowan, is kidnapped as a child and carried abroad. At the sacrifice of her own life Meg Merriles helps Bertram learn his true identity.[12]

This is a very handsome edition of the Meg Merriles pattern mounted on a double base and having acorn and oak leaf decorated coffin-shaped prisms. The New England pressed glass secondary bobeche is another attractive feature of this pair. The flared prism rings of grape clusters and leaves, while seen in the girandole illustration of Starr, Fellows and Company's New York catalogue, were used elsewhere. The twisted tree shaft and deep gilding hints of Boston as the place of this pair's manufacture. These girandoles, therefore, could have been made in any one of the three American centers.

Both the bouquet vase and the "Dog" pattern girandole can be attributed with confidence to Henry N. Hooper and Company of Boston. The bouquet features a red glass liner situated in a conical, pierced holder which is decorated with three masks as is seen on a bouquet with no model number illustrated on the fifteenth page of Hooper's 1858 catalogue. The base is executed in gilded brass which has been embellished with water leaves. The "Dog" pattern girandole is also a composite of several Hooper motives and exhibits that rich, deep gold finish preferred in Boston. At present, only Boston can be documented as having made girandoles featuring the all metal, octagonal step bases. This base as well as the downturned petal prism ring are features of the "Roman Centurion" model illustrated as model number 318 in the Hooper catalogue. A similar recumbent setter-type dog is seen used on the octagonal all metal step base of a single socket girandole illustrated as model number 443 in the same catalogue. The candle cups with foliate decorated sides are one of several variations on this theme found in the Hooper catalogue. Finally, there is the "Dirk Platternick" pattern which is so inscribed with incised upper case letters below the figure. This is a corruption of "Dirk Hatteraick," a smuggler in Sir Walter Scott's novel, Guy Mannering. Hatteraick is the one who did the actual kidnapping of the hero of the novel, Harry Bertram. He is, therefore, depicted in a smuggler's cove. We may be certain that "Dirk Platternick" is really Dirk Hatteraick because of the existence of the "Les Merriles" model, which is a corruption of the spelling of another character in the story, Meg Merrilies.

253. Three Branch Girandole (Centerpiece for an incomplete set in the Old Mortality model), American (Philadelphia), Rococo Revival style, gilded brass, marble and glass, circa 1855. Collection of Garrison Grey Kingsley, Greenville, Delaware.

Hardly legible on the lowest brass portion of this girandole is the crudely inscribed Roman lettered legend, "Old Mortality." It, also, appears on the companion single socket flanking girandoles not seen in the illustration. Another of Sir Walter Scott's novels, Old Mortality, published in 1816, gives the name to this model of girandole.

"Old Mortality" was the nickname of the fictionalized character, Robert Paterson, who traveled through Scotland in the late eighteenth century cleaning and repairing the tombs of the Cameronians. The Cameronians were a sect of strict Presbyterians who defended their religion by force of arms during Charles II's reign. The figure on the ground represents Robert Paterson telling stories about the Covenanters to Sir Walter Scott, who is clad in plaid breeches and sits on a stump.

There is a relationship of this girandole model with the park-like cemetery, "Laurel Hill" established in Philadelphia during the 1840s. The concept was based on that of the Mount Auburn Cemetery in Cambridge, Massachusetts. A complete set of girandoles in this pattern is found in a grotto at the Philadelphia cemetery and was apparently bought for it.

182

254. Pair of Girandoles (Fisher Boy and Girl model), American (made by Archer and Warner of Philadelphia), Rococo Revival style, silver plated brass, marble and glass, circa 1850-1856. H: with ruby overlay peg lamp 20 in. H: with plain peg lamp 18 in. Collection of Garrison Grey Kingsley, Greenville, Delaware.

The Fisher Boy and Girl pattern is the correct period title for this model used in the Starr, Fellow and Company catalogue of 1856. This is another of those subjects that was widely enjoyed and was made with slight variations by all the important manufacturers. This one pair has marked Archer and Warner prism rings and the spun-brass candle cups that the firm favored. Girandoles are frequently employed as supports for peg lamps. Here two spirit lamps of New England origin are shown. The left example is a fine and rare ruby overlay model which contrasts sharply with the more ordinary flattened globe lamp in clear glass.

255. Set of Girandoles (Boy and Girl model), American (probably New York), Rococo Revival style, gilt brass, marble and glass, circa 1845-1861. Five-branch girandoles: H: 20 in. W: 14-¾ in. D: 6 in. Single-light girandoles: H: 15-⅛ in. W: 6-⅝ in. D: 4 in. Courtesy Didier, Inc., New Orleans.

The popular "Boy and Girl" model of girandoles seems to have been made in all three American centers of manufacture. This set is attributed to New York on the basis of the flaring prism ring composed of grape clusters and leaves that precisely match those illustrated on the "Stagg" and "Capture of Andre" model shown in the 1856 Starr, Fellows and Company catalogue. This garniture is removed from the ordinary by virtue of its size—the commanding five-branch centerpiece is rare—and it is of the better quality associated with girandoles having double bases. A negative feature is the so called "Albert" prisms which are not original.

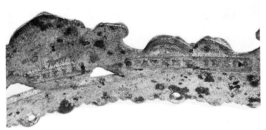

256a. Pair of Girandoles (Boy and Girl model), American (made by Archer and Warner of Philadelphia), Rococo Revival style, gilded brass, marble and glass, circa 1850-1856. H: 14-3/16 in. W: 5-1/8 in. D: 3-1/2 in. Collection of Anglo-American Art Museum, Louisiana State University, Baton Rouge.

What appears to be a rather ordinary variation on the "Boy and Girl" model of girandole is made more interesting by being a marked pair by Archer and Warner. On three separate raised rectangles on the inside of the prism ring the legend, "ARCHER & WARNER/PHILA/PATENT 1850" appears. The drapery lambrequin-like design of the prism rings seems to be unique to the Archer and Warner firm and is an atypical model. The rather precise dating of these girandoles is made from both the patent date and the fact that on 27 November 1856, William F. Miskey joined the partnership and the firm's name changed to Archer, Warner, Miskey and Company. The piece has its original light gold matte finish which is highlighted with brightly finished areas. Note that the candle cups in this pair are spun brass rather than the usual cast brass. The cups are more like those on girandoles made by Starr, Fellows and Co. of New York City. The cable decoration on the bobeche is another feature not usually seen on known Philadelphia-made girandoles. One sleeve-like tin insert remains with this set. Once common and now rare, these crudely made tin inserts assist in the correct fitting of the candles to their cups and facilitate the cleaning of the sockets. The girandoles are shown both with and without prisms and two details feature the maker's mark. The prisms are certainly period but not necessarily original. Note that the buttons or headers are plain rather than matching the "star" or "snowflake" pattern of the prisms, as is usually the case.

256d. Detail of mark, "PHILA./PATENT 1850" on Boy and Girl model girandole's prism ring.

256c. Detail of ARCHER & WARNER mark on "Boy and Girl" model girandole's prism ring.

257a. Three Branch Girandole (Boy and Dog model), American (Boston), Rococo Revival style, gilded brass, marble and glass, circa 1845-1865. H: 17 in. W: 17 in. D: 3-⅝ in. Courtesy M.S. Rau Antiques, New Orleans.

The "Boy and Dog" pattern was one of the most popular models and was made in all three centers of American manufacture. This is a particularly admirable example which possesses most of the hallmarks of the pieces associated with girandoles made in Boston. The original deep gold gilding remains in excellent condition. The prism rings with their vertically placed band of leaves, each separated from the other with vertical beading, and the foliate bobeches on the candle cups featuring palmette decorations both give testimony of Boston manufacture.

The double step marble base with its cast, gilded brass transitional element decorated with foliate motives adds to the statement of quality made by this candleholder. It is enhanced by having prisms of the proper shape and size adorning it.

257b. Detail of the Candle cup and Prism Ring from Boy and Dog girandole

Several aspects of the work associated with Boston manufacturers of girandoles can be observed here. Not only can the palmette decoration of the side of the candle cup and the foliate or scalloped border of the bobeche be seen, but the intentional slight roughness of the casting in that component is also visible. The grainy texture of the casting has a sparkle to it as the light strikes the gilding. The prism ring which is much more elaborately decorated is sharply cast and finished. The candle cups made in Boston appear to be the only ones ornamented with palmettes. These palmettes relate to the palmettes found on the sides of New England-made solar lamps.

185

258. Pair of Girandoles (Boy and Dog model), American (Boston ?), Rococo Revival style, gilded brass, marble and glass, circa 1840-1865. H: 13-9/16 in. W: 5-9/16 in. D: 3-1/16 in. Collection of Anglo-American Art Museum, Louisiana State University, Baton Rouge.

The contrast in color between this pair of "Boy and Dog" girandoles and the three-branch example of the same model is not as extreme as the photograph would lead one to believe. The gilding here is a deep, rich, matte finish gold as opposed to the bright but deep gold color of the three-branch girandole. Both finishes, which are original, express Boston preferences. While both the pair and the three-branch have the same type of prism ring, the pair introduces a new type of candle cup. A band of palmettes is located on the side of each cup below the rather plain bobeche.

The prisms give every indication of being original and show yet another acceptable period arrangement in that two similar types of the many faceted upward tapering spear-head prisms are used in alternating positions. The longer ones are notched about an inch above the spear head and are separated from the prism ring by one button. The shorter unnotched prisms have two buttons between them and the prism ring which make their spear tips hang level with the longer prisms. Evidence is too inconclusive to state that this type of prism was exclusively used on Boston-made girandoles; but this type, which appears infrequently, is usually found on those felt to be of Boston origin.

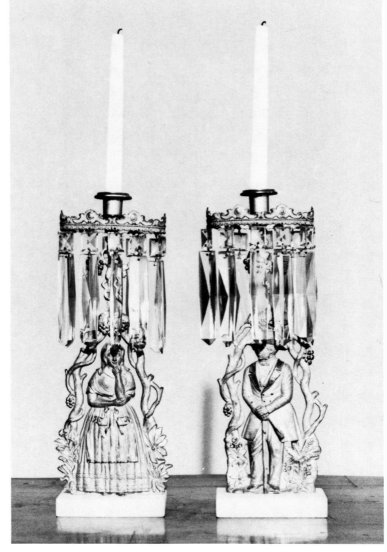

259. Pair of Girandoles (Lady and Gentleman model), American (made by Archer and Warner of Philadelphia), Rococo Revival style, gilded brass, marble and glass, circa 1851-1856. H: 16-3/8 in W: 5-1/4 in D: 3-5/16 in. Collection of The Athenaeum of Philadelphia, Philadelphia, Pennsylvania.

This pair of girandoles marked, "ARCHER & WARNER, PHILA. PATENT 1850" on the inside of the prism ring in the same manner as the "Boy and Girl" model is the "Lady and Gentleman" pattern. A second mark, "ARCHER & WARNER, PHILA./PATENT/1851" appears on the back of the figures. The 1851 in the mark is incised. These feature the same drapery lambrequin-like design prism rings seen on other girandoles made by this company. The candle cups are of the spun-brass variety that this firm seems to have preferred. The gilding is a soft, matte lemon-gold with bright highlights on the lady's dress and on the lapels of the gentleman's jacket. Appropriate and contemporary with the pieces are the coffin-shaped prisms.

260. Three Branch Girandole (Castle model from a garniture composed of this fixture and two flanking single socket models), probably American (Boston), Gothic Revival-Rococo Revival style, gilded brass, marble and glass, circa 1845-1860. H: 16-^{1}/16 in. W: 17 in. D: 4-^{1}/16 in. Collection of J. Donald Didier, New Orleans.

Architectonic subjects never held the popularity of the figural themes with the makers of girandoles. The relatively few models that do feature architectural devices are usually in the Gothic Revival style. The inspiration for this castle model girandole could well have been the inexpensive pottery castles and cottages being produced in great number by the Staffordshire potteries. The two dimensional nature of the pottery was most adaptable to the usual design and casting techniques of the girandole manufacturers.

The candle cups with their palmette decorated sides and the foliate border of the bobeche and the retriculated foliate trumpet-vine prism rings are all seen on signed Bigelow Chapel model girandoles by William F. Shaw of Boston. Couple that to the rich, deep gold finish preferred by Boston makers and the similarity of this model to the Bigelow Chapel pattern and another Gothic Revival model—the so-called "Ivanhoe" model which exhibits the same Boston characteristics—make a Boston attribution most plausible.

261a. Three Branch Girandole (Bigelow Chapel model), American (made by William Shaw, Boston), Gothic-Rococo Revival style, gilded brass, marble and glass, circa 1848-1851. H: 16 in. W: 15-²¹/₃₂ in. D: 3-¾ in. Collection of Anglo-American Art Museum, Louisiana State University, Baton Rouge.

The Bigelow Chapel model is unquestionably the most frequently encountered girandole pattern in the Gothic taste. There are single socket examples and one five-branch model has been seen in the collection of Ronald Bourgeault of Hampton, New Hampshire.

The subject of this model is the Bigelow Chapel in America's first planned, non-sectarian burying ground, the Mount Auburn Cemetery in Cambridge, Massachusetts. Only six miles from Boston and opened in 1831, the cemetery proved to be a favorite place for strolling and was regarded as one of those places to see by tourists to the Boston area.

William F. Shaw was active in Boston from around 1845-1900. His earliest Boston City Directory listing is 1845. In 1848 he moved to his Washington Street address and remained there through 1851. Cast in raised block letters on the back of each chapel is the legend, "W.F. Shaw/270 WASH'N ST/BOSTON/PATENT/DEC 18 1848."

The girandole and the detail of one belonging to Garrison Grey Kingsley have the classic Boston candle cups with palmette decorated sides and floral bobeches as well as a trumpet vine pattern prism ring. A pair of single-socket models illustrated as figure 115a in Katherine S. Howe and David Warren's Houston Museum of Fine Arts 1971 exhibition catalogue, <u>The Gothic Revival Style in America, 1830-1870</u> has cylindrical candle cups with palmette bordered bobeches in the Philadelphia-New York style. Those candle cups are coupled, however, with the Boston style of vertical leaf motif prism rings and the Shaw signature.

261b. Detail of Boston style candle cup and trumpet vine prism ring on Bigelow Chapel model girandole. Courtesy Garrison Grey Kingsley, Greenville, Delaware.

262. Three Branch Girandole (Ivanhoe model), American, (probably Philadelphia or New York), Gothic-Rococo Revival style, gilt brass, marble and glass, circa 1845-1860. H: 17-¼ in. W: 17-¼ in. D: 4-⅛ in. Collection of Anglo-American Art Museum, Louisiana State University, Baton Rouge, Gift of Dr. and Mrs. C. C. Coles.

Girandoles with a knight in a niche have come to be known as the "Ivanhoe" model because it is felt that the characters from the stories so romantically popularized by Sir Walter Scott were the inspiration for this pattern. This example is shown stripped of its prisms so that the blending of the Gothic and Rococo Revival styles can be fully appreciated. The piece has its original light lemon-gold matte and bright finish. The casting is especially sharp and crisp on this example. Observe the diapering directly above the marble plinth, as well as the gougework in the same area and the rosettes above and below the knight.

The standing knight figure, who wears a full suit of armor and holds a tall narrow shield, was separately cast. The style of candle cups, the prism rings with their lovebird finials and the finish suggest Philadelphia or New York as these girandoles' place of manufacture.

261c. Detail of William F. Shaw on the back of Bigelow Chapel model.

263. Pair of Girandoles (Ivanhoe model), American (Boston), Gothic-Rococo Revival style, gilt brass, marble and glass, circa 1845-1860. H: 16-³/16 in. W: 7-⅞ in. D:3-³/5 in. Collection of Anglo-American Art Museum, Louisiana State University, Baton Rouge.

These girandoles, with their double-step bases were the finer and more expensive models when they were new. Their finish has deteriorated over the years so that they are not as important as the previous three-branch example for today's collector. "Marriages" of double and single base girandoles were made during the period of their fabrication as well as at later times. This pair has Boston-style candle cups and prism rings and a few other differences from the Philadelphia-New York model. There is no foliate element in the void below the knight's niche on the Philadelphia-New York model. Note also that the knights in the pair wear domed helmets with a raised band at the base of each helmet in contrast to the flat-topped helmet worn by the Philadelphia-New York made knight.

264. Three Branch Girandole, (Bears and Bees model), American (attributed to Starr, Fellows and Company or Starr, Fellows and Hoffman of New York), Gothic-Rococo Revival style, gilded brass, marble and glass, circa 1856-1865, H: 14-½ in. W: 15-½ in. D: 3-¼ in. Collection of Anglo-American Art Museum, Louisiana State University, Baton Rouge.

The "Bears and Bees" model while not illustrated is mentioned as one of the patterns made by Starr, Fellows and Company on the principal girandole page of their 1856 catalogue. That statement regarding the model, coupled with the use of the flaring prism rings with the grape clusters which match the illustrated girandoles in the catalogue, make this attribution most convincing.

The usual foliate rococo revival branches are united with the Gothic revival style shed complete with imbricated roof, cluster columns and quatrefoils. The shed houses a traditional-style beehive made of rushes which is the chief attraction for a standing mother bear and her cub. Both bears are being attacked by several bees.

The prisms while appropriate and period are composed of two slightly different models.

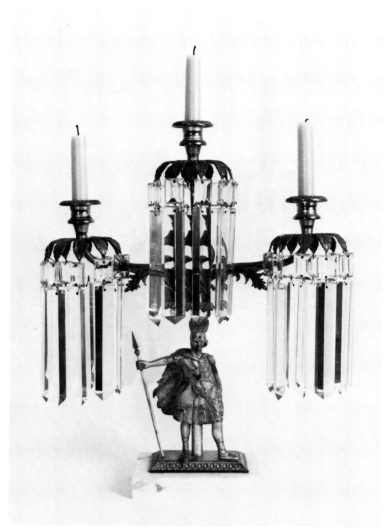

266. Three-Branch Girandole (Warrior model), American, Rococo Revival style, gilded brass, marble and glass, circa 1845-1860. H: 19-¼ in W: 15-⅜ in D: 4-⅛ in. Private collection.

This pattern of girandole and this particular example provide several enigmas for the scholar. The first question is precisely what does the figure represent? At one and the same time, a curious blend of costume and armaments suggest an American Indian and an Anglo-Saxon warrior as the inspiration. The feathered headdress and, certain decorative aspects of the figure's skirt resemble the American Indian influence. The lion skin cape, the shoes and leggings, as well as the formal spear and axe loosely evoke the Middle Ages. Until such time as a document comes to light revealing the period name for the pattern, "Warrior" model will have to suffice.

The second part of the mystery is where did this model originate. The cast candle cups with palmette bordered bobeches and delicate downturned water leaf prism rings support a Philadelphia or New York place of manufacture. The deep matte gold finish with bright highlights and the fact that the girandole was found in Boston points to that city as its place of origin. It could be that this is a design pirated from an original Philadelphia or New York pattern. The reverse could be true as well. It could well have been made in Philadelphia with a deep gold finish for the New England market.

The piece exhibits great quality regardless of whether it was made in Philadelphia, New York or Boston. The casting is precise, the double gilding is superior and the extra long original prisms are the perfect complement for the piece's metalwork.

265. Single Girandole (Bear and Bees model), American (attributed to Starr, Fellows and Company or Starr Fellows and Hoffman of New York), Gothic-Rococo Revival style, gilded brass, marble and glass, circa 1856-1865. H: 14-½ in. W: 5-¾ in. D: 3-¼ in. Collection of James Anderson, New Orleans. Photo by Prather Warren.

This example survives with better gilding than the preceding three-branch model. The mother bear and her cub both covered with bees are much clearer here. Aside from the finish, the only difference between this girandole and the three-branch example is the prism ring. The pierced foliate ring on this piece is identical to that used on the "Stagg" model seen earlier in this chapter. The "Stagg" pattern appears to be unique to Starr, Fellows and Company, which permits the attribution of this "Bears and Bees" girandole to the same firm.

191

267. Three Branch Girandole (Warrior with musket model), American (Boston), Rococo Revival style, gilded brass, marble and glass, circa 1845-1860. Courtesy Ronald Bourgeault Antiques, Hampton, New Hampshire.

A careful study should be made between this girandole and the previous variation of the same pattern. Here the warrior has exchanged the spear for a musket. The figure itself is thicker and more squat in appearance. Rather than the formal rectangular plinth of the latter example, a base of gilded brass in the shape of a rock formation has been created. A most effusive scrolling rococo revival shaft cum branches has been created. The thicker and more heavy-handed Boston type of downturned palmettes form the prism rings. The candle cups are an interesting four-sided foliate shape that resemble certain flower buds opening. The prisms are too short in proportion and are replacements.

268. Pair of Girandoles (Indian Medallion model), American (Philadelphia or New York), Rococo Revival style, gilded brass, bronzed zinc, marble and glass, circa 1855. H: 15-½ in. Collection of Garrison Grey Kingsley, Greenville, Delaware.

The notion of the "noble red man" was certainly well established by the 1850s in the East Coast cities where girandoles and other lighting devices were made. Here the medallion of the Indian bust in bas relief is set against a trophy background all executed in what was referred to as white metal or potmetal and which is zinc. Zinc is used only on occasion in combination with brass or bronze in the manufacture of girandoles. In the manufacture of gasoliers, however, it was the usual practice. Indian medallions quite similar to the ones on this pair of girandoles appear on the pair of gasoliers in the dining room of Stanton Hall in Natchez, Mississippi. The majority of that mansion's gas fixtures survive in situ and are considered to be the work of the Cornelius and Baker firm because of the close relationship between the dining room gasoliers and a surviving design made by J. G. Bruff for the Treasury Building in Washington (See plate 55 in Denys Peter Myers Gaslighting in America: A Guide for Historic Preservation). The striated candle cups and grape leaf and grape cluster prism rings were used in both Philadelphia and New York. The intertwined ivy vines form a striking and not commonly seen shaft or stem for these girandoles.

269. Pair of Three Branch Girandoles (Cherub model), American (Philadelphia or New York), gilded brass, bronzed zinc and glass, circa 1850-1865. H: 17-¼ in. W: 17-¼ in. Collection of Garrison Grey Kingsley, Greenville, Delaware.

Like the previous "Indian Medallion" model, the term "cherub model" is a descriptive name that has been affixed for identification purposes. This pair also features the use of bronzed white metal in the creation of the putti figures which are sculpted in the round. The figures can also be seen as part of gasoliers. The prism rings, candle cups and the intertwined ivy vine match those on the Indian Medallion model.

270a. Garniture Set (Three Branch Cupid's Dream model with flanking single socket models), American (made by Dietz, Brother and Company of New York), Rococo Revival style, gilded brass, marble and glass, circa 1855. Centerpiece-H: 14-⅜ in. W: 17-⅝ in. D: 3-⅞ in. Flanking pieces-H: 14-⅛ in. W: 6-½ in. D: 3-⅞ in. Collection of Anglo-American Art Museum, Louisiana State University, Baton Rouge.

The title "Cupid's Dream" is merely a description of the plinth decoration which features a reclining winged putto with four boys above him. One boy is in a kneeling position and is placing flowers in a basket. Another seated figure holds a sheaf of wheat while the remaining figures stand. This model is neither depicted nor described in the 1860 Dietz catalogue. The legend "DIETZ, BROTHER & CO" stamped on a separated plate has been applied to the back of the foliate shaft. Appearing directly above the name are the cold stamped numerals "24."

The candle cups which are spun sheet brass survive with their original bright and matte finish gilding. The grape cluster and vine prism rings are also made of pressed sheet brass. That same motif is picked up in the cast brass borders which appear on the stepped marble bases.

270b. Dietz Brother and Company Mark on Cupid's Dream Model Girandole

271a. Three Branch Girandole (Roman Centurion model), American (made by Henry N. Hooper and Company, Boston), Rococo Revival style, gilded brass and glass, circa 1845-1868. H: 17 in. W: 16-½ in. Collection of Garrison Grey Kingsley, Greenville, Delaware

The title "Roman Centurion" pattern for this model is based on the subject's costume. Fortunately the subject is illustrated as model 318 in the Henry N. Hooper catalogue which permits the solid attribution to that manufacturer. There are three differences between the illustrated model and the example in the Kingsley collection. The Kingsley piece has grape cluster and leaf downturned prism rings as opposed to the downturned petals model in the illustration. Slightly different, foliate rococo revival branches appear in the catalogue illustration. The catalogue states, and perhaps it is a typographical error, that this model is only thirteen inches tall, rather than the height of seventeen inches for the Kingsley example. Having the Hooper catalogue proves that the more English custom of using a stepped metal base without marble was done by at least one Boston foundry.

271b. Page from SAMPLE BOOK OF LAMPS, CANDELABRA & LIGHTING FIXTURES FOR GAS AND OIL by Henry N. Hooper & Co., Boston, 1858. Courtesy, Essex Institute, Salem, Massachusetts.

The "Roman Centurion" model just discussed is to be seen in the upper right corner. The ornate model No. 601 is the standard for an oil lamp. The solar chandelier shows the repousse palmette decoration which is seen on the fonts of most New England-made solar fixtures. A fascinating aspect of the decoration of this chandelier is the use of male and female masks exhibiting contemporary hair styles.

No. 601.
17 in. high.

No. 318.
13 in. high.

No. 704.   3 Light Solar Chandelier.

273. Five Branch Girandole (Athena model), American (probably Philadelphia), Rococo Revival style, gilded brass, marble and glass, circa 1845-1855. New York State Office of Parks, Recreation and Historic Preservation. Bureau of Historic Sites—Clermont State Historic Site—Taconic Region.

This massive girandole displays all the characteristics of the first quality work done by the Cornelius firm of Philadelphia. The castings are crisp and sharp and the lemon-gold matte and bright finish is well done and in an excellent state of preservation. This model has been termed "Athena" on the strength of the heroic and dignified classical figure. The relationship between this monumental girandole and the magnificent Washington-Franklin example is immediately apparent. The thick marble double bases, the prism rings and candle cups and even the style of prism are the same. On the Athena model double headers or buttons are used to good effect with the prisms on the central candle socket. Both of these models bear comparison with the five-branch, "Daniel Boone" or "Leather-Stocking" model which bears the mark of Cornelius and Company.

272. Three Branch Girandole (Roman Centurion model), American (Philadelphia or New York), American Empire style, gilded bronze, marble and glass, circa 1840-1861. H: 21-¼in W: 17-½ in. D: 6-½ in. Courtesy Eugene D. Cizek, Ph.D. and Lloyd L. Sensat, Sun Oak House, New Orleans.

This example of the Roman Centurion pattern features a less stocky figure than the Boston-made piece of the same subject. The powerful, square, double-step marble base of refined downturned leaf prism rings and cylindrical candle cups point to this being the work of a major Philadelphia or New York firm. The crisp quality of the casting relates this girandole to the Washington-Franklin and the "Athena" models.

274. Pair of Girandole-Bouquets (Classical Muse model), American (attributed to Henry N. Hooper and Co., Boston), Rococo Revival style, gilded brass, marble and glass, circa 1850. H: 15-¼ in. W: 8-¼ in. D: 3-½ in. Collection of Anglo-American Art Museum, Louisiana State University, Baton Rouge. Gift of Mr. and Mrs. Chester C. Coles.

The combination candleholders/flower vases seem to be unique to New England, probably because of the close proximity of large glass houses and foundries. The gilded or ormolu device which holds each starch blue bouquet vase is pierced and decorated with masks and is the same one illustrated in the Hooper firm's 1859 catalogue. The combination of the starch blue vases, the cut prisms and the rich deep gold of the gilding all contribute to a sumptuous effect. The charming muse figures regrettably are partially obscured by the prisms.

275. Pair of Girandoles (Classical Family model), American (Philadelphia or New York), American Empire style, gilded brass, marble and glass, circa 1840-1861. H: 15-7/16 in. W: 5-½ in. D: 3-11/16 in. Collection of Anglo-American Art Museum, Louisiana State University, Baton Rouge.

"Classical Family" is a modern descriptive term applied to this model in lieu of having a period catalogue featuring a labeled example. This is another case of the Victorian merely evoking the past, because the dress is an accurate reproduction of neither ancient Greek nor Roman clothing. Here a youthful male and female support on their shoulders a child holding an upraised torch.

The floral prism ring with lovebird finials and the cast, striated candle cups all suggest a Philadelphia or New York origin for these pieces. Contrast the quality of the casting between this pair and the following pair having the same theme. In the present example fine detail will be noticed in the diaper patterned floor upon which the figures stand as contrasted with the lack of decorative flooring in the next example. The quality differences do not stop with the casting; the prisms and headers are fine examples of the coffin-style of prisms which have been embellished with an oak leaf and acorn design.

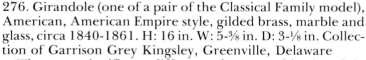

276. Girandole (one of a pair of the Classical Family model), American, American Empire style, gilded brass, marble and glass, circa 1840-1861. H: 16 in. W: 5-⅜ in. D: 3-⅛ in. Collection of Garrison Grey Kingsley, Greenville, Delaware

The most significant difference between this girandole and the variation of the same model previously shown is the prism ring. The antefix-like border surmounting the top of the ring is seen on some Philadelphia-made chandeliers. The Hooper catalogue of 1858 illustrates, however, a brass and glass chandelier as model 376, which could either burn candles or be piped for gas, that has similar prism rings. As was noted in the caption for the other variation of this pattern, the present example is not so lavish a design and the casting is not so fine. One is left with simply saying that it is American.

277. Four Light Bouquet Girandole, American (made by Henry N. Hooper and Company, Boston), Rococo Revival style, gilded brass, amethyst and clear glass, circa 1840-1868. H: 21-¼ in. W: 16-⅓ in. Collection of Garrison Grey Kingsley, Greenville, Delaware.

This exciting fixture is a fine example of how a standard catalogue model could be modified to suit differing tastes and social requirements. This model is illustrated as pattern number 266 in the Hooper catalogue of 1858 as a five branch girandole. In the superb fixture owned by Mr. Kingsley, the Hooper firm exchanged the central branch and candle cup with one of their pierced gilded brass bouquet holders. The vase itself is amethyst colored New England-made flint glass having a handsomely scalloped lip. The original matte and bright gilded finish in the deep gold color favored in Boston survives. The basically triangular, concave foot was inspired by English and French lighting devices of the early nineteenth century. The beaded console supports in the plinth area are beautifully articulated. The combination of the long coffin-shaped prisms on the central shaft with the shorter ones on the flanking branches is especially effective and is probably original.

278. Three Branch Girandole (Spirit of '76 model), American, Rococo Revival style, gilded brass, marble and glass, circa 1855. Courtesy Ronald Bourgeault Antiques, Hampton, New Hampshire

A "Spirit of '76" pattern is noted as being one of Starr, Fellows and Company's models on the unnumbered page illustrating two girandole patterns in their 1856 catalogue. The peg-legged Revolutionary War veteran wearing knee breeches and tricorn hat accompanied by a child wearing a hat with a cockade certainly fits the description. Is the girandole by Starr, Fellows and Company or is it a Boston copy? The prism ring is a style associated with Boston, but the candle cups are in the New York-Philadelphia style.

280. Girandole, mostly American (?), Rococo Revival style, gilt brass and glass. H: 15-½ in. W: 5 in. D: 4-¾ in. The Dornsife Collection, Williamsport, Pennsylvania.

Almost every great collection has a whimsey of some kind or another. This quite charming girandole was made up of various old pieces by Samuel J. Dornsife. Mr. Dornsife refers to this as a "confection" having as its primary component a circa 1890 late Rococo Revival standard which features a winged putto holding a spear. To the upraised putto's arm a modern, turned shaft has been added and a period Rococo Revival candle cup and prism ring appended to the shaft. The final ingredients are six prisms of an indeterminate origin and date and a scalloped glass bobeche which is American and dates to the 1880s.

279. Three Light Girandole, American (attributed to Henry N. Hooper and Co., Boston), Rococo Revival style, gilded brass, circa 1855. H: 17-½ in. W: 15-½ in. D: 6-¼ in. Courtesy Goudeau Antiques, Baton Rouge Louisiana.

It is possible that this candelabrum is the partially torn-out illustration from page ten of the copy of the 1858 Hooper catalogue owned by the Essex Institute of Salem. The foliate candle cups and broad grape cluster alternating with grape leaf prism rings can be seen. There are certainly other vintage pattern shafts in the catalogue. The plinth raised on tripod feet is one of the most interesting ones of American manufacture. Its three principal corners are embellished with single eagle heads on a large monopod talon.

FOOTNOTES FOR GIRANDOLE CHAPTER

1. Oxford English Dictionary (Oxford: Clarendon Press, 1961) Vol. IV, p. 174.

2. Ibid

3. Ibid

4. Ibid

5. Ibid

6. Webster's New International Dictionary (Springfield: G. and C. Merriam Co., 1960) p. 350.

7. Stimpson's Boston Directory, (Boston: Charles Stimpson, 1845), p. 14.

8. For a more detailed synopsis of the story, see Sir Paul Harvey and J. E. Hasetine's The Oxford Companion to French Literature, (Oxford: Clarendon Press, 1959) pp. 544-545.

9. Ulysses G. Dietz Victorian Lighting: The Dietz Catalogue of 1860 (American Life Foundation: Watkins Glen, 1982) p. 8.

10. Ibid, p. 30.

11. Ibid, p. 30.

12. Complete synopsis of the novel can be found in Sir Paul Harvey The Oxford Companion to English Literature, (Oxford: Clarendon Press, 1967) pp. 310-361.

Candle Powered Chandeliers and Sconces

The candle powered chandelier came into more general residential use during the last half of the eighteenth century and during the first half of the nineteenth century before gas became common for domestic use. Wooden and cut glass chandeliers were the most favored materials for domestic chandeliers in Europe, Britain and America during the eighteenth century. At the end of the eighteenth century, the French developed the dish type of chandelier made of patinated bronze and/or ormolu. This type of chandelier had wide influence all across Europe and models displaying regional variations were produced in Austria, the Germanic states, Russia and Scandinavia.

This new form is the logical place to begin the chapter. First comes the discussion of the metallic dish and spherical French chandeliers and the sconces made of iron, wood and gesso dating from the late eighteenth century through the 1880s. Second, come the Russian, Scandinavian, Austrian and other Germanic metal fixtures that follow the French taste. Glass elements were more important in combination with the metal work in those countries of manufacture. Contrast is provided with some of the English work. Third, a good sampling of European and British basket-type metal and glass chandeliers are reviewed, since this is an important new form that evolved during the period. Fourth, the hall lanterns and especially the wonderful examples made for a wide-world market in Britain, the cradle of the Industrial Revolution, are illustrated. Some American-made hall lanterns of the 1830 to 1850 period are included there as well.

Fifth, a large and fairly comprehensive series of cut glass, Anglo-Irish-made chandeliers are presented. These chandeliers in the neoclassical taste were made in large numbers and for such a broad world market, which included the whole British Empire as well as the former American colonies, that they deserve special attention. I have started with a simpler example from the 1770s in a combination of the rococo and early neoclassical styles to provide contrast with the high Adam neoclassical examples which were made from the 1780s forward. Note that throughout this chapter and the rest of this book, the term glass or cut glass is used rather than the word "crystal." Strictly speaking crystal refers to the rock crystal found in nature as opposed to cut glass which is manufactured. Many of these chandeliers have been called Anglo-Irish because of the close

relationship between the English and Irish glass houses. There is no concrete evidence that any of these chandeliers were made exclusively in Ireland. The data points toward pieces of Irish-made glass being used in assembling chandeliers, sconces and table candlesticks in England.

Many English-made glass chandeliers of late eighteenth and early nineteenth centuries are loosely attributed to the Parker and Perry firm. It was one of the biggest firms specializing in the manufacture of glass lighting devices, thus making commentary on that firm's history appropriate at this time. The London firm under its various names and styles was begun by William Parker as early as 1762. Parker was in partnership with Edward Watton during that year, dissolved the partnership in that same year and moved to 69 Fleet Street, property the firm still owned in 1820. The 1771 London City Directory gives the name "William Parker, glass seller, . . . " at that address. In 1784 the name of the company was changed to "William Parker and Sons, glass-manufacturers to H.R.H. the Prince of Wales." The firm's name was changed to Parker and Perry by 1804. By 1830, the name had been changed again to read Perry and Company. The glass used by this firm was made by the famous Whitefrairs works on the north side of the Thames River. The fame of the Parker and Perry Company rests on several well documented chandeliers. The Assembly Rooms at Bath, England have original 1771 chandeliers. In 1937 when the chandeliers were taken down for repair, J. B. Perret discovered the inscription PARKER, FLEET STREET, LONDON engraved inside the bowl of the one located in the Tea Room. As the purveyor of chandeliers to the Prince Regent, the Parker firm supplied chandeliers for Carlton House from 1789 until its dismantling in 1826. Those chandeliers were modified and reinstalled at Buckingham Palace in 1834. The firm of Perry and Company provided the five great Regency style chandeliers for the Throne Room at Buckingham Palace, as well as two more for the two alcoves on the side of the thrones.[1]

---

1. Information on the Parker and Perry firm is to be found in Harry J. Powell Glass-Making in England, (University Press, Cambridge: 1923), pp 150-151 and in E.M. Elville English and Irish Cut Glass 1750-1953, (Country Life, London: 1950), pp 51, 57, 59—One of the Assembly Room chandeliers at Bath, in the rococo taste, is shown as plate 23 and the central chandelier in the Throne Room at Buckingham Palace is shown as plate 24.

Sixth, a short section on British wooden and mixed media chandeliers and sconces of the Regency period separates the early neoclassical glass chandeliers from the later ones in the Regency, George IV, William IV and Victorian styles. American chandeliers in gilt metal and glass are included here. The seventh and final grouping consists of the American tin chandeliers and tin and glass examples made during the first half of the nineteenth century.

281. Sixteen Light Chandelier, French, Consular style, ormolu and glass, circa 1800. Courtesy Nesle, Inc., New York. Photo by Helga Photo Studio.

This is an excellent example of the dish-type chandelier developed by the French in the late eighteenth century. The shallow glass dish itself is ribbed and has a vertical band of two neoclassical borders. The lowest has a palmette and reed motif and the upper one is composed of a series of individual rosettes set within lozenges with foliate devices flanking each lozenge. The latter described border is repeated on the side of the corona which is capped with pierced stylized anthemia. The overall delicacy of this fixture is a prelude to the much more effusive models which evolved during the First Empire and Charles X periods.

282. Six Light Chandelier, French, First Empire style, painted sheet metal and ormolu, circa 1805. Courtesy Nesle, Inc., New York. Photo by Helga Photo Studio.

This unusual chandelier expresses, as well as any chandelier, the French First Empire's ability to achieve perfect thematic harmony using the neoclassical vocabulary. This fixture can be termed the zodiac chandelier. The heavens are represented by the sheet metal or tole sphere which is painted azure and embellished with gold stars. The ormolu band has two vignettes of the signs between candle branches. In this view the Gemini twins and the crab representing Cancer can be seen. The winged griffins of Greek mythology serve as the branches. An anthemion-decorated candle cup rises from each griffin's head and each detachable bobeche is edged with an egg and dart border. The bottom of the sphere is embellished with a sunburst of palmettes which is repeated in the vertical element at the top of the sphere. The small cast corona is decorated with cast anthemia which alternate with palmettes.

French chandeliers were popular with high-style English designers such Thomas Hope. An illustration of a chimney-piece and boudoir in Hope's own home, "The Deepdene" in Surrey, shows a chandelier remarkably similar to this one [see pages 209-210 in Peter Thornton's AUTHENTIC DECOR, THE DOMESTIC INTERIOR 1620-1920, (Weidenfeld and Nicholson; London: 1984]. Mr. Thornton mentions in his caption accompanying these pictures that the chimney-piece could have been acquired in Paris. The same comment can be made about the chandelier.

283. Ten Light Chandelier, French, First Empire style, patinated bronze and ormolu, circa 1810. Courtesy Nesle, Inc., New York. Photo by Helga Photo Studio.

The relationship of the elements in proportion, texture and the masterful repetition of decorative motives make this fixture a superior example of the dish-type chandeliers made in First Empire France. The casting is crisp and sharp and employs in combination several decorative elements especially favored by the French of that period. Rising as the crest for the dish ring are single butterflies alternating with a bouquet of flowers with sheep supports. The candle cups are decorated with a lozenge pattern employed frequently by the French in all decorative work. The medallion-like interlocking rosettes appearing as a band on the concave ring are repeated as the design for the bold chains. The side of the corona is decorated with a band of anthemia which is repeated as a pierced crest.

284. Pair of Two Light Sconces, Continental Europe, or American, Neoclassical style, pine, gilded gesso, gilded iron and tin, circa 1810-1820. H: 13 in. W: 18-¾ in. Courtesy Herbert Schiffer Antiques, West Chester, Pennsylvania.

With their crimped tin drip pan and the folk art quality in the carving of the eagles, there is a possibility of these sconces having been made in America. It is more likely, however, that they were made in France or elsewhere in northern Europe. The gilded iron branches are embellished with wood, gesso and gilded balls and bellflowers which relate to the crafts of that area.

285. Two Light Sconce, French or Continental, *Directoire* style, gessoed and gilded wood and gilded iron, circa 1795-1825. Courtesy Herbert Schiffer Antiques, West Chester, Pennsylvania.

This piece could have been made in provincial France, Switzerland or Italy, but it reflects French aesthetics and choice of materials in the late eighteenth century. From a gouge-work giltwood bar embellished by a raised tablet with an applied rosette, branches and sheaves of wheat rise. Ribbons and bellflower swags fall below. The stems of the wheat sheaves are gilded iron to which gessoed and gilded wooden sheaves and grain pods have been applied. The scrolling branches are also gilded iron which terminate in cylindrical candle cups with round beaded bobeches, all done in gilded sheet iron. The bellflowers are carved, gessoed and gilded wood and run on a stiff wire swag. The ribbons are also giltwood. This is a traditional neoclassical form that could have been made for individuals having conservative tastes as late as 1825.

287. Eight Light Chandelier, French, *Restauration* style, patinated bronze and ormolu, circa 1835. Collection of Mr. & Mrs. Raymond St. Germain, Natchez, Mississippi.

This beautifully designed and crafted lighting device is slightly heavier in feeling regarding decorative detail than its Empire and Charles X predecessors. This is true in the casting of both the anthemia decorated crown and the foliage garnished cornucopia branches. The chains are robust, consisting of alternating shield-shaped, patinated bronze devices and octagonal ormolu ones. Bold ormolu masks cover the bases of each of the branches. The plain surface of the underside of the dish is decorated with a powerfully cast ormolu foliate sunburst and artichoke pendent. The upper part of the dish is covered with a flared conical device which is typical of the French chandeliers made during this period.

286. Sixteen Light Chandelier, French, *Restauration* style, patinated bronze and ormolu, circa 1820-1830. Courtesy Nesle, Inc., New York. Photo by Helga Photo Studio.

This large chandelier which arranges its sixteen lights in two tiers is an example of the technological advances occurring as the nineteenth century progressed. The small candle cups rising directly from the dish of the fixture do accommodate candles; however, the bolder, broader sockets on the branches can provide a suitable support for oil-fired lamps as well as candles. The casting is robust and much heavier than that of French First Empire period. The gilded consoles beneath the corona which are used to hold the decorative chains are especially refined features of this chandelier.

288. Twelve Branch Chandelier, French, *Restauration* style, patinated bronze and ormolu, circa 1835. Collection of Mr. & Mrs. Raymond St. Germain, Natchez, Mississippi.

This is a larger and more sophisticated variant of the *Restauration* chandelier. The corona is of patinated bronze with an applied crest of pierced ormolu anthemia alternating with acanthus leaves. The six strong chains employ links of patinated bronze anthemia alternating with ormolu devices. The plain dish is capped by a simpler splayed, bronze cone having an ormolu crown composed of a beaded border, pierced laurel wreath and an anthemion and palmette crest. The foliate branches have ormolu masks on their underside. At the bottom of the dish is a large circle of ormolu water leaves and palmettes from which an artichoke pendent falls.

289. Six Light Chandelier, Continental (possibly French), *Restauration* style, sheet iron, wrought iron with gilding, circa 1820-1830. Courtesy Bernard and S. Dean Levy, Inc., New York. Photo by Helga Photo Studio.

This type of wrought iron chandelier was popular from France through the Swiss cantons, the German states and Austria, thus making it impossible to pinpoint its country of origin positively. The amphora-shaped shaft clearly dates it into the nineteenth century. Scrolling branches embellished with gilded leaves and rosettes rise from a flange placed before the gilded pendent of palmettes which terminates the shaft. Three gilded lilies partially obscure the hook for the chandelier's chain.

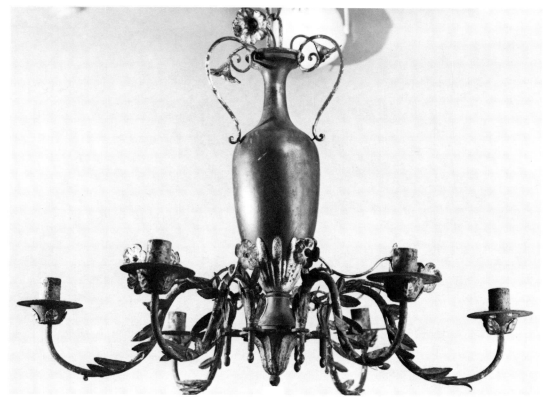

290. Three Light Chandelier (one of a pair), Spanish or Spanish Colonial, (town mark—a lion within a sunburst and maker's mark ?—"BISCINO"), traditional style, silver, late eighteenth—early nineteenth century. H: 8 in. Courtesy Christie's, New York.

The baluster supports three flat, open-worked branches— all harken back to the seventeenth century. In tradition-loving Spain and its colonies in Latin America, early styles continued to enjoy a vogue long after their popularity had faded in more sophisticated artistic centers. Unquestionably, more chandeliers of this general type were made in brass and bronze. With the hordes of silver acquired by the Spanish from the conquest of Mexico beginning in the sixteenth century, however, the Spanish developed a luxurious taste for using silver in place of base metals in many decorative objects. Several pieces of eighteenth century-made Mexican furniture actually have silver hardware. The cylindrical candle cups, central stem and circular drip pans express the stylistic conservatism of the Spanish while utilizing a rich material for construction.

291. Eighteen Light Chandelier, French late Louis Philippe-Second Empire style, ormolu and patinated bronzes, circa 1840-1860. Courtesy Nesle, Inc., New York. Photo by Helga Photo Studio.

This rather exotic chandelier was obviously inspired by the materials and the decorative vocabulary of the First Empire, but here ornaments are employed in new ways. Springing from the plain upper band of the deep base are patinated bronze blackamoor arms, each of which supports a tall three-branch candleholder in the form of a caduceus. The restraint exercised during the First Empire and Charles X periods is missing here in a chandelier where the most sumptuous look was desired by its designer. The confusion of the chains with the branches seen in the photograph does not exist when the fixture is viewed from the floor as was intended.

292. Six Branch Chandelier, French, First Empire style or possibly Empire revival style, patinated bronze and ormolu, circa 1810 or circa 1870. Collection of Eugene D. Cizek, Ph.D. and Lloyd L. Sensat, Sun Oak House, New Orleans.

The full vocabulary of the French Empire is employed in this relatively modest sized fixture. Ormolu swans spring from the low patinated bronze dish which is embellished with rosettes and other foliate pieces in ormolu. Foliate ormolu "C" scrolls which terminate in griffin heads rise from the dish to hold finely cast ormolu cables which serve as chains running to the anthemion decorated corona. A turned shaft of patinated bronze with foliate and beaded ormolu ornaments is placed in the center of the dish. This chandelier has suffered two unfortunate losses. The principal one is that the branches were replaced with hollow reeded tubing when the piece was electrified early in the twentieth century. Also, the piece seems originally to have had ormolu chains which ran from the beaks of the swans to the original branches. With the exception of the replacement branches, the proportions and quality of the casting appear up to First Empire standards. There are, however, some superior examples of fine casting in the First Empire taste made during the Second Empire. Screw technology will usually reveal the true period of the piece unless it has been completely dissembled as this one has.

293. Twenty-four Light Chandelier, French, Second Empire style, bronze and ormolu, circa 1860-1880. Courtesy Nesle, Inc., New York. Photo by Helga Photo Studio.

This outstanding chandelier exemplifies the best of inventive eclecticism occurring in France during the second half of the nineteenth century. This form of chandelier borrows heavily on the style of the First Empire. Its bronze and ormolu hemispherical dish, its ormolu corona, its rod-like chain elements which are joined by graduated spheres, and its pulley system all harken back to that period. While there are some neoclassical decorative devices employed, such as the guilloche band bordering the edge of the lip of the dish, the other decorative motives are largely derived from the Louis XIV period. The bulbous candle cups and even the branches were inspired by the French baroque. The decorative pairs of ormolu "C" scrolls seen on the dish, the cover for the pulley action, the graduated ball connectors on the chains, and the canopy of the corona are other Louis XIV period ornaments. The cartouches which join the chains to the dish are also in the baroque style.

294. Sixteen Light Chandelier, made by E. F. Caldwell of New York City, Empire Revival style, patinated bronze and ormolu, circa 1920. Courtesy Nesle, Inc., New York. Photo by Helga Photo Studio.

The New York firm of E. F. Caldwell specialized in the manufacture of fine quality traditional fixtures during the first thirty years of the twentieth century. This chandelier is one of those inspired by French First Empire to Charles X period models. The rather anemic treatment of the upper corona or crown and the poorly executed chains are deficiencies not seen in pieces made during the early nineteenth century. The overall, bas relief, neoclassical design of the dish is in the manner of the late nineteenth and early twentieth centuries. The dish is missing a decorative element and pendent drop. Additionally, the short broad branches supporting the candle cups appear to be modelled on branches for oil lamps. While in large part the chandelier exhibits its beautiful casting, the piece is not a reproduction of any chandelier made in the early nineteenth century.

295. Four Light Chandelier, Russian, ormolu, clear cut glass and blown turquoise blue glass, neoclassical style, circa 1795-1805. Courtesy Nesle, Inc., New York. Photo by G. Barrow.

This tiered chandelier was probably intended originally to serve as a hall or boudoir fixture. In proportion and inventive use of material it is exemplary. Mr. Albert Nesle suggests that this piece may be the work of the chandelier maker, Zech of St. Petersburg. The prism rings whether of thin sheets of ormolu or ormolu wire are very delicate. The principal prism ring has been engraved with an egg and dart border. A crest of ormolu wire in the shape of a wicket border is attached to that ring and pyriform prisms are suspended from the apex of each wicket. The fixture is a study in the use of graduated pear-shaped prisms. Two pieces of turquoise blue glass are used as elements in the central shaft. The lowest is urn shaped while the upper one is ovoid and is attractively held in place by thin ormolu palmettes. The four ormolu chains which assist in balancing this piece resemble strings of large paper clips. The four foliate candle cups alternate with matching but smaller cups which are the sockets for tall slender triangles of glass having circular faceted finials.

While not outlawing the possibility of this fixture being French, the hemispherically-shaped cut glass bowl is typical of Viennese work and the form was favored in the Germanic and Slovakian areas of Europe. In addition to the pointed diaper pattern, there are the handsome band of cut leaves found on the middle of the bowl, the vertical cut leaves at the base and a laurel wreath border below the lip. The bright and matte finished ormolu of the bezels for the bowl and the domed glass canopy, as well as the candle cups, compliment the piece well. The "S" shaped branches rise from lion masks.

296. Twenty Light Chandelier, Russian, style of Czar Alexander I, ormolu, circa 1810. Courtesy Nesle, Inc., New York. Photo by Helga Photo Studio.

The imperial court at St. Petersburg and the nobles and gentry of Russia during the late eighteenth and nineteenth centuries developed a taste for one of the grandest life styles known in Europe. The importation of foreign architects, designers and craftsmen that began with Peter the Great resulted in a westernized style which retained a distinct Russian accent. The manufacturers of decorative arts in the St. Petersburg area were numerous by the end of the eighteenth century. As with most of the continental European countries, the styles of Bourbon and later First Empire France were the principal design sources.

The Russian and Scandinavian manufacturers took particular delight in the use of pierced support rings decorated with foliate motives. Another form favored by the Russians is the central shaft's elements being in the classical vase shape. A pendent, stylized artichoke is substituted for the usual square stepped base of a vase. A border of palmettes and carefully articulated water leaves issue forth from the mouth of the vase. This idea is echoed by the stylized anthemion and grape cluster motives rising from the corona. The light form of the chains seems to be peculiar to Russia and Scandinavia.

299. Six Light Chandelier, probably Scandinavian, Russo-Scandinavian taste of the Alexander I period, glass and ormolu, circa 1810. H: 40 in. Diam: 30 in. Courtesy Nesle, Inc., New York. Photo by Helga Photo Studio.

This dish-type chandelier in cut glass and ormolu bears resemblance to the previous Austrian example and the succeeding English-made piece as well as to French examples, but it points up Russo-Scandinavian decorative predilections. The thin, stamped gilt-brass corona with prisms is a Scandinavian preference. The broad lobed canopy with the series of prism drops and the six wire chains embellished with faceted jewels of glass is in the Russo-Scandinavian taste. Those chains run from an ormolu disk which is basically hidden by the pyriform prisms that are hung from a recessed prism ring. The chains are connected to an ormolu ring whose sides are decorated with a guilloche band. This ring serves as a bezel for an inverted, ribbed, domical dish as well as being the support for six scroll branches. The branches are screwed to the ring and each screw is concealed with a decorative rosette and that rosette is repeated on the secondary scroll that decorates the upper face of each arm. Each branch has an ornamental bird head with a ring in its beak. The campana-shaped, cut glass candle cups are not too dissimilar from English examples except for the fact that each serrated bobeche/prism ring is a part of the cup and is far broader than English ones. The large glass dish has a lotus-shaped ormolu pendent and an artichoke finial to complete the design.

298. Eight Light Chandelier, probably made in Vienna, in the Franco-Russian taste, ormolu and cut glass, circa 1810-1830. Courtesy Nesle, Inc., New York. Photo by Helga Photo Studio.

Vienna, the seat of the Austro-Hungarian Empire, was another of those melting pots of style. The overall configuration of this dish-type chandelier rests stylistically in First Empire France. The thinner casting and the pierced laurel wreath making the principal ring, as well as the tall double anthemion crest of the corona, all relate to other Viennese work. Compare the cutting on the cornucopia with the cross-hatching of leaves and ellipse in the previous fixture. That shape is repeated in the branches where a cornucopia form emerges from a serpent's tail which is the lower part of each branch. In essence the form is reproduced yet another time in the interlocking swags which crown the ring that holds the dish element.

300. Six Light Chandelier, English, Regency style, glass and ormolu, circa 1820 to 1835. H: 34-½ in. W: 26-½ in. Courtesy Nesle, Inc., New York. Photo by Helga Photo Studio.

The preceding Scandinavian chandelier is a composition of individually beautiful components, but the good proportions of the elements of this English-made example present a unified whole. This is achieved by the use of thirty-six chains composed of graduated octagonal, faceted buttons. The pierced arabesques in ormolu which form the corona provide support for a series of three graduated, octagonal buttons, each of which terminates in tear-drop prisms. This same arrangement is repeated in larger scale on the large moulded ormolu ring, which also functions as a support for the candle arms and the bezel supporting the flattish glass dish cut with flutes. The scrolling ormolu arms support deeply dished diaper-cut prism rings and similarly cut candle cups which have attached bobeches with serrated edges.

301. Six Light Chandelier, Russian or Scandinavian, Alexander I style, ormolu, clear cut glass and ruby glass, circa 1810-1825. Courtesy Nesle Inc., New York. Photo by Helga Photo Studio.

Many of the best characteristics associated with the early nineteenth century Russian and Scandinavian work are to be seen in this chandelier. These include the thinness of the cast components—curved branches, bobeche/prism rings, bejeweled chains and the principal ring. The principal ring is composed of pierced interlocking rinceaux and is surmounted with a trailing branch of delicate leaves and acorns. Another decorative device which was particularly favored by the Russian manufacturers is the ormolu arches which leap from the top of the corona to support sprays of prism drops. Three handsomely curved ormolu supports rise from the back of the large lower ring to hold a sphere upon which the figure of cupid raises his right arm to hold a prism as though it were a lantern.

303. Six Light Chandelier, Russian, Alexander I style, ormolu with clear and red glass, circa 1810. H: 35 in. W: 33 in. Courtesy Nesle, Inc., New York. Photo by Helga Photo Studio.

302. Eight Light Chandelier, Russian or Scandinavian, Alexander I style, ormolu and cut glass, circa 1800-1810. Courtesy Nesle, Inc., New York. Photo by Helga Photo Studio.

This simple chandelier exhibits a great deal of sophistication. The rather thin casting of the ormolu prism rings and the use of wire sprays from which pyriform cut drops fall are Russo-Scandinavian characteristics. Pear-shaped cut glass jewels framed by ormolu bezels are other preferences of the St. Petersburg and Scandinavian-made fixtures. The diaper pattern decoration on both ormolu prism rings is inspired by French Consular and First Empire examples, but is handled in an eastern European way. Note the sawtooth border on the lower edge of the upper prism ring or corona, which has the diaper pattern decoration framed by a brightly burnished ormolu band. Each sawtooth element acts as the support for the graduated series of circular and pyriform drops which are mixed with some small faceted buttons of blue glass. The colored glass is subtly repeated in the pendents falling from the big prism ring and the small pierced ones below the candle cups, as well as in the sprays.

The former owner of this chandelier, Mr. Albert N. Nesle who is regarded as one of the great experts on European lighting devices of the eighteenth and nineteenth centuries, suggests that this *soigne* example is from the St. Petersburg workshop of a manufacturer named Zeck. It certainly is illustrative of early nineteenth century Russian taste with its lavish use of colored glass and its bejeweled wire fronds. While the pierced ring for branches was not unknown in France during this period, the French much preferred the dish-type chandelier. Here the voids in the ring are filled with rosette-shaped cut glass jewels, and graduated faceted oval prisms fall from the lower ring. The baluster-shaped central shaft is largely made of ruby red glass. From an ormolu flange near the bottom of that shaft, ormolu wire vines and foliage which are further enriched with cut glass extend as far as the ring. Two glass jewel bedecked sprays in graduated sizes rise from ormolu neckings on the shaft. A canopy in dish form and executed in red glass set in ormolu has yet more ormolu wires and rosettes with glass drops rising from the dish's inside to complete the chandelier.

214

304. Eighteen Light Chandelier, probably French with Russian additions, First Empire style, ormolu, blue glass, circa 1810. Courtesy Nesle, Inc., New York. Photo by Helga Photo Studio.

In a casual viewing of this fixture, many Russian characteristics should immediately register. The blue glass urn with ormolu wire sprays for faceted glass drops is associated with St. Petersburg work. The series of six triple prisms attached to a central lozenge which has been suspended from the florid ormolu crown is yet another Russian characteristic. Yet when those elements are removed and the heavily cast big prism ring, corona, chains and central pendent ball—all crisply cast—are examined, the style clearly relates to the French First Empire. It is known that the blue glass urn and the spray, which are antique, were added to the piece in this century. The addition of more Russian-style prisms would therefore not be difficult. The lotus-shaped candle cups rising from antefixes placed on the top of the prism ring is another uncommon feature of this chandelier.

305. Six Light Chandelier, Russian or possibly Scandinavian, Neoclassical style, ormolu and iron, circa 1790-1810. H: 55-¼ in. W: 31-½ in. Courtesy Nesle Inc., New York. Photo by Thomas Lawaetz.

The skeletal nature of this chandelier and the stair-step arrangement of swags of prisms up the four vertical members forming the shaft are elements seen on both Russian and Scandinavian-made fixtures. The six curious ormolu and glass canopy-like decorative pendents which fall from chinoiserie scrolls at the head of the shaft are seen on other Russian examples. The openness of the framework and sparseness of prisms perhaps discouraged later owners from wiring it for electricity.

306. Sixteen Light Chandelier, Russian, Alexander I style, ormolu and cut glass, circa 1805-1815. H: 57in. W: 36 in. Courtesy Nesle, Inc., New York. Photo by Helga Photo Studio.

This multi-tiered chandelier is a precursor for all the later tiered chandeliers made in Europe and in America after 1850 that were considered as being in the Russian taste. The lower three graduated tiers of spear-pointed prisms and headers begin with a broad ormolu ring surmounted by a gallery of pierced ellipses. From that ring spring ormolu prongs that join together to form a series of eight large leaf shapes. The voids formed between the prongs that make the leaf shapes are ingeniously filled with a pattern of faceted glass buttons. From the tip of each leaf an ormolu wire branch rises that divides into two scrolling arms which support one candle cup prism ring each. Dropping first as pendents on faceted glass chains from each leaf tip in an alternating arrangement are flat lozenge-shaped cut glass elements from which three prisms with accompanying headers fall; second, a pierced circular ormolu frame falls in the same manner, from which spearhead prisms with double headers fall.

Joining the principal lower section of the chandelier to the upper three graduated tiers are four bejeweled chains which have three sets of horizontally placed chains arranged in swags. Those vertical chains are connected to the lowest of the three graduated ormolu prism rings. All the upper prism rings employ multiple buttons with each spearhead prism. The uppermost prism ring is actually a double ring with a section in between pierced to appear as a band of leaves. To the top of that ring, eight scrolling ormolu wires have been soldered. From each tendril-like wire, in a slightly larger scale and on longer chains, the same sort of pendents seen in the lower section are repeated.

216

307. Eight Light Chandelier, Russian, Alexander I style, cut glass on ormolu frame, circa 1815-1825. Courtesy Nesle, Inc., New York. Photo by Helga Photo Studio.

The pierced central ormolu ring of this fixture has rinceaux motives filling in the voids in the ring. Both serpentine and circular ormolu elements are attached on the same level to the ring and from all these rings tapered spearhead prisms fall. The simple inverted bell candle cups and simple prism rings rise from the principal ring and the auxiliary rings. The teardrop prisms seen there are repeated in horizontal pairs attached to four decorative curved ormolu arms which are equidistantly spaced. The central shaft is simply decorative and consists of ormolu beads and reels on either side of a scalloped glass flange. The three chains running from the principal ring to the tiered corona are composed of linked circular ormolu bezels into which faceted cut glass is set. The corona has a central ring which supports more spearhead prisms, as well as ormolu wire vines which hold spearhead prisms and are connected to every other wire with swags of faceted glass buttons.

308. Eight Light Chandelier, Russian, Alexander I style, ormolu and cut glass, circa 1810-1820. H: 45 in. Diam.: 38 in. Courtesy Nesle, Inc., New York. Photo by Helga Photo Studio.

This tiered Russian chandelier employs devices seen in the two previous fixtures in slightly different ways. Here the wire-like tendrils of ormolu support horizontally placed teardrop prisms, and the wires in turn hold the faceted glass chains and canopied prism rings and prisms. An exciting new neoclassical feature is the use of a set of four ormolu paterae whose voids contain a sunburst of prisms each radiating out from a stamped ormolu rosette. These paterae are fastened halfway up the central supporting shaft. Each patera has additional spearhead prisms attached to its lower side and groups of prisms emerge ray-like from the upper edge.

217

309. Sixteen Light Chandelier, Russian, Alexander I style, ormolu and glass, circa 1820. H: 44 in. W: 39 in. Courtesy Nesle, Inc., New York. Photo by Taylor and Dull.

The heavier proportions of this fixture suggest a date late in Alexander I's reign as its time of manufacture. From beneath the lower of two rather broad prism rings (one with a gallery) each of eight branches swoop downward and make contact with the top of a neoclassical mask. From there each branch curves upward to terminate in a cylindrical candle cup with bobeche cum prism ring below. While four of the branches have single lights, they alternate with those branches having two smaller arms attached to the lower side of the principal bobeche, thus forming a group of three branches.

An unusual and very Russian feature of this piece is the way in which on a horizontal plane, graduated button-type prisms descend between the eight principal branches. They stop when they reach the swags of ormolu which run from mask to mask. Cast rinceaux are a part of those swags. From the lower edge of the ormolu swags, spearhead prisms with headers are suspended.

310. Eight Light Chandelier, probably Russian, period of Nicholas II, patinated bronze and ormolu, circa 1830. Courtesy Nesle Inc., New York. Photo by Helga Photo Studio.

The proportions of this chandelier lack the refinement of the pieces made during the opening years of the nineteenth century and, it is more heavily ornamented than those fixtures. The thin casting of the foliate crest on the dish element and on both the upper and the lower corona suggests a Russian or eastern European origin for this fixture. The overly delicate chains fall from wire-like scrolls which are another Russian-Scandinavian preference.

Particularly inventive and graceful are the neoclassical figures which fly out from the dish to serve as the branches. Flowing from the arms of each figure is a wishbone-like element to which each bobeche and candle cup is screwed.

311. Twelve Light Chandelier, French, First Empire style, ormolu and glass, circa 1805-1810. Courtesy The Historic New Orleans Collection, The Kemper and Leila Williams Foundation, New Orleans.

About 1800, some unknown French lighting device manufacturer developed the "basket" type of chandeliers. From the great central ring which supports the branches, chains of graduated circular prisms are run to a much smaller spoked wheel or ring. While this model's metal parts are ormolu, other models employ painted sheet metal. This form was widely emulated by continental and British manufacturers; however, this model has a combination of features that clearly mark it as French. The crisply cast, cornucopia-form branches which terminate in serpents' heads that spring directly out from the great ring is the manner most preferred by the French. The ring itself is delicate but stoutly cast. Each branch is attached to a rosette on the ring and pairs of circular cut glass jewels are inset between them. Forming a crest on the ring are two alternating castings. One crest motif is a putto with foliate and floral supports and the second consists of pairs of cornucopias. The corona's ring or band repeats on a reduced scale the use of decorative pairs of inlaid cut glass jewels. Rising from the top of the ring are heavily cast anthemia in the best French neoclassical tradition.

219

312. Twelve Light Chandelier, English, Regency period in the French Empire taste, ormolu and glass, circa 1805. H: 43-¾ in. Diam: 28 in. Courtesy Boscobel Restoration, Inc., Garrison-on-Hudson, New York.

While not a part of the original furnishings of Boscobel, this is the very type of chandelier that the well-to-do American merchant or planter of the Federal period could have selected for either a town or country dwelling. Contrasting this chandelier with the previous French example will show that the English makers were certainly in debt to French designers, but this fixture is in no way inferior to the French lighting device in either concept or manufacture. Both chandeliers are roughly of the same size; however, the English example has thinner scrolling branches which terminate in ormolu prism rings and sockets which are decorated with simple mouldings. The broad spearhead-type prism is a type preferred by Anglo-Americans for chandeliers and not by the French. The corona's crest is composed of stylized Bourbon fleurs-de-lis, which were not in favor with the Napoleonic regime in France. The sides of the corona ring and the large ring supporting the branches are decorated with finely cast interlocking circles—each of which contains a rosette.

313. Six Light Chandelier, (one of a pair), probably Scandinavian, in the French First Empire taste, cut glass circa 1805-1815. Collection of the Hermann-Grima House, New Orleans. Courtesy the Christian Women's Exchange.

The pair of chandeliers gracing the salon and dining room of the Hermann-Grima House appear too skeletal to be French. The use of cut glass jewels raised on thin wires covered with glass beads at both the branch ring level and the corona is certainly a decorative device favored by the Scandinavians. The branch ring is a brass rim from which faceted rectangular prisms are hung. The large cut glass bobeches look like canopies from English Adam-style chandeliers which have been inverted. They and the brass candle cups which they hold rest directly on the ring which is also not typical of French work. The basket element on this pair of chandeliers is especially attractive in that the final prisms in the graduated chains are rectangular and attached to a cut glass bezel containing a circular faceted jewel. This pendent or boss is perfectly related to the jewels on the two rings.

314. Hall Lantern, English, Neoclassical style, gilt brass and glass, circa 1800. Courtesy Herbert Schiffer Antiques, West Chester, Pennsylvania.

This hexagonal hallway fixture grew out of the more elaborately decorated passageway devices dating back to before the middle of the eighteenth century. Touches of elegance are seen in the arched ribs which rise to the central knop which is surmounted by a foliate ring to receive the hook and chain. Each of the ribs has one cast water leaf soldered to its lower, outer edges and there are six spool and acorn pendents which serve as feet when the lantern is on a table for cleaning. Another constructional clue to its late eighteenth-early nineteenth century date is the long wire hinge as opposed to the wrought hinges seen on the earlier lanterns. The English core cast brass chamber candlestick dating from circa 1795 to as late as 1850, while pleasant, has nothing to do with the original way this lantern was illumined. A shaft can be seen dropping from the hemispherical knop at the head of the lantern. From that shaft a small two or three light chandelier would have been suspended, protected from drafts sent down halls by the opening and closing of doors.

315. Single Light Hall Lantern, English, Neoclassical style, gilt brass, glass, circa 1785-1810. Courtesy Herbert Schiffer Antiques, West Chester, Pennsylvania.

In addition to the straight-sided hexagonal and octagonal hall lanterns, hall lanterns with four tapering sides were made in various qualities during the late eighteenth and early nineteenth centuries. The basic form was adapted from the covered street lamps on poles. This lantern is a highly refined example blending the rococo design elements in its base with the highly neoclassical motives of the lip. The cast scrolling feet and pierced foliate elements were cast and applied to the plain base of the lantern. Each upper terminal corner is embellished with an applied cast satyr head. Rising above each head to form pivotal points on the crest is a single anthemion. The rest of the crest is not unlike a gothic crenellation in that it consists of a line of trifoliate motives. The chains in this case are replacements and the lantern is missing its smoke bell.

221

316. Single Light Hall Lantern, English, Adam style, glass and gilded brass, circa 1795-1815. Courtesy Bernard and S. Dean Levy, Inc., New York. Photo by Helga Photo Studio.

This fine example has three beaded rings on its ventilator which are repeated on a larger scale as a part of the bezel. The pierced swags of flowers that are a part of the bezel are in the best Adam or neoclassical taste.

317. Single Light Hall Lantern, English, Adam style, glass and gilded brass, circa 1795-1815. Courtesy Bernard and S. Dean Levy, Inc., New York. Photo by Helga Photo Studio.

Some of the most attractive of the hall lanterns feature the inverted, tapered bell form of shade. These usually were intended for a single candle placed in a socket in the ventilator. The bezel holding the shade conforms to the ventilator's simple reeded borders and simple hooks for the splendid chains composed of neoclassical baskets of flowers. This lantern has lost its smoke bell, which is unfortunately the first casualty in lanterns of this type.

318. Wall Lantern, English, Adam style, lead, iron, ormolu and glass, circa 1790-1810. Courtesy Nesle, Inc., New York. Photo by Helga Photo Studio.

This type of hanging fixture would have been originally attached in sets to the walls of great Adamesque halls. An especially attractive element of this lighting device is the half-ovoid, frosted, blown glass shade which has been copper-wheel engraved with Royal Garter Badges. The rather simple lead frame for the shade has been embellished with neoclassical ormolu devices which include heavily cast artichoke-like finials, rosettes, an ovoid fruit pendent and exciting delicately cast drapery swags with tassels. The frame ascends literally to a regal ormolu crown. There is a loop ring at the head of the crown which is hooked to the gilded iron eagle-head terminal pendent of the arched standard. This arched section is further decorated with well-articulated and gilded cast iron foliage on the lower back of the arch and an arabesque in the same material springs from the front of the curve and terminates in a large rosette.

319. Hall Lantern, English, Adam style, glass and ormolu, circa 1790-1805. Courtesy Bernard and S. Dean Levy, Inc., New York. Photo by Helga Photo Studio.

Ignore the improper foliate and floral branches placed in this fixture for electrification and this lantern can be appreciated as a superior representative of the hall lantern in the Adam taste. The generous shade is a true inverted bell shape. The shade's bezel consists of an egg and dart moulded ring with four magnificent ram's heads placed equidistantly to serve as hooks for the chains. The hooks proper are actually delicately cast ropes which are looped around the rams' horns. The ormolu base consists of palmettes with a foliate and fruit pendent.

320. Single Light Hall Lantern, English, Neoclassical style, glass and gilt brass, circa 1800. Courtesy Bernard and S. Dean Levy, Inc. New York. Photo by Helga Photo Studio.

The shade is in the form of an inverted dome or straight-sided bell with a flaring lip. The flaring lip allows for the use of an offset cast bezel with pierced arches and a bold beaded border. The beaded border is repeated twice in a reduced scale on the ventilator. The hooks for the chains are well sculpted griffin heads which project from the bezel.

321. Single Light Hall Lantern, English, Regency style, copper-wheel engraved glass and stamped brass, circa 1805-1815. H: 28in. Diam. of lip: 10in. Courtesy Bernard and S. Dean Levy, Inc., New York.

Stamped brass furniture mounts and elements for lighting devices were introduced in the late eighteenth century. The florid nature of the decoration on both the bezel and ventilator dates this fixture to the early nineteenth century. The floral and foliate engraving on the glass greatly enhances the quality of this lantern. Griffin-head hooks for the chains appear on the side of the bezel.

323. Hall Lantern, English, Regency style, frosted and copper-wheel engraved glass, gilt brass and iron, circa 1815-1825. Collection of Mr. & Mrs. Raymond St. Germain, Natchez, Mississippi.

This large lantern having the great cast iron and gilded eagle in flight was probably intended for the American market. The inverted dome shade is completely frosted and copper-wheel engraved with laurel swags. Its bezel is stamped and gilded brass, while the ventilator at its base is cast.

322. Hall Lantern, probably English, Regency style, glass and gilt brass, circa 1810. Lambdin Collection, Natchez, Mississippi.

Numerous hall lanterns with blown glass inverted dome and bell-shaped shades were created for use in British, British colonial and American houses of the late eighteenth and early nineteenth centuries. Many of the better quality ones featured copper-wheel engraved grape clusters and vines such as this one or other motives. This example does not have the usual brass ventilator at the bottom and is therefore atypical. Caution should be taken by the prospective purchaser of aquamarine glass bell-shaped hall lanterns with no ventilators, because they are usually French *cloches* (belljars for protecting small plants) that have been adapted into lighting devices. The English glass at hand is supported by a stamped brass band which has griffin-like hooks attached to chains which connect to a bezel directly below the smoke bell. The electrified three-branch device is modern, but is a successful way to achieve the original effect of candles with electricity.

325. Hall Lantern, probably American, Empire or Grecian style, gilt brass, frosted and copper-wheel engraved glass, circa 1835-1845. Lambdin Collection, Natchez, Mississippi.

This is a variation on the previous lantern. Here the stamped bezel has interlocking foliate arabesques and a fleur-de-lis crest. An oak leaf pattern in repousse embellishes the ventilator. Especially well articulated leaves serve as the hooks for the chains.

324. Hall Lantern, probably American, Empire or Grecian style, gilt brass, frosted and copper-wheel engraved glass, circa 1835-1845. Collection of Mr. & Mrs. John Callon, Melrose, Natchez, Mississippi.

This hall lantern is a good example of a very common type of fixture having a bulbous shade in what modern Americans term the American Empire style, but was termed "Grecian" by nineteenth century English-speaking people. Here the frosted shade is cut with flowers and stylized foliage. The bezel holding the shade is pierced with a foliate motif and three leaf-shaped hooks spring from it and the chain holders. A decorative brass ventilator with a spool finial appears at the bottom of the shade. All of this style of fixture could have been installed originally with either candle cups for candle illumination or with a font and burner for whale oil.

226

326. Six Light Chandelier, English, transitional style of Rococo to Neoclassical, glass and silvered brass, circa 1770. Courtesy Nesle, Inc., New York. Photo by Helga Photo Studio.

This chandelier is the immediate ancestor of the neoclassical or Adam-style chandelier. While perhaps the overall feeling is rococo, there are some subtle hints of the high neoclassical style that is becoming popular in England during the 1770s. The blown glass urn-shaped principal element on the shaft soon becomes a faceted glass urn in the 1780s. None the less, this timid urn replaces the balusters and series of balls seen on most rococo glass chandeliers. The candle cups are blown urn-shaped ones which by the 1780s become cut and have crenellated lips. The cabled branches and particularly those with the snake-headed decoration are more in the Adam tradition. With the Adam-style chandeliers there are swags or festoons of prisms running between the branches.

327. Twelve Light Chandelier, English, Georgian style, glass and silvered brass, circa 1780. Courtesy Nesle, Inc., New York. Photo by Helga Photo Studio.

Clearly this is an English-made chandelier complete with Van Dyke candle cups, star-shaped prism rings and pear-shaped prisms cut in the British manner. It is, however, an English chandelier with a slight Italian accent. The upper tier of decorative scrolls which loop inward and frame pyriform drops is not in the usual English tradition. The chief decorative element of the upper shaft is in the shape of a bulbous Middle Eastern or Chinese water jar which would have been a little old-fashioned in the then emerging neoclassical period.

Opposite page:

328. Ten Light Chandelier, Anglo-Irish, Adam style, glass and silvered brass, circa 1780-1795. Courtesy, Nesle, Inc., New York. Photo by Helga Photo Studio.

This is a slightly more simplified model of the Adam-style of chandelier. The most distinctive feature on the shaft is the faceted baluster component. There is a canopy at the top and bottom of the chandelier and a faceted hemispherical dish to support one tier of six scrolled branches and the upper tier of four smaller scrolled arms. The candle cups are the old-fashioned cylindrical shape on Adam star-shaped prism rings. A restrained but elegant use is made of the swags of glass chains and pyriform drop prisms.

Opposite page:

329. Ten Light Chandelier, Anglo-Irish, Adam style, glass and silvered brass, circa 1780-1795. Courtesy Nesle, Inc., New York. Photo by Helga Photo Studio.

An interesting decorative motif is the presence of snake scroll glass chain supports in this variation of the Adam-style chandelier. The "S" shaped branches are clear but are actually hexagonal and arranged in two tiers. The usual Van Dyke candle cups, star-shaped prism rings, urn-shaped principal element on the shaft, two canopies and swags of glass chains all appear here.

330. Eight Light Chandelier, Anglo-Irish, Adam style, glass and silvered brass, circa 1780-1790. Courtesy Nesle, Inc., New York. Photo by Helga Photo Studio.

This neoclassical chandelier achieves its beauty with a modicum of pyriform-shaped prisms. The principal elements of the shaft—faceted vase, dish for the branches and faceted ball pendant—are all clearly visible. The upper tier of scrolling snake-headed branches is especially robust. From the tip of each snake head four prisms fall. The second prism in each of those series of drops is round and faceted and is the connecting element for cut, drapery-like swags. Each faceted candle branch terminates in a Van Dyke candle cup which sits atop a star-shaped prism ring. Only two graduated, pear-shaped prisms fall from the center of the ring, leaving the tips of the stars unobscured.

331. Four Light Sconce (one of a pair), English, Adam style, glass and ormolu, circa 1790. Courtesy Nesle, Inc., New York. Photo by Helga Photo Studio.

This sconce exhibits all the decorative devices associated with the high Adam style. Two tiers of scrolling, faceted arms rise from a faceted half-round which is attached to an oval ormolu backplate. The outer edge of the backplate is beaded, and a reeded bracket support for the glass half-round has been soldered to it. From the half-round a spear with saw-tooth cuttings on its terminal edges rises to a domical, faceted canopy which has finger-like projections from which graduated pyriform prisms fall. Holding the canopy in place is a very graceful cut glass urn. Pairs of chains of faceted pear-shaped prisms run from the underside of the canopy to the star-shaped bobeches of the upper tier of branches. Falling from the front of that canopy is a series of pyriform and patera-shaped cut prisms. At the level of the backplate, two chains of pyriform prisms swoop downward and then up to connect to the bobeches of the upper tier of branches. The candle cups are of the Van Dyke type and are coupled with the usual star-shaped bobeches. Screwed to the underside of the bracket on the backplate is a partially fluted plumb-bob-shaped device to which a canopy, in the same design as the upper canopy, is attached. The usual graduated, pear-shaped prisms fall from the canopy as well as a central pendent in the form of a faceted artichoke.

332. Two Light Sconce (one of pair), English, Adam style, glass and silvered brass, circa 1785. H: 32 in. W: 18 in. Courtesy Nesle, Inc., New York. Photo by Helga Photo Studio.

Sconces of this sort were made in sets to go with matching chandeliers. This example is impressive because of its size, quality and the number of uncommon features it possesses. The vertical backplate element is composed of a tall spear having a canopy in a pagoda roof shape from which graduated pyriform prisms are hung. The spear is crowned with a rayed, eight-pointed star finial. In place of a third branch another shorter spear rises on the face which is topped with a reduced pagoda roof canopy and a smaller number of graduated pear-shaped prisms. A pair of faceted "J" scrolls emerge from a basket-like element at the bottom of the base. Both pyriform prisms and faceted glass swags or festoons are suspended from the "J" scrolls. The cabriole branches also spring from the basket and provide beneath their star-shaped prism rings a place of attachment for the glass festoons. There are four of the faceted festoons in all running between the backplate, the branches and the base for the face's decorative spear. Aside from the fact that the preceding chandelier has Van Dyke candle cups and the sconce has cylindrical candle cups with a different type of scalloping, they would pair nicely.

333. Twenty-four Light Chandelier (one of a pair), Anglo-Irish, Adam style, glass and silvered brass, circa 1780-1790. Courtesy Nesle, Inc., New York. Photo by Helga Photo Studio.

This variation on the large Adam style chandelier employs the highly successful formula which was developed by the late eighteenth century British chandelier manufacturers. There is a large canopy at the top with numerous drops and swags of prisms which screen the upper shaft. The large faceted urn is the shaft's major component and it is exposed to full view. A faceted baluster provides filler between the base of the urn and the large hemispherical dish from which the branches spring. Twelve shorter branches rise in an upward scroll, while twelve larger faceted branches swing downward. All branches terminate in Van Dyke candle cups having star-shaped prism rings from which graduated pyriform prisms hang. Swags of prism chains run from branch to branch on both tiers. The lower canopy looks like a cascade to which pear-shaped prisms were added. The pendent drop is a faceted mallet.

334. Seven Light Sconce, English, Adam style, glass, plain brass and silvered brass, circa 1790. Courtesy Nesle, Inc., New York. Photo by Helga Photo Studio.

This is a rather unusual piece in that it is half of a small chandelier complete with a brass trefoil swinging loop at the top and a hook for it to be attached. The faceted half canopy has the expected pyriform prisms employed as drops and in swags attached to cut patera prisms. The shaft is composed of faceted half-balusters and half-urn. The dish for the branches is in half, too, but has a backplate to be attached to the wall for both support and balance. The plain scroll arms terminate in Van Dyke candle cups and the star-shaped prism rings are equipped with more pear-shaped drop prisms.

335. Twelve Light Chandelier, English, Adam style, clear and green glass, silvered brass, circa 1780-1800. Courtesy Nesle, Inc., New York. Photo by Helga Photo Studio.

Long before the days of the British Raj, English-made goods were very much in vogue with the rulers of the Indian princely states. The British East Indian Company was only too happy to accommodate the desires and taste predilections of the maharajahs and other upper class Indians. This chandelier with its Bristol green arms, prism swags, faceted urns and other shaft elements is a fine example of the clear and colored glass chandeliers and sconces made for Indian palaces. The Raj ended in 1947 and the Republic of India was established in 1950—events that have resulted in the dissolution of most of the princely states. Since that time, hundreds of Anglo-Irish chandeliers and sconces, such as this one, have come to western countries, the United States in particular.

No concession to Indian taste, save the green color, has been made in this typical Adam-style chandelier. Two tiers of "S" branches springing from a central dish on the shaft, star-shaped prism rings, Van Dyke candle cups, the urn on the shaft and the canopies at the top and bottom of the chandelier, along with many swags of glass chains are the Adam design formula.

336. Eight Light Chandelier, Anglo-Irish, Adam style, glass, silvered brass and brass, circa 1790-1805. Courtesy Nesle, Inc., New York. Photo by Helga Photo Studio.

In this model, having relatively few prisms, the arrangement of the shaft elements in a typical Adam-style chandelier can be well seen. Even in this rather reserved pattern, the use of the pyriform prisms in graduated sizes is a key ingredient in the overall success of the design. The shades with their copper-wheel engraved anthemion borders would have been popular in the hotter areas of the British Empire as well as in the well-to-do residences of the former southern colonies in the United States. The candle cups are vented brass sockets that can support both the candle and the glass shade.

337. Twenty Light Chandelier, Anglo-Irish, glass and silvered brass, circa 1780-1800. Courtesy Nesle, Inc., New York. Photo by Helga Photo Studio.

This large and important chandelier and others in its basic pattern are nothing less than one of the great triumphs of the Anglo-Irish designers and manufacturers of glass chandeliers of the latter part of the eighteenth century. The shaft's focal elements are the faceted urn which rises above the branches and the canopy that is supported on a cut obelisk. From that canopy two interlocking swags of faceted pyriform prisms fall with additional chains dropping down from the rosettes which serve as connectors for the swags. The other most visible parts of the shaft are the domical lower canopy to which graduated pear-shaped prisms are attached. The shaft is completed with a faceted globular pendent.

Two tiers of faceted "S" shaped branches originate from a barely visible dish on the shaft. Each branch terminates in a Van Dyke candle cup having diaper-pattern faceted and star-shaped prism rings which support more graduated pendents of pyriform prisms. The concept of the double swags of glass prisms connected by rosettes and having pear-shaped drops, as seen on the upper canopy, is repeated in a larger scale running from the star-shaped prism rings.

338. Three Light Sconce, English, Adam style, giltwood, painted porcelain, glass and brass, circa 1790. Courtesy Nesle, Inc., New York. Photo by Helga Photo Studio.

While not the best articulated example of this rather uncommon form, the piece does have a great deal of charm. The circular giltwood backplate is ornamented with beading and gadrooning and frames a polychrome painting of a sprig of flowers on a white ground. The potty, giltwood, spread eagle finial holds a ring in his beak from which two swags of brass chains fall. A double swag of chains is suspended from horizontal, rectangular blocks projecting from the center of the side of the frame. The chains connect to a similar projecting block on the bottom of the frame. The three branches also originate from those projections. Each branch consists of a strangely disfigured female bust. Van Dyke candle cups, star-shaped bobeches and pyriform prisms complete the picture. In reality, this piece is an interesting variation on the convex looking glass which has branches.

236

339. Single Light Sconce, English, Neoclassical style, glass and brass mounted on mahogany, circa 1790-1810. Courtesy Joe Kingdig, York, Pennsylvania.

The sconce with its splendid heavily cut hurricane shade makes the point about the cheap quality of gilding used on many brass objects made in England during the late eighteenth and early nineteenth centuries. This gilding would wear out and hand polishing would be required. Note that the backplate for the sconce and the branch for the smoke bell are different. This could have happened originally or be a later marriage. A hierarchy of conditions is established with the foliate decorated and cable bordered plate of the sconce proper and the plain circle of the plate for the smoke bell. The mahogany backing board is modern. There are examples, however, used in India particularly, where the sconces were originally mounted on a board.

340. Eight Light Chandelier, English, Adam style, glass and ormolu, circa 1800. Courtesy Nesle, Inc., New York. Photo by Helga Photo Studio.

Two important new features are to be noted in this chandelier which dates from the end of the eighteenth and beginning of the nineteenth century. The first is the ormolu band decorated with classical designs set within roundels that borders the lip of the hemispherical dish supporting the branches and the urn-shaped device in the middle of the shaft. The second new feature is the use of chains of pyriform prisms which fall all the way from the upper canopy to the star-shaped prism rings. The rest of the chandelier is of excellent quality, but is in the conventional Adam-style. The quality of the ormolu is superior and is very possibly from the Soho Works of Matthew Boulton near Birmingham.

341. Twelve Light Chandelier, English, Adam style, glass and brass, circa 1800. Signed by DeLaFosse. Courtesy Nesle, Inc., New York. Photo by Helga Photo Studio.

This chandelier is a handsome, atypical form in late eighteenth century English-made glass chandeliers. Urns, balusters or balls or a combination of those elements usually form the highly visible central shaft. Here the shaft is almost totally obscured by the twelve long curving canes of glass which are the arms of the piece. These branches drop from brass sockets which are screwed into a brass flange that is in the middle of the shaft. Also rare are the decorative "J" shaped decorative arms that spring from upper sockets of the same element that holds the candle branches. The large "J" branches are in a reverse position to the candle branches and hold alternating arrangements of faceted glass drops, as well as support the swags of chains that run from "J" branch to "J" arm. Terminating the candle arms are the typical Van Dyke candle cups and star-shaped prism rings. The pyriform drops and swags of chains are in the normal late Georgian mode. Characteristic of the English work of this period are the domed glass canopies seen at the head and base of the shaft. They are graduated in size with the lower one being smaller and having chains of graduated pear-shaped prisms dropping from its edges as well as a faceted globe pendent falling on a brass chain from its center. In addition to the upper canopy being larger than the one at the base, it has glass chains and swags in the same configuration as those on the "J" arms, but reduced in scale.

238

343. Eight Light Chandelier, English, Regency style,
giltwood and glass, circa 1810. H: 53 in. Diam.: 31 in. Courtesy Nesle, Inc., New York. Photo by Helga Photo Studio.

Many stylish chandeliers made in England and to a lesser
extent in the Germanic countries during the early nineteenth century were made of carved wood which was gessoed
and gilded and combined with faceted glass. Here a large
ring composed of continuous bands of graduated beads
serves as the support for both the candle cups on the upper
side and for the faceted tear-drop prisms falling from the
bottom. The lathe-turned candle cups are in the campana-
urn pattern and alternate on the ring with pairs of antefixes
which flank solitary lotus urns. Hidden by the ring and
prisms is a spoke-like arrangement which radiates out from
a central fluted column as the real support for the ring. The
column rises to the giltwood double-tiered corona. The upper part of the corona has water leaves alternating with rosettes as its decorative finial. Tear drop prisms fall from that
upper ring, while chains of faceted glass buttons drop from
the lower ring to join the backside of the great giltwood ring.

342. Twelve Light Chandelier, English, Regency style, glass
and silvered brass, circa 1815. H: 53 in. Diam.: 33 in. Courtesy, Nesle, Inc., New York. Photo by Helga Photo Studio.

The Regency characteristics of this chandelier, with its interesting arrangement of eight branches in pairs on the upper tier alternating with four single branches on the lower
tier, are immediately apparent. The dish-shaped bobeches
are cut with palmettes and that design is repeated on the larger dish that supports the upper branches. The shaft is a slender, faceted baluster having a small canopy at the bottom and
none at the top. A metal ring which holds sockets for
branches is concealed behind three large cut glass roses.
Connected to the sockets on the underside are the four large
"J" shaped candle branches. Springing from the upper socket are eight more florid "J" branches which support swags
of prisms. The upper part of the shaft displays another Regency form, a ball with cone very much in the shape of an
argand lamp shade.

344. Eight Light Chandelier, attributed to William Holland, London, England, Regency style, gilt-gesso on pine, iron wire and chain and gilded pewter, circa 1807. H: 34-½ in. Diam.: 38-½ in. Courtesy, Boscobel Restoration, Inc., Garrison-on-Hudson, New York.

Amongst the stellar objects gracing the upstairs sitting room of Boscobel is this stunning chandelier made from an interesting combination of materials. Suspended in mid-air on a chain dropping from the center of the corona is a carved, gessoed and gilded Mercury in flight. The messenger of the gods stretches his left hand heavenward to extend a cup, while his other hand holds a flask. The corona, with its star crowned finial elements, as well as the branch ring are turned and carved of wood which has been gessoed and gilded. The stars and anthemia applied to the great ring are gilded pewter castings. The scrolling branches with foliate devices in the English taste are made of gilded iron.

345. Six Light Chandelier, English, Regency style, gilt-gesso on pine, iron, brass, and glass, circa 1820-1830. H: 36 in. Diam: 22 in. Courtesy Rosedown Plantation and Gardens, St. Francisville, Louisiana.

Giltwood chandeliers which were much in vogue for residential use all over Europe throughtout the seventeenth and eighteenth centuries began to be less used in the nineteenth century. Their popularity did not decline, however, in northern Europe and Britain until the 1830s. In its graduated three-tiered arrangement and the way in which the prisms are attached directly to the underside of the branches to form swags, Russian and Scandinavian influence is seen. The restraint and economy of decoration are in the British tradition. The chandelier is almost entirely made of gilt gesso on pine. The three tiers are attached to a central cylindrical shaft of giltwood. The two lower tiers have moulded giltwood frames to hide their brass prism rings. Progressively larger anthemia serve as crests for each tier. Only at the corona is there no moulded giltwood crest. There, a flat metal flange serves both as a prism ring and a place to mount the giltwood anthemia crest. Attached to the lowest tier are the scrolling branches of iron wire which has been gessoed and gilded. The flared and reeded candle cups are the finishing touch on this fixture. This model of candle cup appears on some candle lighting devices made later by the Boston firm of Henry N. Hooper and Company.

346. Convex Looking Glasses with Two Branches, English, Regency style, gessoed and gilded deal, ebony and brass, circa 1810. H: 36 in. W: 21 in. Courtesy Herbert Schiffer Antiques, West Chester, Pennsylvania.

While not usually considered a lighting device in the latter part of the twentieth century, looking glasses with sconces were very definitely regarded as lighting devices in the past. The mirrored surfaces helped to double the candle power. Convex looking glasses which provide a distorted image must have been chiefly regarded as decorative pieces and lighting devices first. There are many variations on this general theme. The convex mirror is framed by a reeded bezel of ebony and that is framed by a circular scoop moulding whose trough is embellished with twenty-seven giltwood balls applied with wire pins to the frame. Separately carved humorous, dolphin-like fish flank a grotto of rocks which provides a plinth for the spread-eagle finial. Giltwood foliage forms the companion pendent at the base. Scrolling wire arms covered with gilded gesso make the arms to which the beaded brass bobeche and candle cup are attached.

347. Convex Looking Glass with Two Branches, English, Regency style, ebony, gessoed deal ebonized and gilded, iron and brass, circa 1815. Courtesy Herbert Schiffer Antiques, West Chester, Pennsylvania.

This convex mirror is framed in a reeded ebony bezel which is surrounded by a gilded bead moulding and ultimately by an ebonized convex moulding with four gilded neoclassical neckings placed equidistantly. The usual foliate support is seen at the base in ebonized wood with the principal pendent leaf gilded. An unusual plinth of twisted vines terminating in foliage provides support for a spread eagle finial posed in profile grasping a gilded ball. The branches are iron which has been gessoed in a spiral twist and gilded. The candle cups' cylinders have a broad reeded border. The bobeches are missing and as is the case with many giltwood pieces much of the gilding has had to be restored.

348. Two Light Sconce, English, Regency style, giltwood and gilded iron, circa 1810-1830. H: 13-¼ in. W: 14 in. D: 6-¾ in. Courtesy Herbert Schiffer Antiques, West Chester, Pennsylvania.

Sconces in the bouquet or basket of flowers form are unusual. The design was probably originated by the French late in the reign of Louis XVI. The candle cups and bobeches of giltwood are most like those on English wooden chandeliers of the Regency-George IV period, allowing the assumption that this piece was fabricated in England. The more florid use of flowers and fruit in the basket is also nineteenth century rather than eighteenth.

349. Three Light Sconce (one of a pair), English, Regency style, glass and ormolu, circa 1810-1820. Courtesy Nesle, Inc., New York. Photo by Helga Photo Studio.

This large sconce and its companion are illustrative of the high quality multi-media work being done by the makers of lighting devices in Regency England. The scrolling ormolu arms are reeded and have supporting foliate arabesques and rosettes. The round backplate is embellished with palmettes. The ormolu candle sockets also hold cylindrical shades which have tapered bottoms. The upper part of the shades is copper-wheel engraved with a foliate border. The edges of the dish-shaped cut glass bobeches or prism rings are cut in scalloped shell motives. This same bobeche appears on numerous argand lamps as do the graduated, faceted, circular drops above the eight-sided long prisms with multifaceted tips.

350. Twenty-four Light Chandelier (one of a pair), English, Regency style, glass and ormolu, circa 1820-1830. H: 70 in. Diam.: 46 in. Courtesy Nesle, Inc., New York. Photo by Helga Photo Studio.

This splendid chandelier and its companion were formerly part of the contents of Devonshire House in London before being acquired by William Randolph Hearst. Mr. Hearst, in turn, sold them to the Nesle firm. Originally made for candles, the piece has been electrified.

A number of differences are apparent between this chandelier and those in the Adam style. Almost the entire shaft is hidden by the cable-cut bobeches, as well as four vase-form ornaments which are interspersed among the lower branches. Those vases and the vase on the central shaft are cut to look like palm leaves. The four vases are fitted into an ormolu socket of palm leaves, while an ormolu band decorated with gougework and lion masks divides the principal vase on the shaft. Festoons of prisms are held by a ring in each lion mask. The ormolu corona displays Russian influence and is shaped like a palm tree from which hang large pyriform prisms and festoons of prisms.

351. Twelve Light Chandelier, English, early Victorian style, clear and colored overlay glass and gilded cranberry glass, circa 1840-1855. H: 66 in. Diam: 41-⅜ in. Collection of the Mississippi Governor's Mansion. Courtesy of the Mississippi Department of Archives and History, Jackson.

The contrast of the cranberry red and white overlay on the shaft and bobeches as well as the gilded, cranberry shades needs to be seen in situ in the Front Rose Parlour of the Governor's Mansion to be appreciated. This is the type of chandelier that would have been made either for candles or gas in that period of transition from candles to gas. The flattish "S" shaped branches, the use of overlay glass, the series of balusters in the shaft and the canopy arrangements, as well as the use of the "Albert"-type prisms, are all clues to the date of this piece.

352. Twelve Light Chandelier, English (attributed to the firm of Perry and Company of Grafton Street, London), early Rococo Revival style, glass and brass, circa 1830. H: 44 in. Diam: 36 in. Courtesy Herbert Schiffer Antiques, West Chester, Pennsylvania.

This chandelier plays upon certain eighteenth century rococo themes, but uses them in new nineteenth century ways. The shaft's cut glass ball, for example, does not stand alone in the eighteenth century manner, but rather has apertures into which the solid glass scrolling arms are fitted to be screwed into the central metal shaft. The plain, solid glass shafts are proof that this fixture was made for candles and not piped for gas. The deeply cut canopies and prism rings originated in the nineteenth century. This chandelier also has more prisms than was the fashion in the 1750s and 1760s.

253. Eight Light Chandelier, English, William IV style, brass and glass, circa 1830-1840. Courtesy Nesle, Inc., New York. Photo by Helga Photo Studio.

This chandelier with its numerous chains of faceted prisms conceals a very skeletal frame and grew out of the Regency style. It represents the transition from candle-lighted fixtures to gas fixtures. Gas as a fuel for illumination was already well established in English centers when this piece was made, and while this piece does have hollow arms, the cut glass bobeches and sabot-shaped candle cups appear original. This simply exhibits good retailing sense. The device could be sold to the customer as a candle chandelier with the option of an easy conversion to gas should the client's residence later be piped for gas.

A new decorative device, which seems to have emerged during the 1830s and which would be popular for glass chandeliers during almost the rest of the century, is cut glass stars placed on threaded brass shafts which can be screwed to both the branch ring and the corona. During the late 1830s the slow transition from the use of the tear-drop prisms seen here to the spearhead or "Albert"-type of prism for chandeliers and sconces began.

354. Twelve Light Chandelier, English, early Victorian style ormolu and opaline glass, circa 1845. Collection of Mr. & Mrs. John Callon, Melrose, Natchez, Mississippi.

The chandelier survives with its original matte and brightly burnished gilt finish and is a particularly handsome example of the early Victorian style of chandelier. The six chains are a boldly cast series of loops punctuated with rosettes and clusters of foliage. The simple crown is greatly enriched with gilded foliate "C" scrolls. Three huge gilded leaf forms serve as the support of the blue opaline vase which rises in the center of the chandelier between the chains. The use of actual flowers and foliage inside the house for decoration had been restrained in earlier periods. As the nineteenth century progressed, more and more natural flowers, vines and other foliage were brought into the house. Even chandeliers could have places for massive bouquets, such as the vase seen here. The chandelier has two tiers of plain prisms completing its base. Straight brass rods run from a central ring to support the cut glass prism rings, campana-shaped brass candle cups and cut glass bobeches. The hollow brass rods employed as the branches indicate that the English manufacturer intended for this model of chandelier to be readily adapted to burn gas.

355. Six Light Chandelier, English or American, William IV style, cast and stamped brass and glass, circa 1845. Collection of Garrison Grey Kingsley, Greenville, Delaware.

This charming small chandelier with the bouquet holder could be either English or American. If it is American, it has the type of candle cup which the Boston manufacturers copied from the English. The branches, candle cups and prism rings are cast, while the majority of the shaft is composed of elements stamped from sheet brass. The owner of this chandelier is one of the most knowledgeable dealers in the field of nineteenth century lighting and thanks to his efforts, attention was brought to a chandelier of similar design and construction that bore English registry marks. While antique, the red glass bouquet holder and the appropriate lobed glass drip pans were added by the present owner. This chandelier was designed for use in a fairly low ceiling room. It has cast foliate chain links alternating with circular ones which form the three chains which lead directly from the fixture to the stamped brass ceiling boss.

356b. Detail of one of the pair of twenty-four branch chandeliers attributed to Henry N. Hooper and Company. Shown without prisms.

356a. Twenty-four Light Chandelier (one of a pair), American (probably made by Henry N. Hooper and Company, Boston), Gothic Revival style, ormolu and glass, circa 1840-1850. Courtesy The Historic New Orleans Collection, the Kemper and Leila Williams Foundation, New Orleans.

This chandelier and its mate probably comprise the finest extant set of American-made candle chandeliers in the Gothic Revival style. Arranged in two tiers of eighteen and six branches, they exhibit several characteristics associated with the Hooper firm. The use of masks on the branches of the middle and upper tier and the foliate candle cups are all known in Hooper's work. The deep gold gilding is original and of the type preferred by the Boston makers.

356c. Detail of masks, candle cups and prism rings of one of the twenty-four light chandeliers attributed to Henry N. Hooper and Company.

357. Three Branch Wall Bracket, probably made by Henry N. Hooper and Co., Boston, Rococo Revival style, matte and bright gilded brass, circa 1855-1865. Collection of Garrison Grey Kingsley, Greenville, Delaware.

Wall brackets such as this would have been used originally in both public and private ballrooms, lecture halls or almost any room that had a gallery and would require more lighting than that provided by ceiling fixtures. This example has everything including an American eagle finial. The attribution to the Hooper firm is made on the basis of the bearded mask with foliate crown that is seen in the Hooper catalogue of 1858, as well as on the strength of the foliate candle cups. The double gilding is of the rich, deep gold color preferred by Boston manufacturers.

358. Candle Bracket (one of a set of four), American (Philadelphia), Rococo Revival style, gilt brass, circa 1844. H: 4-¼ in. W: 4 in. D: 11-½ in. Collection of Rosedown Plantation and Gardens, St. Francisville, Louisiana.

These revolving brackets were customarily made to be mounted on upright pianos, cheval looking glasses and on looking glasses attached to dressing stands or chests-of-drawers. The bracket seen here is mounted on an unusual chest-on-chest-on-chest in the Gothic Revival style. This chest is a part of an extraordinary bedroom set made on commission from a group of Henry Clay's friends by Crawford Riddell of Philadelphia, in anticipation of Clay's being elected President of the United States in 1844. When Clay did not win the election, the owner of Rosedown Plantation, Daniel Turnbull, bought the set and put up a new wing on Rosedown to accommodate the high post bed which rose to a height of thirteen feet and two inches. In addition to the previously mentioned chest, the cheval glass also has a set of the rococo revival style branches, which were undoubtedly made by the Cornelius firm or an equally good Philadelphia foundry. The branches look like branches from girandoles and the downturned leaf prism rings are equipped with their original, plain three-sided prisms.

359. Bracket (one of a pair), American (probably Philadelphia), Rococo Revival style, gilt brass, circa 1840-1860. H: 8 in. D: 7 in. Courtesy Rosemont Plantation, Woodville, Mississippi.

This bracket and its mate survive with their matte and bright gilded surfaces in almost mint condition. The naturalistic swivel arm in the shape of oak branches complete with leaves and acorns would have been regarded as rustic by their original Victorian owners. It is quite possible that there was originally a prism ring between the end of the branch and the candle cup.

360. Eight Light Chandelier, American (probably Pennsylvania or New England), Federal style, tin, circa 1805-1835. Courtesy the Index of American Design, National Gallery of Art, Washington D.C. Drawing by Elmer Rudisill Kottcamp.

From the later colonial period forward there were numerous tinsmiths in Britain's American colonies, especially in the northeastern area from Pennsylvania to what is now Maine. While the majority of these devices were made for public places such as churches, taverns, and court rooms, some were made for residential use. The majority that survive date from approximately the first thirty years of the nineteenth century. Here the central ring has been repoussed with rosettes while the corona has a chevron pattern punched into it which is framed by pairs of moulded repousse lines. The branches run in a cabriole pattern from the crimped drip pan or bobeche first touching the large ring and then proceeding to join the inside of the corona. Two more pieces of flat tin form a dome above the corona. Through the center of the dome a wrought wire hook is attached for hanging the fixture to the ceiling.

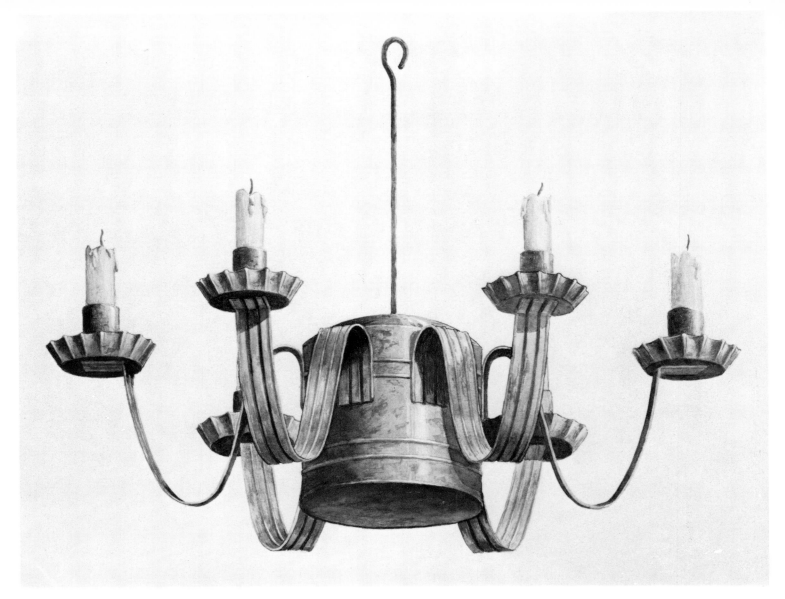

361. Six Light Chandelier, American (probably New England), tin, circa 1810-1830. Photograph courtesy the Index of American Design, National Gallery of Art, Washington, D.C.

With the "early American Revival" that began in the 1940s, numerous reproduction tin chandeliers and sconces have been made to provide illumination for interiors featuring pine, maple and cherry furniture. The design of this fixture is simplicity itself, and it and similar models were made by hundreds of tinsmiths in New England, New York, Pennsylvania and the older sections of the Midwest. The shaft is a cylinder with two pairs of raised rib borders at the top and bottom. The cylinder has a low domical top and an iron rod with a hook serves in lieu of a chain. The branches are flat "S" scrolls having the ribbed border. The attached bobeches are made of crimped tin and are fitted with cylindrical candle cups. A word of caution should be offered to the restorer of old houses who feels that these chandeliers can be authentically used in abundance for illumination. The vast majority of this type of chandelier that survives having a solid provenance came from churches, taverns and other public places.

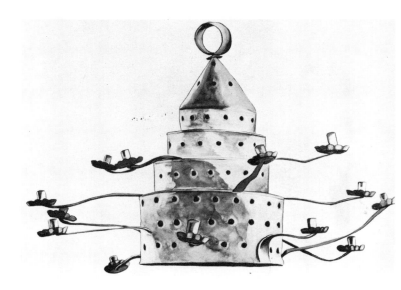

362. Three Tiered Chandelier, American (New Mexico), tin, circa 1850. Drawing by E. Boyd. Photograph courtesy the Index of American Design, National Gallery of Art, Washington, D.C.

This chandelier reinforces the statement made in the previous caption regarding the original use of these tin fixtures. Probably made in the vicinity of Santa Fe, it was used in the Roman Catholic church at Canocito. It also serves as a reminder of the early Spanish settlement of the Southwest which dates back to the early seventeenth century. The tinsmithing tradition was well established by the Spanish settlers of Mexico when they began to colonize what is now New Mexico. Fourteen branches can be seen in this drawing and it is apparent that some arms have been lost, even though there was not a great deal of concern for absolute symmetry as would have been the case with Anglo-American-made pieces. Three graduated, pierced drums rise as the shaft to hold the flattened branches. A final decorative drum having a conical top and loop ring for the chain completes the piece.

363. Sconce, American (probably Pennsylvania), traditional or folk style, tin, early nineteenth century. Photo courtesy the Index of American Design, National Gallery of Art, Washington, D.C.

Tinware was a great specialty of the Pennsylvania Germans. This wall sconce is similar to many made of brass in continental Europe. This device could be used in two ways since no candle cups are provided. It could hold up to six candles, which would be affixed to the trough with their own tallow, or one or more betty lamps could be placed in the trough. The sheet tin black plate has been cut in the form of six tombstones. Each one is framed with a stylized laurel border and rosettes executed in repousse.

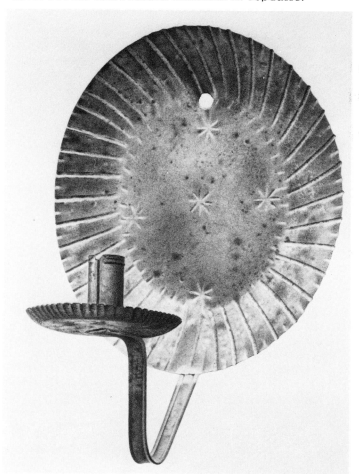

364. Single Light Sconce, American (New York or New England), traditional or folk style, tin, circa 1810-1850. Photo courtesy the Index of American Design, National Gallery of Art, Washington, D.C.

Many sconces of this type were made either wholly from tin or having pieces of silvered glass installed as reflectors. This example has a reflector with ribbed border and the back has been made more interesting with the four chased stars.

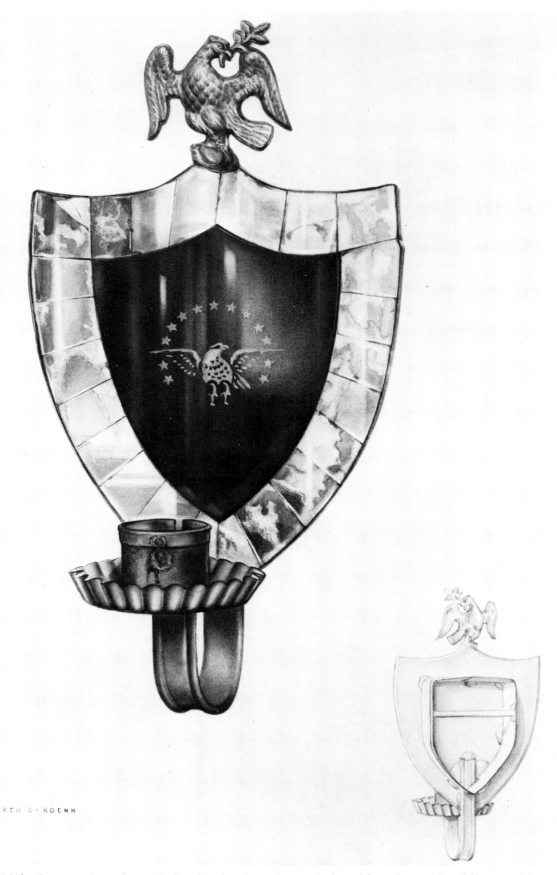

365. Single Light Sconce, American, Federal style, tin, mirrored glass, blue glass with gilding, and brass, circa 1810-1820(?). Photograph courtesy the Index of American Design, National Gallery of Art, Washington, D. C. Drawing by Alfred C. Koehn.

While this sconce was found in Illinois, it was most likely made somewhere between Pennsylvania and Massachusetts. Without seeing the actual object, it is hard to judge whether the piece is authentic or was made at the beginning of the early American craze during the 1920s. The shield-shaped tin backplate holds an escutcheon in blue glass which has been stencilled with a gilded American eagle and thirteen stars. This has been surrounded by pieces of mirrored glass. A "J" shaped branch has been soldered to the back of the shield-shaped plate and there is a scalloped drip pan and cylindrical candle socket. For support, a secondary raised escutcheon has been soldered to the back. Unquestionably old, the gilt brass eagle holding an olive branch in its beak can be seen in English brass founders' catalogues, where they appear on balls and were intended as finials for clocks and other tall case pieces of furniture.

Glossary

Acanthus   A form of ornamentation patterned on the leaf of a prickly herb which is native to the Mediterranean region, used as a decoration on various neoclassical and Victorian lighting devices.

Antefix   An ornament at the eaves concealing the ends of the roof tiles of Greco-Roman architecture. Antefix-like elements appear on some lighting devices.

Anthemion   A classical, stylized honeysuckle decoration which is usually employed as a band of consecutive anthemia or alternating with other classical motives.

Argand lamp   A lamp having a cylindrical wick allows a current of air to pass to both inner and outer surfaces of the wick and results in more even combustion and a brighter light. Named for its inventor Amid Argand, a Swiss scientist, who created the burner in 1782-83.

Betty lamp   A simple boat-shaped oil lamp having a projection to hold a wick. These lamps probably originated in Germany and were popular in eighteenth and nineteenth-century America.

Bobeche   Attached or detachable drip pan fitted to the candle cup of a candleholder and made of metal or glass.

Bocage   A by-form of the old French word *boscage* meaning woodlands. Used in the decorative arts to describe rich foliate devices in ceramics or metal.

Bougie   A wax candle or light from the North African town of the same name which carried on a trade in wax.

Bouillotte lamp   A term used in American decorative arts to refer to a type of French-style (Louis XVI to Empire) table lamp made of gilt brass and burning two to four candles which are protected by an adjustable painted metal shade.

Cabling   A decorative rope-like border principally on metal objects and in architecture.

Cabochon   A convex oval ornamentation of any material, but similar in design to smooth, convex, oval precious or semi-prescious stones.

Cabriole   A convex/concave curved leg which terminates in a decorative foot.

Caduceus   A decorative motif seen on neoclassical fixtures inspired by a herald's staff which has two entwined snakes and is surmounted by a double winged finial.

Calix   A footed Grecian drinking cup with a broad low bowl. The form was reinterpreted by some neoclassical lighting device makers in the standards of their fixtures.

Campana   An inverted bell-shaped, frequently used as candle cups.

Caryatid   A draped female figure supporting an entablature. These figures serve as inspirations for lighting device standards of the eighteenth and nineteenth centuries.

Chased   Relief decoration raised by surface hammering of the metal. The term is also applied to the finishing given to cast or repousse work, allowing rough-ness or projections to be filed or cut away.

Chinoiserie — Decorative motives inspired by Chinese designs.

Contrapposto — From the Italian, meaning "opposed"; in art this refers to the human figure so positioned that the upper portion of the body moves or twists in one direction and the lower in an opposed direction.

Corona — A crown, usually pierced and often seen used as a finial element on neoclassical chandeliers and at the head of supporting chains for such chandeliers.

Fasces — A decorative border modeled on the standards carried by ancient Roman lictors. It consists of a bundle of rods or reeds bound together with ribbons. In its most classically correct form, the reeds surround an axe whose blade projects at one end of the reeds.

Font — A closed element found in many shapes, which is used to hold oil for lamps.

Gadroon — A hammered or cast border ornament composed of radiating flutes or reeds of curved or straight form. This border is used principally on the lips and feet of drinking vessels and on the edges of dishes, plates and candlesticks.

Girandoles — Used in the American sense to refer to candlesticks and candelabra made of metal and having crystal prisms. (See complete discussion of the term in the girandole chapter.)

Knop — A small rounded protuberance which can be faceted and is used decoratively on the standards or shafts of candleholders.

Lambrequin — Used in the United States to refer to a decoration that is like the scalloped or pointed valances placed over windows or doors. Lambrequin-like decora-

tions are infrequently seen on lighting devices.

Mallet — A descriptive term for a shape used in the decorative arts and best visualized in the shape of a bowling pin.

Ormolu — A term derived from the French "or moulu" meaning "ground gold." Originally it was gold or gold leaf which was ground up for use in gilding brass, bronze or other metals. By the latter part of the 19th century, the term referred to an alloy of copper, zinc and tin, having the color of gold. In this text, it is used to refer to gilded brass or bronze.

Ovolo — A quarter-ellipse

Paktong — An alloy of copper, zinc and nickle resembling silver and discovered by the Chinese. Its formula is nearly the same as "German silver."

Palmette — A fan-shaped ornament based on the formalized palm leaf.

Patera — A round or oval ornament either flat or in bas relief, usually having gouged or pie- shaped wedges arranged in a sunburst configuration.

Plinth — In the decorative arts, a lower square or drum-shaped element of the base of a shaft or standard.

Porphyry — A rock consisting of crystals of the mineral feldspar which is embedded in a compact dark red or purplish mass of surrounding rock. This material is seen used in the shafts of some of the finest European lighting devices.

Putto or putti — Representation of a chubby cupid-like boy or children either nude or in swaddling bands.

Pyriform — Pear-shaped

Quoin — An architectural term referring to dressed stones at the corners of buildings laid so that their faces are alternately large and small. Similar features occur oc-

254

casionally in the more architectonic lighting devices as decorations on plinths.

Rabbet

A channel, groove or slot (usually of rectangular section) cut along the surface of some material and intended to receive the edge or end of another piece or pieces— example, the rabbet of a picture frame receives the edges of the glazing.

Repousse

Relief ornament that is hammered from the under or inner side of silver or other metals. Sharpness of form is usually given by surface chasing of detail and outline.

Rinceau

A stylized ornament, usually in low relief, consisting of a scrolling stem with stiff acanthus leaves, which is derived from classical Roman architecture.

Rocaille

Having shells, scrolls and foliate decorations in the manner of the French, Louis XV or rococo style.

Sinumbra

A nineteenth-century oil lamp having an annular ring oil reservoir below the rim of its glass shade. Since the location of the reservoir is away from the flame, little or no shadow is cast. This is unlike fixtures with large oil fonts located below or above and to the side of the burner, which did cast large shadows. The term originates with the Latin, "sine umbra," meaning "without shadow."

Smoke bell

An element, usually made of glass, placed above the flame of a hall lantern or chandelier to trap carbon, thus preventing smudged ceilings. Late eighteenth and early nineteenth-century smoke bells are customarily dish-like while those made from about 1830 forward are bell shaped.

Tangs

A grasping device consisting of a tongue-like piece of metal used to join a shaft to a base— a common method of joining bases to shafts in the making of nineteenth-century candlesticks.

Van Dyke Candle Cup

A campana-shaped glass candle cup whose scalloped bobeche is a part of the socket. Primarily used on Anglo-Irish chandeliers and sconces of the late eighteenth century.

Index

Acanthus
    definition, 253
Adam, Robert, 100, 127, 143
"Albert" prism, 172, 178, 183, 245, 248, 343
    definition and illustration, 19
Andre, Major John, 152, 166
Antefix
    definition, 253
Anthemion
    definition, 253
Apollo, 105
Archer and Warner, 151, 155, 183, 184, 186
Archer, Warner, Miskey and Company,
    184
Argand, Ami, 17
Argand lamp
    definition, 253
Arnold, Crawford, 152
Arnold, General Benedict, 166
The Art-Journal Special Issue, 149, 150
Athena model girandole, 195
Authentic Decor, The Domestic Interior (1620-1920), 202

Baccarat Works, 38
Back-cut Prism, 45, 46, 82
    definition and illustration, 19
Baker, Isaac F., 162, 175
Baker, Robert C., 152
Baker, William C., 152
Barnum, P. T., 158
Basket of Flowers model girandole, 162
Beckford, William, 59
Bears and Bees model girandole, 190, 191
Beehive Candlesticks, 73-75, 78
Bertram, Harry, 181
Bell metal, 53
Betty lamp
    definition, 253
Bigelow Chapel model girandole, 187-189
Binn, Thomas, 21
Birds model girandole, 172
Biscino, 207
Blackamoor model girandole, 12
Blake's Patent model girandole, 138, 159
Blake, William, 159
Messers. Blews and Sons of Birmingham and
    London, 150
Bobeche
    definition, 253
Bobeche,
    American, 20
    Glass, 20, 171
    Victorian style, 20
Bocage
    definition, 253
Boone, Daniel, 175
Boston and Sandwich Glass Company, 4
Bougie
    definition, 253
Bouillotte lamp
    definition, 253
Boulle, Andre-Charles, 111
Boulton, Matthew, 61, 118, 126, 237
Boulton, Matthew and Plate Co., 126
Bouquet girandole, 197

Boy and Dog model girandole, 171, 185, 186
Boy and Girl model girandole, 180, 183, 184,
    186
Bracket
    American, 248, 249
    Candle, 248
    Rococo Revival style, 248, 249
    Wall, 248
Brighton buns, 55
Broad spear-tip or "colonial" prism
    definition and illustration, 20
Bruff, J. G., 192
Buck and Doe model candelabra, 138
Bush, Robert, 51
Byron, Lord, 175

"C" prism, 158
    definition and illustration, 20
Cabling
    definition, 253
Cabochon
    definition, 253
Cabriole
    definition, 253
Caduceus
    definition, 253
Cafe, John, 62
Caldwell, E. F., 209
Calix
    definition, 253
Cambaceres, Jean-Jacques, 21
Campana
    definition, 253
Cancer, 202
Candelabra
    Adam style, 119, 121-124
    Alexander I-Nicholas I style, 114
    American, 5, 13, 133, 135-140
    American Empire style, 133
    Anglo-Irish, 119
    Austrian, 115, 117
    Bohemian, 46
    Brass with gilding, 5, 13, 118, 121, 135-141,
        144
    Bronze with gilding, 96-103, 106-112, 117,
        119, 124, 125, 133, 134, 138
    Buck and Doe model, 138
    Charles X style, 103
    Consular style, 96, 109
    English, 118, 119, 121-130, 132-134, 140
    First Empire style, 97-104, 106, 114, 115
    First Empire-*Restauration* style, 107
    French, 96-114, 140, 141
    George III style, 125
    George IV-Victorian style, 132
    German, 114-116
    Glass, 46, 104, 105, 113, 119, 121-125, 127, 130,
        132, 134, 136, 137, 144
    Iron, 141
    Lily model, 141
    Louis XIV Revival style, 111
    Louis XVI style, 96, 113, 117
    Louis Philippe style, 103
    Neoclassical, 113, 115, 118, 123, 124, 126
    Ormolu, 100, 104, 105, 110, 111, 113-115, 122,
        137, 143

    Porcelain with ormolu, 106, 113, 123
    Regency style, 125-130, 132
    Renaissance Revival, 112, 140
    Restauration style, 105-108
    Rococo Revival style, 5, 13, 46, 109, 110, 116,
        117, 133-139, 141
    Russian, 114, 117
    Scandinavian, 113, 114, 123
    Second Empire style, 109-111
    Silver, 109, 115-117, 126-129, 133, 134
    Silverplated copper, 132
    Stone, 114, 118, 125
    Wooden, 125
Candle Bracket, brass, 248, 249
Candle Shades
    American, 64, 65
    American Empire style, 65
    Neoclassical style, 64
Candlesticks
    Adam style, 49
    Adam Revival style, 67
    Amber, 50
    American, 4, 51, 53, 57, 70-75, 77, 81, 85-88,
        144
    American Empire style, 70, 81
    Baroque Revival style, 44
    Beehive model, 73-75, 78
    Belgian, 41
    Bohemian, 46
    Brass, 24-27, 30-34, 37, 44, 47-49, 52-58, 63,
        64, 69, 72-80, 85-90, 92
    Bronze, 9, 27, 28, 30, 35, 36, 87
    Cast Iron, 33, 34, 36, 72, 76, 77, 86
    Chinese, 84
    Consular-Empire style, 27, 55
    Continental, 47, 86
    Copper, 65, 67
    Diamond Princess model, 79
    Directoire style, 23, 26
    Directoire-Consular style, 24, 25
    Dutch, 44
    Empire Revival style, 47
    English, 35, 37, 49-59, 61-64, 66, 67, 69, 71-80,
        84, 85, 88
    Federal, 57
    First Empire styles, 9, 26, 28, 30, 31
    French, 9, 23-28, 30-40, 55
    General, 21-152
    George IV style, 62
    George IV-William IV style, 55, 67
    Georgian, 69
    Georgian Revival style, 80
    Glass, 4, 28, 38, 43, 46, 49, 50, 64-67, 72, 81,
        85
    History of, 21-22
    "Hogscraper", 17, 71
    Italian, 41
    King of Diamonds model, 79
    Louis XV Revival, 39
    Marble, 23, 63, 84
    Middle European, 43, 44
    Neoclassical style, 41, 43, 44, 50, 52-57, 63, 70,
        72
    Ormolu, 38, 39, 49, 63, 66
    Pewter, 44, 49, 51, 54, 70, 71, 81, 90, 92
    Polish, 43

Porcelain, 39, 40, 84
Pot Metal (Zinc), 86
Pulpit model, 69
Queen of Diamonds model, 79
Regency style, 55, 57-59, 61, 63, 64, 66
Renaissance Revival, 43, 85, 87, 88
Restauration style, 31-35, 37
Restauration-Louis Philippe style, 35, 36
Retardataire Baroque style, 51
Rococo Revival style, 38, 40, 46, 86, 144
Russian, 44
Silver, 41, 43, 47, 48, 52, 59, 61, 62, 67, 91
Spanish, 42
Tin, 51, 71, 92, 93
Traditional style, 51, 71, 78
Victorian, 72, 77-79, 84
William IV-Victorian style, 69, 73-76
Wooden, 51, 63, 64
"Capture of Andre" model girandole, 156, 163, 164, 166, 167, 183
Carleton, William, 156
Caryatid
    definition, 253
Castle model girandole, 187
Chambersticks
    American, 91-93
    American Empire style, 91
    Dutch, 90
    English, 90-93
    French, 47
    Italian, 48
    Neoclassical, 48, 90, 91
    Restauration style, 47
    Scandinavian, 48
    Traditional style, 90, 92, 93
    Victorian style, 93
Chandelier
    Adam style, 228, 231, 232, 234, 235, 237, 238
    Alexander I style, 212-214, 216-218
    American, 16, 209, 246, 247, 249, 250
    Anglo-Irish, 228, 231, 232, 235, 236
    Brass, 16
    Bronze, ormolu or gilded brass, 121, 202, 203, 205, 206, 208-210, 212-220, 246-248
    Candle Powered, general, 199-252
    Continental, 207
    Czar Alexander I style, 211
    Empire Revival style, 208, 209
    English, 213, 220, 227, 228, 234, 237-240, 243-246
    Federal style, 249
    First Empire style, 208, 215, 219, 220
    Franco-Russian taste, 212
    French, 12, 202, 203, 205-209, 215, 219
    French Empire taste, 220
    Georgian style, 228
    Glass, 16, 210-220, 243-246
    Glass and silvered brass, or ormolu, 227-239, 243-247
    Gothic Revival style, 16, 247
    Louis Philippe-Second Empire style, 208
    Neoclassical style, 211, 216
    Nicholas II period, 219
    Regency style, 213, 220, 239, 240, 243
    Restauration, 12, 205-207
    Rococo Revival style, 244
    Russian, 210, 211, 213-219
    Russo-Scandinavian taste, 212
    Scandinavian, 212-214, 216, 220
    Second Empire style, 208, 209
    Sheet metal or tin, 202, 249, 250
    Silver, 207
    Spanish, 207
    Transitional style of Rococo to Neoclassical, 227
    Victorian style, 243, 246
    Viennese, 211, 212
    William IV style, 245, 246
    Wood, iron, 240
Chased
    definition, 253
Cherub model girandole, 193
Chevreul, Michel-Eugene, 21
Chinoiserie

    definition, 254
Chippendale, Thomas, 153
Classical Family model girandole, 196, 197
Classical Muse model girandole, 8, 196
Claude-Michel, 106
Clermont, 170
Clodion, 106
Coffin-shaped prism, 155, 159, 160, 168, 176, 178, 186, 197
    definition and illustration, 18
Coker, Ebenezer, 62
"Colonial Lady" model girandole, 175, 176
Colonial Officer model girandole, 175, 176
Coningsby, 153
Contrapposto
    definition, 254
Convex Looking Glasses
    English, 241
    Regency style, 241
Cooper, James Fenimore, 5, 175
Cornelius and Baker, 16, 77, 162, 175, 176, 192
Cornelius and Company, 133, 156, 157, 161, 175, 176, 178, 195, 248
Cornelius and Son, 162
Cornelius, Baker, and Company, 162
Cornelius, Christian, 155, 156, 162, 175
Cornelius, Robert, 162
Cornucopia model girandole, 164
Corona
    definition, 254
Couchant Hound model girandole, 173
"C" prism
    definition and illustration, 20
Cradock, Joseph, 62
Cristalleries de St. Louis, 38
Crouch, J., 94
Crystal Palace Exhibition, 147, 149, 150
Cupid, 102
Cupid's Dream model girandole, 193

Daguer of Barcelona, 43
Damascene model girandole, 159
Daniel Boone or Leather-stocking model girandole, 175, 195
The Deerslayer, 175
"Diamond Princess" model candlesticks, 79
Dietz and Company, 153, 155, 158, 161, 171
Dietz, Brother and Company, 158, 180, 193
Dietz, Ulysses G., 155, 180
Dirk Platternick model girandole, 181
Disraeli, Benjamin, 153
Dog model girandole, 181
Dolphin model girandole, 156
Don Juan, 175
Dugoure, Jean-Demosthene, 103
Dunham, Rufus, 70

Edison, Thomas Alva, 17
"Elizabethan Couple" model girandole, 171, 180
Essex Institute, 155, 164, 171, 198
Etude de la Nature, 177
Evangeline and Gabriel, 177
Extinguisher, 93

Faberge, Carl, 117
Farrell, Edward Cornelius, 129
Fasces
    definition, 254
Fellows, Hoffman and Company, 155, 164, 166, 168
Fierce Lion model girandole, 172
Fisher Boy and Girl model girandole, 183
Fiske, J. W., 86
Font
    definition, 254

Gadroon
    definition, 254
Garrard, Robert, 134
Gaslighting in America: A Guide for Historical Preservation, 192
Gay-Lussac, 21
Gemini twins, 202
Gentleman and Cabinet-maker's Director, 153

George Washington/Benjamin Franklin model girandole, 157, 195
Girandole
    Brass, 5, 8, 12, 156-162, 164, 166, 168-172, 175-199
    Bronze, 161, 163, 172, 173, 178, 195
    definition, 153, 254
    general, 153-198
    glass, 5, 8, 12, 156-164, 166, 168-173, 175-198
    model names
        Athena, 195
        Basket of Flowers, 162
        Bears and Bees, 190, 191
        Bigelow Chapel, 187-189
        Birds, 172
        Blackamoor, 12
        Blake's Patent, 138, 159
        Bouquet, 197
        Boy and Dog, 171, 185, 186
        Boy and Girl, 180, 183, 184, 186
        Capture of Andre, 156, 163, 164, 166, 167, 183
        Castle, 187
        Cherub, 193
        Classical Family, 196, 197
        Classical Muse, 8, 196
        Colonial Lady, 175, 176
        Colonial Officer, 175, 176
        Cornucopia, 164
        Couchant Hound, 173
        Cupid's Dream, 193
        Damascene, 159
        Daniel Boone or Leather-stocking, 175, 195
        Dirk Platternick, 181
        Dog, 181
        Dolphin, 156
        Elizabethan Couple, 171, 180
        Fierce Lion, 172
        Fisher Boy and Girl, 183
        George Washington/Benjamin Franklin, 157, 195
        Indian Medallion, 192, 193
        Ivanhoe, 187, 189, 190
        Jenny Lind, 158
        Lady and Gentleman, 186
        Les Merriles, 181
        Little Eva, 156
        Lyre, 160
        Old Mortality, 182
        Paul and Virginia, 177
        Recumbent Doe, 169-171
        Recumbent Stag, 169-171, 180
        Rip Van Winkle, 177
        Robinson Crusoe, 156
        Roman Centurion, 180, 181, 194, 195
        Romeo and Juliet, 171, 180
        St. John the Baptist, 158
        Scottish Dancers, 179
        Setter, 164
        Spirit of '76, 201
        Stagg, 163, 164, 166, 168, 183, 191
        Sultan, 178
        Sultana, 178
        Three Light, 198
        Trophy, 167
        Urn, 163
        Vase, 161
        Warrior, 171, 191
        Warrior with Musket, 171, 192
    Potmetal (zinc), 192
Gleason, Roswell, 70
The Gothic Revival Style in America, 1830-1870, 188
Grazioni, Guiseppe, 41
Greenhill and Company, 145
Griffith, 92
Guy Mannering, 181

Hannam, T., 94
"Hawkeye", 175
H. B. in Augsburg, 115
Hearst, William Randolph, 243
Hennell, Jr., Robert, 134

Hogscraper candlesticks, 17, 71
Holland, William, 240
Henry N. Hooper & Co., 8, 13, 85, 86, 133-137, 139,
    140, 155, 156, 159, 163, 164, 169, 171, 177, 180,
    181, 194, 196-198, 240, 247, 248
Hope, Thomas, 61, 202
Hopper, Humphrey, 63, 125
Horus, 101

Indian Medallion model girandole, 192, 193
Interlocking "C" and Star Prism
    definition and illustration, 20
Irving, Washington, 153, 177
"Ivanhoe" model girandole, 187, 189, 190

Jenny Lind model girandole, 158

"King of Diamonds" candlesticks, 79
Knop
    definition, 254

Lady and Gentleman model girandole, 186
Lambrequin
    definition, 254
Lamp
    American, 150, 151
    American Empire style, 151
    Armorial-Palmer patent lamp, 150
    Brass, 145-148, 150-152
    Candle, 144, 145, 149-151
    English, 145-148, 151
    French, 144, 145
    Glass, 4, 146-148
    Iron, 145, 146, 150
    Louis XVI style, 144
    Neoclassical style, 145, 151
    Marble, 151
    Oil, 4
    Ormolu, 144, 145, 147, 148
    Palmer Patent, 146-148, 150
    Rococo Revival style, 147
    Transitional style, 145
    Victorian, 150
    "Vine-wreath foot"—Palmer Patent, 150
    William IV style, 146
    William IV-Victorian style, 148
Lantern
    Adam style, 222, 223
    American, 226
    Empire style, 226
    English, 221-225
    Engraved glass, 224-226
    Glass and brass, 221-225
    "Grecian style", 226
    Neoclassical style, 221, 224
    Regency style, 224, 225
Laurel Hill Cemetery, 182
Leather-Stocking Tales, 175
"Les Merriles" model girandoles, 181
LHF of Lemberg, 43
"Lily" candelabra, 141
Lind, Jenny, 158
"Little Eva" model girandole, 156
Livingston family, 170
L. K. of Vienna, 117
Looking Glasses with branches, wood, brass, 241
Loveridge & Co., H. W. Hampton, England, 92
Lustre
    American, 81, 82
    Anglo-Irish, 81
    Bohemian, 45
    Brass, 81
    English, 82
    Glass, 45, 81, 82
    Rococo Revival style, 45
    Victorian style, 45, 81, 82
    William IV-Victorian style, 81
Lyre model girandole, 160

Mallet
    definition, 254
Many-Faceted Straight or "Georgian" prism, 173
    definition and illustration, 18
Medusa, 115

Meg Merriles, 181
Mercury, 97, 240
Milly, 21
Minerva, 97
Minoret, 31
Miskey, William F., 184
Modified coffin-shaped prism, 176, 181, 196
    definition and illustration, 18
Morgan, Joseph, 21
Mount Auburn Cemetery, 188
Myers, Denys Peter, 192

Napoleon I, 28, 109, 127
Napoleon, Louis, 109
Natty Bumppo, 175
Neptune, 129, 133
New England Glass Company, 4
Nike, 97, 98, 103
19th-Century America: Furniture and Other
    Decorative Arts, 175
Nubian blackamoors, 99, 100

Old Mortality model girandole, 182
Ormolu
    definition, 254
Ovolo
    definition, 254

Paktong
    definition, 254
Palmer & Co., 146, 148
Palmer, William, 146, 147, 149
Palmette
    definition, 254
Pan, 30
Parker and Perry, 199
Parker, William, 199
Parker, William and Sons, 199
Parsons, John & Co., 52
Patera
    definition, 254
Paterson, Robert, 182
Paul and Virginia model girandole, 177
Paul et Virginie, 153, 177
Pegasus, 97
Perkins, Richard, 51
Perry and Company, 199, 244
Plain "Albert" prism, 155
    definition and illustration, 19
Plinth
    definition, 254
Pompeii, 109
Porphyry
    definition, 254
Potts, Mr. of Birmingham, England, 147, 149
Prism
    "Albert", 19, 172, 178, 183, 245, 284, 343
    Back-cut, 19, 45, 46, 82
    Broad spear-tip or "colonial", 20, 157, 191,
        192, 195
    "C", 20, 158
    Coffin-shaped, 18, 155, 159, 160, 168, 176, 178,
        186
    Interlocking "C" and Star, 20
    Many-Faceted Straight, 18, 173
    Modified Coffin-shaped, 18, 176, 181, 196
    Plain "Albert", 19, 155
    Spear-point, 19, 164, 186
    Star and Snowflake, 20, 155, 159, 161-164, 166,
        175, 177, 180, 183-185, 188-190, 193, 194,
        196, 197, 201
    Straight spear-tip, 18, 155, 179
Pulpit model candlesticks, 69
Putto or putti
    definition, 254
Pyriform
    definition, 254

"Queen of Diamonds" candlesticks, 79
Quoin
    definition, 254

Rabbet
    definition, 255

Recumbent Doe model girandole, 169-171
Recumbent Stag model girandole, 169-171, 180
Reid, William K., 62
Repousse
    definition, 255
Rich, Obadiah, 91
Richardson of Stourbridge, 150
Richardson, Thomas, 159
Rinceau
    definition, 255
Rip Van Winkle, 153, 177
Rip Van Winkle model girandole, 177
"Robinson Crusoe" model Girandole, 156
Robinson, Dean, 157
Rocaille
    definition, 255
Rockingham Works, 84
Roman Centurion model girandole, 180, 181, 194,
    195
Romeo & Juliet model girandole, 171, 180
Rorke, Edward & Co., 89
Rosedown Plantation, 27, 38, 63, 105, 114, 130,
    159, 240
Rosel of Barcelona, 43
Ruggio, Joe, 71
Rushlight Club, 71

St. John the Baptist model girandole, 158
St. John the Baptist, 158
St. Louis Glass House, 105
Saint-Pierre, Bernardin de, 153, 177
Sample Book of Lamps, Candelabra and Lighting
    Fixtures for Gas and Oil, 164, 171, 194
Sconce
    General, 199-252
    Adam style, 231-233, 236
    American, 204, 251, 252
    Brass and glass, 237, 242, 252
    Continental, 204
    Directoire style, 204
    English, 231-233, 236, 237, 242
    Federal style, 252
    French, 204
    Neoclassical, 204, 237
    Regency style, 242
    Traditional style, 251
    Wood, iron, tin, 204, 207, 216, 242, 251
Scottish Dancers model girandole, 179
Scott, Sir Walter, 179-182, 189
Setter model girandole, 164
Shakespeare, William, 180
Shaw, William F., 154-156, 187-189
Sinumbra
    definition, 255
Sketchbook, 177
Smith, George, 61
Smoke bell
    definition, 255
Snuffer-on-Tray, 93
Soho Factory, 118
Spear-point prism, 164, 186
    definition and illustration, 19
Spirit of '76 model girandole, 201
Staffordshire pottery, 84, 158, 187
"Stagg" model girandole, 163, 164, 166, 168, 183,
    191
Star and Snowflake prism, 155, 159, 161-164, 166,
    175, 177, 180, 183-185, 188-190, 193, 194, 196,
    197, 201
Starr, Fellows and Company, 153, 155, 156, 162-
    164, 166, 168, 181, 183, 184, 190, 191, 201
Starr, Fellows and Hoffman, 190, 191
Storr, Paul, 43, 59, 61, 128, 133
Straight spear-tip prism, 155, 179
    definition and illustration, 18
Stroud, William, 91
Sultan model girandole, 178
Sultana model girandole, 178

Tangs
    definition, 255
Thomire, Pierre-Philippe, 97, 98, 103
Thornton, Peter, 202
Three Light Girandole, 198

258

Torchere
    Adam style, 143
    English, 143
    First Empire, 143
    French, 143
    Glass with ormolu, 143
    wooden with ormolu, 143
"Trophy" model girandole, 167

Urn model girandole, 163

Van Dyke style Candle Cups

definition, 255
    49, 50, 119, 121, 122, 130, 231-234, 236, 238
Vase model girandole, 161

"Warrior" model girandole, 171, 191
Warrior with Musket model girandole, 171, 192
Watton, Edward, 199
Wax Jack
    Brass, 95
    English, 94, 95
    Neoclassical style, 94
    Regency style, 95

Silver, 94
Silverplate on copper, 94
William IV-Victorian style, 95
Wedgwood Factory, 123
Wickes, George, 62
W. P. of Berlin, 116

Zech of St. Petersburg, 210, 214

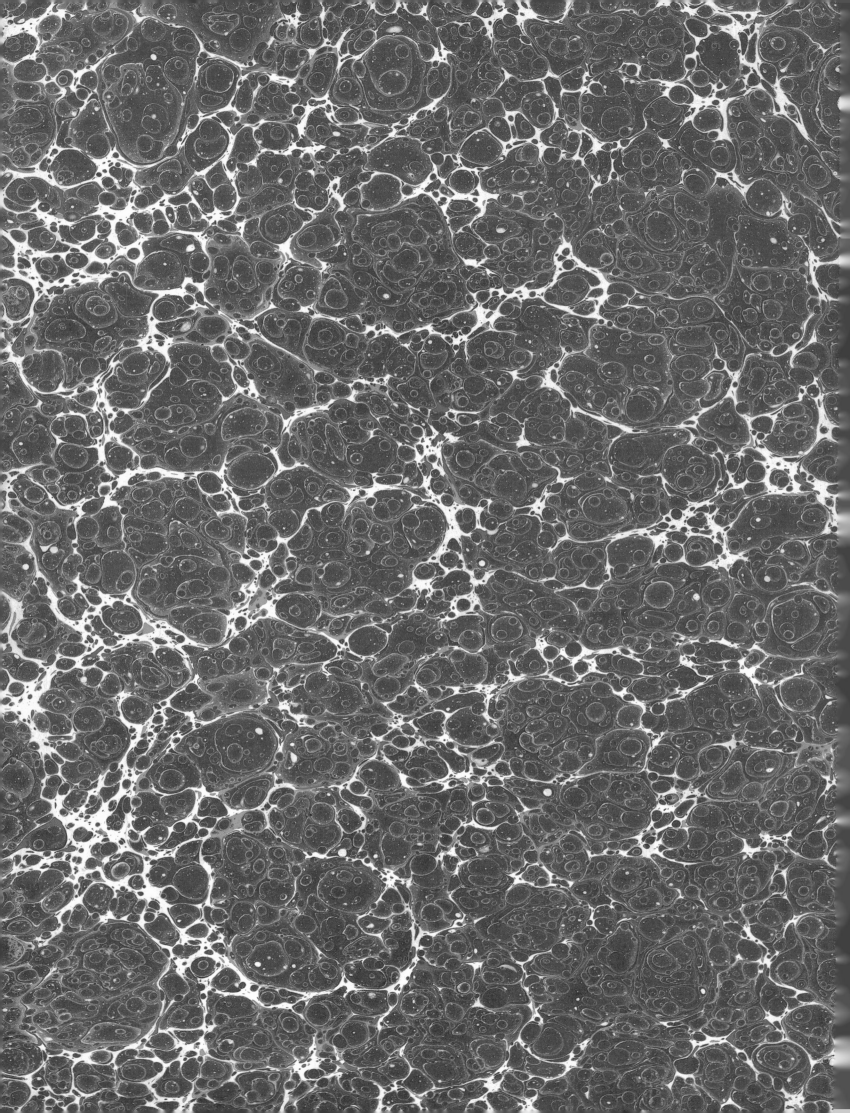